Mixed or single-sex school?
Volume II: Some social aspects

Mixed or single-sex school?

Volume II
Some social aspects

R. R. Dale

Reader in Education, University of Wales, Swansea

London   Routledge & Kegan Paul
New York Humanities Press

First published in 1971
by Routledge & Kegan Paul Ltd
Broadway House,
68–74 Carter Lane,
London EC4V 5EL
Printed in Great Britain by
Butler & Tanner Ltd,
Frome and London
© *R. R. Dale 1971*

ISBN 0 7100 7024 1

Contents

Tables

Tables

Appendix Tables

Figures

xii

Introduction

This volume concludes the presentation of those research results which compare co-educational and single-sex secondary schools in their influence on the social and emotional development of pupils and which examine various attitudes of pupils to these schools. Necessarily teachers play their part and are reflected in the results, but the focus is on the pupils and ex-pupils. It was expected that the present material would make two moderately-sized volumes, but it has proved possible to publish it in a single large one. A third, last volume is projected on the influence of the two types of schooling on academic attainment, and a concluding section of this will present a miscellany of papers relating to co-education containing material which is outside the scope of the previous books.

During the twenty-four years since the first of these researches was commenced there has been in the world a gradually increasing momentum in the trend towards co-education in secondary schools.[1] In the early years of the work a high-ranking delegation of Russian educationists visited the University College of Swansea, enquiring among other things about co-education. The writer's guarded reply that up to then the results of his research were in favour of co-education though it was too early for a definitive pronouncement, may or may not have influenced their decision, but soon after the delegation's return to Moscow it was announced that the Russian educational system was reverting to co-education! Step by step, as a result of several enquiries among their teachers and pupils, more and more of the Swedish secondary schools have, since the 1920s, become co-educational. Soon after the Second World War Japan changed over to this system and in France the experimental 'classes nouvelles' set up in the 1950s tended to be concentrated in co-educational *lycées*. The interest shown in the subject in Italy has prompted an Italian publishing firm to ask permission to translate the first volume of this work into Italian, and even the

---

[1] This short sketch is not intended to be a history of co-education. Readers who are interested in this aspect should consult W. A. C. Stewart, *The Educational Innovators* (2 vols, London, 1967–8), or B. A. Howard, *The Mixed School*, (1928) (to 1926 only).

Roman Catholic Church, for long a bastion of the single-sex school, now takes a distinctly less rigid attitude.

The State schools of the United States have from the first been for boys and girls together, and, much nearer home, the Scottish schools are traditionally co-educational. In Wales under the Intermediate Act of 1889 many schools had to be built for the two sexes together because of the sparseness of the population, and the same policy was applied in the rural parts of England after the Balfour Act of 1902. Because of the prestige of the best independent boarding and the direct grant schools (lumped together incongruously and somewhat illogically as the 'public schools'—but all then single-sex), some of these co-educational municipal grammar schools were split into two single-sex ones where the increase in population and demand for education made an additional school necessary. This tendency—it could hardly be called a policy—was mainly to be found between about 1925 and 1950, and was even given a little official support in the Hadow Report (1926) and the short-lived Pamphlet No. 1 'The Nation's Schools', issued by the Ministry of Education in 1945. During the last decade, however, the proportion of co-educational secondary (including grammar) schools has been increasing rapidly and in 1968 there were 3,345 mixed compared with 2,231 single-sex schools (Statistics of Education 1968). The grammar schools cannot be separated from the others because of the existence of comprehensive schools, but the trend is to be seen at its strongest in the latter, of which 576 are mixed and 169 single-sex. Recently this tide of change has even reached a few parts of the central stronghold of the single-sex tradition—the public schools.

Though this research has for many years produced results which were favourable to co-education it would be wrong to dismiss the work of the single-sex grammar schools as bad; on the contrary, there was much that was admirable and they established a fine tradition. The findings contained in the two volumes point towards co-education as a means of improving this service to the community. Co-education, however, is not an automatic indication of perfection, and its success will depend, like that of the single-sex schools, on the quality of the men and women serving in such schools.

As with the single-sex type, co-educational schools have their own special problems. Several of these are mentioned in the text, including the need for a reasonable balance between the number of men and women on the staff. A similar problem is occurring with the pupils of some areas in that there is a heavy preponderance of girls in the junior and middle school, arising from a policy of merging boys and girls in a common list in the 11-plus examination or perhaps in some other equivalent instrument of selection. If the examination or its equivalent is weighted too heavily on the verbal side (and if the arithmetic is dominated by the 'mechanical' kind to the virtual exclusion of problem arithmetic), then the girls may gain regularly each year appreciably more than their 50 per cent of places and thus outnumber the boys in the local co-educational school. This is bad for the school and unfair to the boys in so far as the better performance of the girls is probably due partly to their more advanced maturity—a lead which will gradually disappear in the grammar school—and partly to the nature of the examination. Moreover, as the pupils grow older in grammar school and university so the performance of the boys improves in relation to the girls'. In fact in mathematics and the physical sciences boys are soon well in the lead early in their grammar-school life. It might be said that this point should have been reserved for the next volume, in which attainment is to be the main theme, but it is presented here to avoid the delay that would ensue, and also because such an imbalance, if large and continuous, could have an adverse effect on the social life of the school and perhaps (in a more subtle way) on the emotional adjustment of the pupils.

A much more speculative thought is the possible effect of co-educational schooling in reducing the over-aggressive attitudes of the male in the international field. Under Stalin, a few years before the Second World War, the Russians changed from a largely co-educational system of schooling to one which was, where possible, single-sex, because they believed it easier to inculcate a militaristic spirit into their boys in this way. The Nazis also stressed single-sex education for similar reasons. In a world which may depend for its existence on the damping down of aggression this is a topic which is well worth research, however unlikely the theory may seem to some.

The preparation of this book and of the previous volume has been materially assisted at various times by the financial aid of the Department of Education and Science, and by a generous grant from the Leverhulme Trust which enabled the writer to have leave of absence from university teaching and administration for some eight months—including the 'long vacation'. Sincere thanks are extended to both these bodies. Similarly thanks are tendered to those local education authorities, heads, staffs and pupils of schools, principals, staffs and students of Colleges of Education who co-operated so whole-heartedly in the research in spite of their other heavy commitments, and to the members of the advisory committee who gave valuable advice at the start of the Schools project. There is a great debt to be acknowledged to three colleagues, Mr H. Rothera, Mr D. Sharp and Dr P. Miller, who put aside important

3

work of their own in order to give the writer the benefit of their advice on the manuscript.

Finally, thanks are due to my successive research assistants Miss J. MacDonald and Mr G. Lyons for their hard work in the preparation and administration of tests and classification of data; to Dr Patrick Miller for his able assistance with statistics and to Mrs M. Viner for her willing and skilled help in computer programming. Special thanks are due to my secretary, Mrs R. M. Lewis, for her considerable contribution to the preparation of both volumes; her very efficient secretarial work and the insight and accuracy with which she carried out innumerable statistical tests kept the research moving steadily along even when the writer's other duties would otherwise have brought it to a halt.

Earlier versions of Chapters 2, 3, 4, 17 and 18 have appeared in the *British Journal of Educational Psychology* and parts of Chapter 16 in *Occupational Psychology*.

The investigations

The research on which this volume is based is derived from those enquiries which were described fully in Chapter 1 of the first volume of the series.[1] The present chapter repeats in a shortened version the account of the procedures and samples in order to make this book independent of the earlier volume, but some changes are made to bring the chapter more into relevance with the new material. However, those readers who do not wish to bother with these details are urged to turn at once to Chapter 2, where the account of the results begins.

This book examines the attitudes of pupils and ex-pupils towards their lives in co-educational or single-sex secondary schools, including their attitudes towards their fellow-pupils. The most important part of the research is probably that which assesses the reactions to school life of those pupils who had experience in both single-sex and co-educational schools. There is an exploration over a wide field of attitudes, rather than a study of one attitude in depth, a choice deliberately made because it seemed appropriate to a survey of unknown territory. The size of the field dictated the technique of research. Attitude scales, in which a large number of questions are asked on a single attitude, were considered inappropriate because of the number of attitudes investigated. This seemed to call for a questionnaire approach, but some of the virtues of the attitude scale were added by making each question in itself a miniature scale. For example, ex-pupils were asked, 'Was your life in school Very happy/Happy/Jogging along/Rather unhappy/Very unhappy?' and they could choose their answer from any one of these points of a linear scale. Throughout the book these judgments are called estimates. An important addition was that the principal questions were usually followed by a few blank lines on which respondents were invited to state reasons for their answer. These are termed the comments or free responses. They proved to be a rich source of additional information, though time-consuming

[1] Dale, R. R., *Mixed or single-sex school?* Vol. I, Routledge & Kegan Paul, 1969.

in analysis. They deepened the understanding of the estimates made, gave an excellent idea of the reliability and seriousness of the answers and also enabled the respondents to protest against any ambiguity or looseness in the question and to qualify their estimates. The evidence derived from these comments, and also from the estimates, in spite of its limitations, has implications for education which reach far beyond the comparison of co-educational and single-sex schools.

The request for these comments or free responses was a technique common to most of the surveys, and the method by which quotations were selected from them is described now to avoid repetition. For those items regarded as the most important the number of replies selected from each category of comment was kept in proportion to the total for that category, except where this would have produced such a small number of comments that they would have been inadequate to illustrate the argument. The co-educational and single-sex samples were always treated alike unless this procedure gave inadequate illustration to the arguments for single-sex schools. Sometimes, however, selection of comments in proportion to the total was considered unnecessary, the classified Tables themselves having set out the proportions of responses in the various sections and whether they were favourable to co-education or not. The responses were then chosen because of their interest, their humour or their contribution towards an insight into the minds of the pupils. Whatever the procedure is, this is clearly stated to avoid giving a wrong impression. A method considered and rejected was selection of the responses randomly; this would have been more scientific but it would have produced a much less interesting book and almost certainly a less useful one.

Not all the survey procedures are described fully in the following section; those which are of a minor character are given as they arise in the text, and one which affects only one chapter is given in that place. The others are outlined here to avoid the repetition that might have been necessary where the findings of an enquiry are scattered through many chapters. The investigations are divided into those concerning ex-pupils and those concerning pupils, but when they examine the same topic, which is quite frequently, the results are assessed together in the same chapter.

The ex-pupils

The three surveys which come under this heading used as subjects students who were training to be teachers. Before describing each of them in detail it is convenient to mention some important aspects of the samples which are common to all three enquiries.[1]

The use of student-teachers has both advantages and disadvantages. The subjects are adult, interested in education, responsible and have a wider experience of schools than have other ex-pupils of similar age. The use of the same type of persons as representatives of both co-educational and single-sex schools also helps to put the two kinds of school on an equal footing. A further safeguard is that one of the surveys consisted only of ex-pupils who had attended both a co-educational and a single-sex grammar (or technical) school. On the other hand certain disadvantages are present. The student-teachers cannot be said with certainty to represent all types of grammar school ex-pupils, though the differences in attitudes between the co-educated and single-sex educated ex-pupils of the research samples are so marked as to make it seem unlikely that these would disappear or even be reversed if the attitudes of the remainder of the ex-pupils were ascertained. If the student-teacher ex-pupils consider prefects in single-sex schools to be much more officious than those in co-educational schools, it seems highly improbable that the other ex-pupils would find no such difference. Some of these results also receive support from a small-scale investigation among sixth-formers, who are at least a wider cross-section of the ex-pupils than are the student-teachers.

In the previous volume it was shown that the high proportion of co-educational colleges in the Second College survey had no undue influence on the estimates, nor did the college courses in general (including teaching practice) *reverse* the preference of more than a negligible number of students for co-educational or single-sex schools. Though the theoretical preference of an appreciable number of ex-pupils for co-education was *strengthened* by their college experience, this influence is likely to have been much less when the ex-pupils were asked specific questions about their experience in the schools they attended; for example, 'Do you think the school's concern with the out-of-school conduct of the pupils was excessive?' This opinion receives some support from the estimates of those ex-pupils (rather more than half the men and slightly less than half the women) who said their college course had made 'no change' in their attitude. Yet one will await with some interest results obtained from entirely different samples.

We now turn to the description of the surveys. The questionnaires themselves, however, are given in *Appendix 1*.

[1] A more detailed discussion of the samples will be found in *Mixed or single-sex School.'* Vol. I, Chapter I.

(i) *The First College survey*

This was a first, exploratory survey, made to see whether there appeared to be a prima facie case for investigation. As it concerns only Chapter 11 it is described there.

(ii) *The Second College survey*

The Second College survey used a more detailed questionnaire than that of the First College survey, covering a number of the points at issue between the opposing schools of thought. It was sent to those colleges of education and university departments of education that were willing to co-operate, with the request that it should be administered to students in large groups. Sixteen colleges and five departments agreed, and although one college and one department failed to observe the group administration the return of forms was almost 100 per cent. The students were limited to those who had attended secondary grammar or technical or comprehensive schools ; if they had attended such schools for less than one year they were removed from the sample. Almost all had been day pupils and no separate analysis was made for boarders. In order to encourage students to write frankly and to minimize possible external pressure or undue influence, replies were made private and anonymous and directions about this were issued to the questionnaire administrators. Provision was made for those who had attended more than one school of either type. Questions were designed to make a first exploration into such aspects as happiness in school, the state of pupil–teacher relationships, type of school preferred, effect of school life on relations with the opposite sex, attitude to the opposite sex in general, marriage and parenthood, and, for minor reasons, attitude to games and (for women) domestic subjects. As exactly the same questions were asked about the co-educational and the single-sex school the possibility of bias in the questions was reduced. Students were asked to make judgments by means of a five-point scale, e.g. Very happy/Happy/Jogging along/Unhappy/Very unhappy. Requests were also made for free comments in relation to six of the more important questions. The percentage of ex-pupils who selected each value was calculated, and the distributions for co-educated and single-sex educated were compared by the Chi-square test.

For a representative part of the sample, data were secured on parental occupation. Almost 2,000 students participated, scattered throughout England and Wales, so the replies must express opinions about many hundreds of secondary schools (excluding secondary modern). Nine of the colleges were mixed, three were for men and three for women, the proportion of students from mixed colleges being twice those from single-sex colleges. There was no Roman Catholic college and such students are therefore under-represented. The percentage of College of Education students in the sample at 81.7 is only slightly smaller than the 85 per cent in the whole student-teacher population, taking as a basis the number of trainees entering each year.

The written replies again showed that the students had a highly responsible attitude to the investigation. The previous discussion about college samples applies to this inquiry, notably that the college course and experience would not be expected to create any appreciable bias which would influence the comparison between co-educational and single-sex schools, as most of the questions were on the life of the school the students had attended.

(iii) The Third College ('Both schools') survey (1965-6)

The Second College survey suffered from the disadvantage that the great majority of respondents had attended only one type of grammar school. At the time this survey was made the number of students who had been pupils at both a co-educational and a single-sex grammar or technical school would probably have been too small to have formed a satisfactory sample, but the recent re-organization of secondary education has been increasing these numbers appreciably.[1]

As its name implies, this third ('Both schools') survey therefore consisted of an inquiry among ex-pupils who had attended both a mixed and a single-sex secondary school, excluding those from secondary modern schools because in that case other unwanted variables would have been brought into action, such as comparative prestige, equipment, building and staffing. The respondents were students in Colleges of Education, and are not therefore a representative sample of *all* ex-pupils of these schools. We wrote to 169 colleges and received offers of co-operation and completed forms from 71, distributed in random fashion all over England and Wales; of these, 5 were men's colleges (out of 10), 29 were women's colleges (out of 72) and 37 were mixed (out of 88). These figures show no heavy imbalance and for reasons already stated it was not considered necessary to persist until a similar proportion of each type of college was reached. There was, however, through no fault of our own, an under-representation of Catholic colleges (one men's and two women's out of two men's, eight

---

[1] Bilateral and comprehensive schools are included in the sample.

women's and one mixed), and the number of students from each of these colleges was also low (20 in all). This last fact may be due to Catholic families tending to be of lower social class and therefore obtaining a low percentage of grammar school places; another reason may be that Catholic families do not move about the country from one school to another as much as Protestant families. To put the matter into proper perspective, the addition of merely one R.C. women's college—and possibly the mixed for good measure—would correct the slight imbalance. Even if the missing R.C. students were to be appreciably different in their judgments compared with Protestant students (and the differences shown by the 20 in the sample are in fact heavily in favour of mixed schools), the impact of their small numbers on the average 'scores' of the 795 respondents (620 women and 175 men) would indeed be negligible. A corrective factor is that many Catholic students attend non-Catholic colleges.

Colleges were asked to administer the questionnaire (see *Appendix 1*) to the students in large groups under examination conditions, with emphasis on anonymity, privacy and the great importance of the work. To minimize undue influences in any direction the student was asked to place his completed form in an envelope and seal it before handing it in. Most of the colleges observed the request for group administration and returned all the forms completed. A few distributed the forms to individual students and found it administratively too difficult to ensure that each student obtained one and then to collect it when completed. With the many calls on the time of the staff this is understandable and thanks are certainly due for the high degree of co-operation obtained. The number of 'abstentions' is, however, not definitely known, but it would be so small as to have no material effect on the comparison of the two types of school, even if the nature of the replies had been different, and no reason can be given why they should differ. Any 'abstention' would be an abstention from both the mixed and the single-sex school statistics, because the student attended at least one of each.

It will be seen that the first part of the questionnaire (in *Appendix 1*) asks for judgments relating to the co-educational school attended, and the second makes, in most instances, identical requests about the single-sex school attended, the exceptions being questions and statements which were applicable only to a mixed school. If a student had attended two schools of the same type (as well as one of the other) his or her estimates for the two former schools were included, on the principle that the research was assessing schools rather than individuals and the more schools that were assessed the more reliable the results would be. Eighty-four of the 620 women and 27 of the 175 men had attended three schools. Of this sub-sample 45 women had attended two single-sex schools and 39 two co-educational schools, while the corresponding figures for the men were 15 and 12. There is no bias apparent in these figures but there exists the possibility that ex-pupils who had attended three schools might tend to have more severe personality difficulties and, e.g. have a greater incidence of delinquency, than those in the main sample, and that this might have a distorting effect on the results. Though such distortion was considered unlikely in view of (a) the relatively small numbers in the sub-sample, (b) the almost equal proportions who had attended either two single-sex or two co-educational schools, and (c) the usually large differences in opinion which were found in the main sample about the two types of school, the possibility was checked by analysing in detail the replies of the women's sub-sample to six of the principal questions. The analysis compared their replies about single-sex schools with those about co-educational schools, and then compared the results from this sub-sample with those from the main body. The chief feature which emerged from the exercise was the closeness of the verdict of the 'three schools' sub-sample and that of the 'two-schools' (i.e. main) sample, and the continuance in the former of the preference for co-educational schools which is such a feature of the parent sample.[1] If we take this statement as a background, we find in the 'three-schools' sample a *slightly* higher vote on the favourable side, e.g. atmosphere 'very pleasant', for both single-sex and co-educational schools, though the exclusion of the 'three-schools' ex-pupils would have resulted in no change in the findings. The same is true of another slight difference between the two samples—that the 'three schools' group produced more than its proper share of the 'unfavourable' votes, e.g. 'very difficult to make friends' (girls' schools), 'a little difficult to make friends' (co-educational schools), 'atmosphere rather unpleasant' (co-educational schools), 'rather unpleasant' and 'very unpleasant' (girls' schools); the same tendency continued for both girls' and co-educational schools in the replies about happiness—the sub-sample having a slightly greater proportion who were 'rather unhappy' or 'very unhappy'. The numbers involved at this unfavourable end of the scale are, however, so small and the effect is so similar for the two types of schools that the net result on the survey findings is negligible. A reasonable explanation of this trend at the unfavourable end might be as suggested at the outset—that the 'three schools' sample would be likely to contain a

---

[1] The results of the main and sub-samples were almost identical for the item on type of school preferred.

small proportion of pupils who had been compelled to change schools because of their own temperamental difficulties—a larger proportion than in the 'two schools' sample; but the relatively high vote of the 'three schools' sample at the positive end of the scale shows that these pupils with personality difficulties can be only few in number.

We now return to the description of the survey procedure. Examples of the items used are, 'Do you think that the school atmosphere was Very pleasant/Pleasant/Neutral/Rather unpleasant/Very unpleasant?'; 'The prefects were officious'; 'The presence of the opposite sex of pupil had a good influence'; and 'Which did you prefer, the mixed or single-sex school?' A number of the items were deliberately repeated from the Second College survey.

The students were requested, as with the previous questionnaires, to give judgments or estimates on a five- (sometimes seven-) point scale, such as Agree strongly/Agree/Doubtful/Disagree/Disagree strongly, and were frequently asked to comment. They usually gave reasons for their preferences and where necessary stated any reservations. This process brought to notice three faults that had escaped the pilot run, namely that three of the fifty-five questions contained ambiguities; these questions have been discarded. The nature of the free replies again showed a high degree of responsibility among the students.

The variables for which data were obtained were: Type and sex of secondary schools attended (even if more than two), length of attendance, order of schools attended, boarder or day pupil, occupation of parent, sex, age, length of stay at College of Education, and what type of college, and information on the situation of the school playing field. Schools were coded as either 'first' or 'last', those in the middle being classified as 'first' unless the pupil had a year in the sixth form.

The pupils

(i) The Schools project (1964 and 1966)

This research differed from those already described, by using pupils at school as subjects and by the administration of paper and pencil tests of personality as well as a questionnaire. Up to this point the surveys had dealt only with teachers and ex-pupils—apart from several minor inquiries—hence the project sought to assess the experience of the children in the schools. The ex-pupils had the advantage of being more mature and perhaps better able to make judgments and were removed from the immediate pressure of school loyalties, but for the pupils there was no time gap to affect the memory, or further experience (such as in Colleges of Education) to influence the judgment. On the other hand the ex-pupils of the 'Both schools' survey were better able to make their judgments as they had attended both a co-educational and a single-sex school.

The study was longitudinal, testing the same pupils twice, with two years in between the testings. Two regions—the West Riding and South Wales—were chosen by representatives of the department of Education and Science, subject to the local authorities' approval. The Welsh branch of the department and the West Riding Education Authority then selected the grammar schools, endeavouring to match each co-educational school with a boys' and a girls' school for social background. This produced 42 schools, in which objectively selected samples of pupils aged 11 plus and 15 plus were tested during September and October 1964, and again during 1966, in May in Wales, and in September in Yorkshire. The samples consisted of 20 boys and 20 girls of each age (i.e. 80 in all) from every co-educational school, 20 boys of each age from every boys' school and 20 girls of each age from every girls' school, making an initial total of 2,240. (Pupils were selected alphabetically.)

The tests included a questionnaire (see *Appendix 1*) rather similar in type to those used in the previous surveys, but repeating only the key items and endeavouring to obtain assessments in new areas such as pupil–pupil relationships, exploring whether the presence of the opposite sex had any influence on attitudes to school subjects and to schoolwork, comparative attitudes to the opposite sex, comparative prevalence of bullying, and comparative ease of social relations with the opposite sex, etc. Like the ex-pupils, the pupils were asked to make judgments based on a five-point scale, and were given the opportunity to make free responses, but this facility was much extended in the 1966 version of the questionnaire and important questions were added. Only those items which are relevant to the topics of this book are given in *Appendix 1*. Parts of the results of several paper and pencil tests of personality are also omitted from consideration as either irrelevant to the present theme or as not being of sufficient importance.

In the assessment of aspects of school life, about which pupils might either be sensitive or easily affected by open or subtle pressures and therefore fearful of going against accepted loyalties, good administration of tests is essential. To do their best to ensure this the researcher and his assistant travelled to each school in 1964 and 1966 to administer the tests in person, the researcher taking the boys and his assistant the girls. This was designed to ensure standardization of the testing of each sex, but unfortunately the woman assistant had to leave after a year and was succeeded by a man, thus breaking the standardization for the girls. Though this affected both co-educated and single-sex educated girls it could possibly have made it somewhat harder for the latter to admit to their troubles etc., when a man was present, though the presence of men on the staffs of all but one of the girls' schools might have diminished this effect. In the event the atmosphere during the testing was almost invariably excellent, as is shown by the seriousness of the written replies and the quite remarkable regularity of the patterns produced by the results.

One set of 1964 results includes all 42 schools, but the longitudinal survey of the same pupils over the two years, to which reference may occasionally be made, discards not only the leavers and absentees (from both 1964 and 1966 results), but also two sets of the 'tripled' schools. One set was in Yorkshire where the two single-sex schools of the triple became co-educational, causing the exclusion of the corresponding co-educational school; the other was in South Wales where a wrong administrative decision caused a comprehensive co-educational school to be substituted at very short notice because the school originally selected had an inadequate number of pupils of the right age. During the testing at this school several pupils had to be withdrawn from the sample because they could not read sufficiently well and others were obviously doubtful cases. A later examination of the I.Q. scores showed them to be much below the average of any other school, and as it was the only comprehensive school of the 42 it was omitted from the results, with the two single-sex schools tripled with it for social background. This exclusion was equitable on the objective criterion established at the outset— equality of social background, as the proportion of working-class pupils in the co-educational school was definitely greater than that in the relevant single-sex schools.

The study was originally designed as a pilot study, preparatory to the taking of a national sample of schools, and had consequent limitations imposed on it by restrictions of time and money—the sample of 14 schools of each type, ultimately reduced to 12, though useful, is none the less small. The tripling of them for social background helps to allay fears that the three samples might not be on reasonable terms of equality, but recourse must be had to the general pattern of the results from all of the surveys for confirmation or otherwise. It would be foolish not to recognize that there are many different reasons why schools can be good or bad, and the chance inclusion of two or three very bad—or abnormally good— schools in one of the samples could seriously affect the results. The danger, however, was foreseen and can be taken into account in the final weighing up of evidence. What was not foreseen was that several heads, perhaps for administrative convenience, did not adhere sufficiently strictly to the administrative procedure for the selection of the sample, nor ensure that all selected pupils who were present in the school at the time of the more important second testing took the test. Though these faults would be unlikely to have a large effect, especially in a longitudinal research, they gave rise to some uneasiness. Lest this should be misunderstood the writer pays tribute to all the heads for their warm welcome and their forbearance about the upset to school routine.

As the occupational class distribution of the parents of the pupils has a bearing on the results presented in a number of chapters, it is given here. The schools were matched in triples for social background, but this did not quite result in equality of the samples; as shown in Table 1.1 the single-sex schools had a slightly higher occupational class entry in the full 1964 sample. The co-educated girls of the full schools project sample had also a slightly lower intelligence score than the girls from girls' schools (Table 1.2); the average scores of the opposing boys' groups were equal at age 15; the boys from boys' schools had a slight superiority at age 11. In the longitudinal samples the girls in girls' schools retained their lead, but the average scores of the boys from boys' schools and those from co-educational schools were virtually the same.

TABLE 1.1 *Occupational class composition of the schools sample (1964)*[1]

	Occupational class of pupils' parents											
	1		2		3		4		5		Totals*	
	N	%	N	%	N	%	N	%	N	%	N	%
Girls Co-ed. schools	81	14·5	152	27·1	230	41·1	74	13·2	19	3·4	560	100
Girls' schools	90	16·1	143	25·5	241	43·0	56	10·0	25	4·5	560	100
Boys Co-ed. schools	70	12·5	130	23·2	274	49·0	55	9·8	27	4·8	560	100
Boys' schools	74	13·2	164	29·3	249	44·5	47	8·4	20	3·6	560	100

* Includes a few unclassifiable. The analysis is based on occupations and follows the classification used in the Early Leaving Report, viz: class 1 Professional, managerial, executive; class 2 Clerical occupations; class 3 Skilled occupations; class 4 Partly skilled; class 5 Unskilled.

[1] The occupational class distribution of the longitudinal sample is in Table A.1. (i.e. Table 1 in *Appendix 2*).

TABLE 1.2 *Average intelligence scores of the schools sample (1964)** (H.S.P.Q. 'B' factor, maximum 10)

	Co-educational schools	Single-sex schools
Boys—11+	7·09	7·18
15+	7·91	7·90
Girls—11+	6·98	7·29
15+	7·87	8·12

* There are 280 in each of the eight groups. The difference between the co-educated girls and those from girls' schools is statistically significant both at 11 plus and 15 plus.

The scores of the longitudinal samples are in Table A.2. There the differences between the girls' groups are in the same direction but only that at age 13 plus is statistically significant.

(ii) The 'Check' questionnaire (1966)

As some of the early results showed smaller differences between the two girls' groups than those expected from previous work a supplementary investigation was carried out amongst all girls of one relevant age group (i.e. those who were 13 plus in 1966) who had not been included in the original samples. This was partly to test the validity of the project samples from each school. A fifteen-minute questionnaire containing the more important questions and a few additional ones was administered to large groups in each girls' school by a research assistant and in the co-educational schools by the writer. This is given with the other questionnaires in *Appendix 1*. In all there were 1,122 girls from 24 schools, and they provide an additional large sample against which to compare the results from the original inquiry. The occupational class composition of the 'Check' sample was as follows:

TABLE 1.3 *Occupational class composition of the 'Check' sample*

	Occupational class of pupils' parents										
	1		2		3		4		5		
	N	%	N	%	N	%	%	N	%		Totals*
Girls in co-ed. schools	88	19·6	95	21·2	184	41·0	51	11·4	22	4·9	449(100)
Girls in girls' schools	149	22·1	152	22·6	289	42·9	54	8·0	23	3·4	673(100)

* Includes 15 unclassifiable.
NOTE: One of the girls' schools of the project had become co-educational and had to be excluded, together with its 'matched' co-educational school.

The data in Table 1.3 show again that in spite of the tripling of schools for social background there remains a small but definite occupational class advantage to the girls' schools. Though this is too small to have more than a slight effect on the results, various analyses of the data according to the occupational class of the fathers of the respondents show that the direction of this effect will be, if anything, in favour of the single-sex schools.

Various other smaller inquiries provided useful supporting evidence but are not sufficiently important for their procedure to be given here. We now move on to the results, which commence with those appertaining to the happiness or unhappiness of pupils and the pleasantness or otherwise of the school atmosphere. The statistical test used to assess the statistical reliability of the differences found in this and succeeding chapters is always Chi-square unless otherwise stated.

2

Happiness in school:
(a) the estimates

We have all heard of 'The whining schoolboy, . . . creeping like snail Unwillingly to school', but we like to think that such creatures are scarcer now than they were in those far-off days when the lines were written. Our memories of schooldays are strong; most of us would agree with Byron:

> 'The schoolboy spot
> We ne'er forget, though there we are forgot,'

and we would dearly wish our children's schooldays to be happy. What forces, then, act upon a child to make him happy, or unhappy, at school? We have little precise knowledge about this, but we can make a number of shrewd guesses—and perhaps a few doubtful ones. This chapter doesn't attempt to unravel the complexity of the situation, but merely presents the estimates of several large samples of pupils and ex-pupils about the degree of their happiness in co-educational and single-sex grammar schools. Chapter 3 will enlarge the picture by examining the reasons given in the free responses for these estimates of pupil happiness. First in chronological order, comes the Second College survey.

The Second College survey

In the Second College survey some 2,000 student-teachers in Colleges of Education and University Departments of Education answered the question, 'Was your life in school, viewed as a whole, Very happy/Happy/Jogging along/Rather unhappy/Very un-happy?' They were asked to underline the answer which was true for them. The results are in Figure 2.1.

The most noticeable feature is that few of these ex-pupils (who would have been at least fairly successful in school work) were rather unhappy or worse. On inspection there is no practical or statistically significant difference between the proportion of these 'unhappy' individuals in mixed schools and that in single-sex

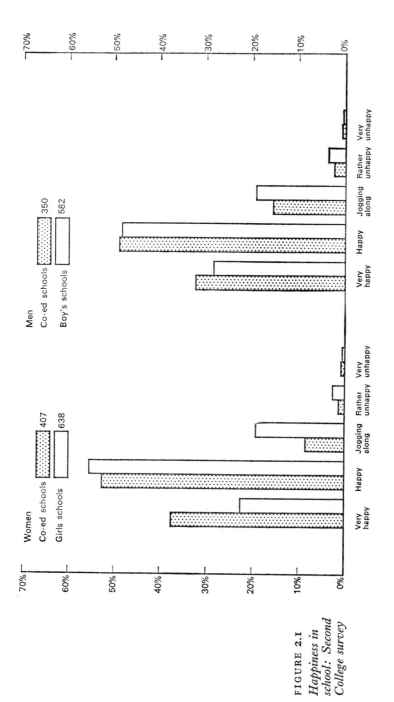

FIGURE 2.1
*Happiness in
school: Second
College survey*

19

schools. On the opposite side, however, there is a decided difference between the co-educated and single-sex educated women, the former being more positively happy when at school than the latter. This greater happiness is to be seen in the 15 per cent superiority in the 'very happy' section and in the 11 per cent fewer who admitted to have been only 'jogging along'.[1] The 3 per cent superiority of ex-pupils of girls' schools in the 'Happy' category redresses the balance only slightly. Though the trend for the men is

TABLE 2.1 *Happiness in school (female ex-pupils)—type of college*
Second College survey

Happiness estimate	Ex-pupils of co-educational schools				Ex-pupils of girls' schools			
	Mixed colleges		Women's colleges		Mixed colleges		Women's colleges	
	N	%	N	%	N	%	N	%
Very happy	89	37.4	49	38.9	93	20·5	30	25.4
Happy	128	53·8	64	50·8	250	55·2	69	58·5
Jogging along	16	6·7	13	10·3	95	21·0	18	15·2
Rather unhappy	4	1·7	0	0	15	3·3	1	0·9
Very unhappy	1	0·4	0	0	0	0	0	0
Totals	238	100	126	100	453	100	118	100

TABLE 2.2 *Happiness in school (male ex-pupils)—type of college*
Second College survey

Happiness estimate	Ex-pupils of co-educational schools				Ex-pupils of boys' schools			
	Mixed colleges		Men's colleges		Mixed colleges		Men's colleges	
	N	%	N	%	N	%	N	%
Very happy	35	24·6	44	38.9	56	23·7	58	29·4
Happy	74	52·2	54	47·8	120	50·8	97	49·2
Jogging along	29	20·4	12	10·6	49	20·8	34	17·3
Rather unhappy	3	2·1	3	2·7	11	4·7	8	4·1
Very unhappy	1	0·7	0	0	0	0	0	0
Totals	142	100	113	100	236	100	197	100

[1] The difference between the women's overall distributions for mixed and girls' schools is statistically highly significant (> ·001).

the same as for the women, the difference between the two men's groups is not statistically significant.

The full discussion of these results is reserved until the end of the chapter, after comparable results from other surveys have been presented, but an important question arises which is best dealt with here. Did the two-to-one preponderance of students from mixed colleges of education help to produce the favourable results for co-education? The answer is given in Tables 2.1 and 2.2.

ANALYSIS BY TYPE OF COLLEGE

In these Tables there is certainly no evidence that the two-to-one ratio of students from mixed compared with single-sex colleges is biasing *this sample* in favour of co-education; curiously enough there is some trend in the opposite direction. The co-educated women who were in women's colleges rated themselves as slightly happier at school than did the co-educated women who were in mixed colleges, and the women educated at girls' schools who were in women's colleges also rated themselves as slightly happier at school than the similarly educated women who were in mixed colleges; as the latter difference is a little greater than the former the net result is a total women's sample which has a negligible built-in bias towards co-education, i.e. a virtual equality. On the other hand the co-educated men in mixed colleges gave estimates of happiness in school which were appreciably lower than the estimates of similar men in men's colleges, and while the men from boys' schools also gave lower estimates when they were in mixed rather than men's colleges, this difference was clearly smaller; the net result here is that the over-representation of mixed colleges resulted in a bias acting *against* co-education in the happiness estimate.

The 'Both Schools' survey

The large-scale survey previously described might be criticized because the students who were giving their estimates about happiness in school had usually experienced only one type of school and therefore could not validly compare the two under consideration. Another survey was therefore made, again with intending teachers because of the great difficulties of getting other representative— and co-operative—samples, but this time the students were those from Colleges of Education only, who had attended both a co-educational and single-sex grammar school; it was called the 'Both schools' survey. There were returns from 71 institutions representative of hundreds of schools (though public schools will probably be under-represented) and in the replies each student was able to compare his or her experience in one or more single-sex and mixed schools. The questions used were often the same as those used in the previous survey but there were many additions. Here we are concerned with the same question on happiness as that asked in the Second College survey.

FEMALE EX-PUPILS

The results for female ex-pupils are presented in Figure 2.2. The order in which the schools were attended was thought to be a variable of importance; the data are therefore divided in accordance with the theory into co-educational first and co-educational last, and the single-sex schools likewise.

The verdict of these students is clear-cut. If for women we combine first and last schools because, surprisingly, there is little difference between them, we find that well over half of the women said they were 'very happy' while co-educated, but only a quarter gave the same estimate for their girls' schools. At both types rather more than a third were 'fairly happy'. Six per cent gave a 'jogging along' estimate for their mixed school, but 20 per cent at their girls' school. Three times as many were unhappy at the girls' than at the mixed school (117 to 38).

MALE EX-PUPILS

The men were equally emphatic, as may be seen in Figure 2.3. If we combine first and last schools more than 9 out of every 10 of the men said they were happy at the mixed school—half of them 'very happy' and half 'fairly happy', but only a quarter of the total said they were 'very happy' in their boys' school and a third estimated 'fairly happy'. In the middle of the scale only 10 out of 186[1] said they were 'jogging along' when co-educated, but nearly 1 in 5 when they were in the boys' schools. At the bottom end, whereas 1 in 27 were unhappy in the mixed schools, this increased to almost a quarter in the boys' schools. A consideration of first and last schools separately shows that this is a variable which needs watching, the last schools receiving higher estimates for the happiness of boys than the first schools (the girls showing little change), but both sexes estimated that they were much happier at the co-educational schools.

---

[1] The number is greater than 175 because a few students had estimates for more than one school of the same type.

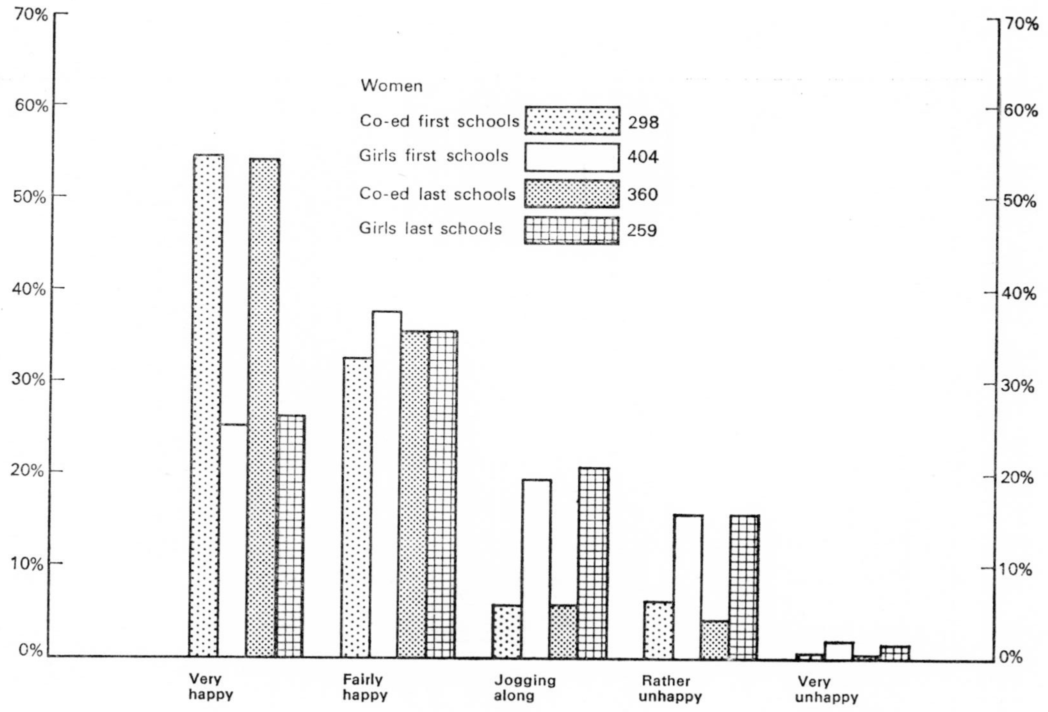
70%
60%
50%
40%
30%
20%
10%
0%
Women
Co-ed first schools 298
Girls first schools 404
Co-ed last schools 360
Girls last schools 259
Very happy
Fairly happy
Jogging along
Rather unhappy
Very unhappy

FIGURE 2.2

Happiness in school (women): 'Both schools' survey

24

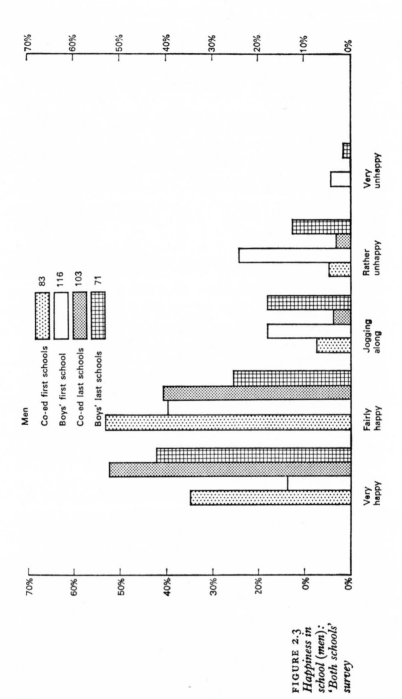

FIGURE 2·3
Happiness in
school (men):
'Both schools'
survey

Social class

In spite of these apparently decisive results it is possible that they could be produced by variables other than those which have so far been under consideration. One of these variables is the social class of the pupils; if one type of school were predominantly upper and the other type predominantly lower class this could produce a difference in the respective estimates of happiness in school. In order to avoid overweighting the text with Tables the full results have been placed in *Appendix 2*, Tables A.3 to A.4. Here it is merely recorded that *in this sample* there is no clear trend associating degrees of happiness with categories of parental occupational class for the female ex-pupils except some tendency for those from classes 3, 4 and 5 in co-educational schools attended last to be a little less happy than ex-pupils from the other occupational classes, manifested by interchange between 'very happy' and 'happy' rather than by any increase of neutral or negative estimates. Co-educated female pupils have a clear lead over those educated in girls' schools, in every class. No occupational class analysis was made of the male ex-pupils' estimates as the sub-divisions of the sample would have been too small.

Things are not always what they seem, and the lack of a clear association between parental occupational class and ex-pupil estimates of happiness at school might be due either to the tendency for these ex-pupils to be moving towards the same class, i.e. the teaching profession, or to the more highly selected nature of the working-class group.

Pleasant situation of school

Another variable which might affect the happiness estimates is the degree of pleasantness of the situation of the school. The respondents were asked, 'Do you agree or disagree with the following statement about your [co-educational/single-sex] school: "Pleasant situation of the school"?' Respondents could choose between, 'Agree strongly/Agree/Doubtful/Disagree/Disagree strongly', as in Table 2.3. The analysis is again limited to the women as their greater numbers give a more dependable result.

Table 2.3 shows that the co-educated women class their schools as slightly more pleasantly situated than do the women educated in girls' schools, but this difference is not statistically significant. It is certainly too small to have produced the large difference in happiness estimates between ex-pupils of co-educational and girls' schools, and may even have been caused by the greater happiness of the co-educated ex-pupils at school causing them to classify

TABLE 2.3 *Pleasantness of school position (women)*

'*Both schools*' survey

Estimates about pleasant situation of school	Replies about co-educational schools				Replies about girls' schools			
	First schools		Last schools		First schools		Last schools	
	N	%	N	%	N	%	N	%
Agree strongly	93	31·0	132	36·7	110	27·2	83	31·9
Agree	134	44·9	168	46·7	165	40·7	124	47·7
Doubtful	43	14·4	39	10·8	66	16·3	26	10·0
Disagree and disagree strongly	29	9·7	21	5·8	64	15·8	27	10·4
Totals	299	100	360	100	405	100	260	100

NOTE: The difference between co-educational and girls' schools is not statistically significant, both for first and last schools: Chi-square, however, is sufficiently high to make further analysis desirable.

the situation of their school buildings in a rather more favourable category. On the other hand there may be a real—though small— overall difference. To test for the possible effect of this the happiness scores were classified within the categories concerning the situation of the school, as in Table A.5 (*Appendix 2*) which also allows for social class, and in Table A.6 which dispenses with the social class breakdown after it had been proved to be unnecessary. A perusal of Tables A.5 and A.6 shows that whatever the category of pleasantness the co-educated pupils were the happier, and that this latter variable was much more powerful than 'pleasantness of situation'.

'*Amalgamated*' schools

The last variable to be examined is a relatively minor one, the existence of a small sub-sample of 'amalgamated' schools among the main sample of co-educational schools. In the first volume of this work these amalgamated schools were consistently shown to be given rather less favourable estimates than those given to the normal co-educational schools, where the boys and girls had grown up in school together. This finding has practical implications for present policy in comprehensive education, as some authorities are planning (or have already commenced) *single-sex* junior high schools and *co-educational* senior high schools, thus creating the problem of suddenly merging classes of adolescent boys with classes of adolescent girls. Whether this less favourable verdict extends to other aspects of social life will be one of the minor themes of this volume (see Chapter 20), and a beginning is made with the estimates for happiness in Table 2.4.

TABLE 2.4 *Happiness of ex-pupils (female): Amalgamated versus remaining 'co-educational last' schools*

Both schools' survey

Estimates of happiness in school	Replies from ex-pupils of amalgamated schools				Replies from ex-pupils of other 'co-educational last' schools			
	About their amalgamated schools		About their girls' schools		About their co-educational schools		About their girls' schools	
	N	%	N	%	N	%	N	%
Very happy	45	48·4	25	26·9	150	56·2	76	24·4
Fairly happy	38	40·9	45	48·4	89	33·3	108	34·8
Jogging along	7	7·5	12	12·9	14	5·2	66	21·2
Rather unhappy	2	2·1	11	11·8	13	4·9	52	16·7
Very unhappy	1	1·1	0	0	1	0·4	9	2·9
Totals	93	100	93	100	267	100	311	100

The data show that the women from amalgamated schools were rather less happy as pupils than were the rest of those who attended a co-educational school last, though the difference is not statistically significant; amusingly enough they were, perhaps by contrast, significantly happier in their girls' school than the rest of the 'girls' school first' sample.

The small sub-sample of men from amalgamated schools were also slightly less happy at school than those who were in normal co-educational schools, but as might be expected from such small numbers the difference was far from statistically significant.

The Schools project

The question on happiness set to the pupils of 42 grammar schools (original 1964 sample) was changed slightly from that set in previous inquiries, the first category of happiness being changed from 'very happy' to 'happy'. This was probably a mistake in judgment as it seemed to make the scale a less sensitive instrument for the samples on whom it was to be used, and might have been anticipated because a principal difference between the co-educated and single-sex educated groups in the surveys already described was in the appreciably higher proportion of the co-educated who endorsed 'very happy' as opposed to 'fairly happy', and some of this distinction between the two groups may have become blurred with the modification of the 'very happy' category to merely 'happy'.

The tables (A.7 to A.10) giving the results about school happiness in the schools project have been placed in *Appendix 2* as their data are so inconclusive, and there is so much other material to be presented. There are two principal ways of looking at the results, one being to regard all eight comparisons as separate entities, and the other to consider the research as four longitudinal studies through time (with only 'before' and 'after' testing).

The first way compares samples of girls from co-educational schools with samples of girls from girls' schools, at the ages of 11, 13, 15 and 17, and correspondingly for boys. None of the differences is statistically significant; six of them give the co-educated pupils as a little happier, one gives the boys' school as slightly happier and one comparison produces virtual equality. In other words the general direction of the difference is in line with the findings of the other surveys but the amount of it is much smaller. The nearest approaches to statistical significance were in favour of co-educated boys aged 11 plus and 13 plus, co-educated girls aged 17 plus, and slightly below the lowest of these, boys aged 17 plus in boys' schools.

Viewed longitudinally there was no major change in any group. Minor ones were that the slightly greater happiness scores of the co-educated 15-year-olds over the group from girls' schools became greater at the age of 17, but it was still not quite statistically significant; also that the virtual equality of the two boys' groups aged 15 changed by the age of 17 into a slight, not statistically significant, lead for those in boys' schools. Analysed in this way no difference can be seen in the effects of the two types of school, but the method has the limitation that it does not allow for any initially greater happiness which a group maintains though does not increase.

It was mentioned in Chapter 1 that the researchers were uneasy about the representativeness of the samples because some heads had not realized how rigidly the administrative instructions for the selection of pupils should be enforced, and that the researchers therefore checked this representativeness by giving the 'Check' questionnaire to the whole of the 13 plus age group, excluding the project pupils of two years previously. It was found that with this much larger group the co-educated girls estimated they were distinctly happier at school than the girls from girls' schools (the

28

results are given in full in the next section). It seems therefore that the project samples of girls aged 11 and 13 were somewhat biased against the co-educational schools compared with the relevant school population aged 13 plus. For practical and financial reasons it was not possible to use the 'Check' questionnaire with the three other groups; they also might have been affected. This illustrates why it is so much better to take an overall view of a number of surveys rather than rely on one.

Yet another factor is the intelligence levels of the opposing groups. In the previous chapter it has been reported that there were statistically significant differences in the average intelligence scores (on a small scale of only ten items) between the co-educated girls of both 11 plus and 15 plus, and the corresponding groups from girls' schools in favour of the latter, and it is presumed that the happiness of pupils would be aided by the ability to master the academic work and reduced by any inability to do so.

The 'Check' survey

In the 'Check' survey, made in 1966 to test the representative nature of the sample in the schools project, all those girls of the 11 plus age group who had not been included in the Schools project sample were asked to complete a short questionnaire which included the question on happiness in school. The results are given in Table 2.5.

TABLE 2.5 *Happiness in school (girls)*

'Check' questionnaire

Estimates of happiness in school	Replies from girls aged 13 plus in			
	Co-ed. schools		Girls' schools	
	N	%	N	%
Happy	234	52·1	291	43·2
Fairly happy	189	42·1	320	47·6
Jogging along	16	3·6	53	7·9
Rather unhappy	8	1·8	9	1·3
Unhappy	2	0·4	0	0
Totals	449	100	673	100

NOTE: The co-educated girls are happier (statistical significance beyond ·01 level).

Readers will see that the difference between the co-educated pupils aged 13 plus and those educated in girls' schools is wider than that for the comparable samples drawn from this age group for the schools project. Whereas the co-educated girls in the Schools project gave happiness estimates that were only marginally better than those of girls in girls' schools, here the difference increases appreciably to become highly significant statistically, bringing it more into line with the findings of the previous surveys. As the 'Check' survey was made with a much larger number of pupils (over 1,100) without the necessity of having pupils selected as a sample of their age group within each school, it is also much more reliable. As it is possible to make only surmises about the reasons for the difference between the two results the matter is pursued no further except to emphasize again a principal theme of the previous volume—that in difficult work of this kind, with so many variables and with the necessity of ensuring that the true results are protected from distortion by the strong emotions sometimes aroused, the only safe procedure is to secure a consensus from a number of surveys, while realizing that an occasional departure from this consensus is not unlikely.

The 'Check' questionnaire was not administered to any other age group of girls, nor was it thought profitable to give it to the boys.

Discussion

As it is the object of these books to present results on many topics and from several surveys, the discussion seeks merely to summarize and to indicate a few major points. It seems that girls in general are happier in co-educational secondary grammar schools than in girls' secondary grammar schools. Bilateral grammar-technical schools would be included, and it is the writer's opinion that the statement would also hold good for secondary modern and secondary comprehensive schools, because of the basic social similarities involved, but this has not been proved. Few girls appear to be 'Rather unhappy' or 'Unhappy' in either type of school, but the major difference appears to be in the higher proportion of girls in co-educational schools who endorse the first category (i.e. 'very happy') in the college surveys.

The two groups of males are closer together, though the 'Both schools' survey, where students had experience of both types of school, shows that they estimated that they were much happier in their co-educational than in their boys' school, even when order of school was held constant.

Certain factors contaminate the sample of normal co-educational grammar schools and reduce their estimates slightly, namely the inclusion of amalgamated and comprehensive schools. The slightly greater pleasantness of situation of the co-educational schools (as estimated by the ex-pupils) may work in the opposite direction.

These factors have, however, been examined and have been shown to be only minor influences.

The reasons the students gave for their opinions will be set out and discussed in the next chapter, but it should be indicated here that although the pupil's happiness is very important, and his possible unhappiness at school perhaps more important than anything, critics could still argue that the price to be paid for happiness could be too great if it were for example at the cost of indiscipline. Others would say that the cost is also too great if the happiness is accompanied by a lower academic standard. The argument about academic attainment has, however, been thrashed out in another place (Dale, 1962a, 1962b and 1964), and the balance of that argument cannot be said to be on the side of the single-sex schools.

3

Happiness in school:
(b) the free responses

In the preceding chapter the estimates of the ex-pupils and
pupils about their happiness in school were examined; in the
present chapter the free responses are added. The estimates give a
reasonable accuracy while the free responses, not as reliable quan-
titatively, produce both greater depth and human colour, remind-
ing us that we are not concerned merely with grey statistical
abstractions, but with living boys and girls who are our children
and other people's children. We seek the greater happiness and
well-being of Jack and Jill and their children after them, though
we would agree that there are other criteria to be kept in mind.

The results of the various surveys will be presented in the same
order as the estimates of Chapter 2, commencing with the Second
College survey.

The Second College survey

The students' estimates showed that co-educated women thought
they were happier at school than did those who were educated at
girls' schools, but we want to know why they were of this opinion.
These reasons were supplied by the free responses which the
students were requested to give after their estimate, and both
men's and women's are included, though as the difference between
the two men's groups was smaller these are less interesting and
they are therefore given less space.

Owing to a lack of clerical assistance the analysis of the free
responses was limited to the first 1,546 respondents whose forms
were returned before a supplementary stage was added to the
inquiry. Slightly less than half of these contained a comment, and
only with the ex-pupils of boys' schools did the proportion rise
slightly above one-half. The answers revealed a difficulty that
had not shown itself in the pilot testing, namely that a few ex-pupils
had trouble in assessing their happiness throughout their secondary
school life because it either fluctuated so much, or was very

different in the lower school compared with the upper. Of the 115 'old girls' of mixed schools who made comments, 13 expressed this difficulty. Of the similar 182 ex-pupils of girls' schools there were 8 who found the lower school happier, and 15 who were discontented with their sixth-form life; on the other hand there were 32 who were happier in the upper school or sixth form. Only a small proportion of these said they had difficulty in making an overall evaluation and none of them failed in fact to give a judgment. The full classification is given in Table 3.1.

TABLE 3.1 *Classified comments on happiness in school*

Second College survey

School education	Male students		Female students	
	Co-ed. (148)	Boys' (230)	Co-ed. (115)	Girls' (182)
Pupil/staff relations happy	25	39	35	22
Pupil/staff relations unsatisfactory	8	19	6	8
Atmosphere good	20	15	26	21
Atmosphere unpleasant	1	1		2
Discipline good			1	2
Discipline too strict		3	1	11
Societies and sports enjoyable	17	31	15	10
Societies too few	3	5		2
Friendships	21	27	23	27
Work enjoyable	10	19	16	10
Work difficulties*	13	22	7	14
Happiness varied	1	5	2	3
Lower school happier		2	2	8
Upper school happier	11	30	5	32
Sixth form discontent		4	4	15
Mixed school happy	4		4	
Personal difficulties		6	2	
Others	24	33	15	23
Totals (of comments)	158	261	164	210

* 'Work difficulties' includes finding school work not interesting or difficult, the pressure of examinations and excessive homework.

The 1,546 completed forms yielded nearly 700 comments (about 800 when classified, because some included two aspects). When these were divided among the four main groups and classified into ten categories of comment, the resulting numbers in the sub-groups were inevitably small. There is also, in spite of precautions, some subjectivity entering into the classification of closely related categories. The Table is, therefore, published not as something conclusive, but as a tentative qualitative illustration of the quantitative results in the previous chapter.

FEMALE EX-PUPILS

If we compare the two groups of female students we find a few clear trends. Those from mixed schools appear, on the whole, to have experienced rather happier relations between pupils and staff than did those who were in girls' schools—though very few of either group said that those relations were unsatisfactory. There may be some measure of support for this in the later comments on the school atmosphere and in those of the previous volume on school discipline, but there may be two opposing views about such a thorny question as discipline. Perhaps the presence of men on the staffs of mixed schools may have influenced these replies, in which case the situation may now be changing somewhat, as more and more girls' schools are appointing a small proportion of men to their staffs. Whatever the reason, we have to record that, whereas four in ten of the comments from women ex-pupils of mixed schools were favourable,[1] the proportion from girls' schools was little more than two in ten; similarly, whereas less than 7 per cent of the comments from the female ex-pupils of mixed schools were adverse, the percentage was 17 from girls' schools. The mixed schools also do better in the comments on work and in the relative lack of sixth-form discontent. It might seem that the girls' schools have an advantage in that a greater proportion of their ex-pupils say they were 'happier in the upper school', but this is merely in apposition to their less happy experience in the lower school; the ex-pupils of mixed schools appear only rarely to experience this variability, or they find the change so slight that they are not impelled to comment.

Female ex-pupils who attended both types

Among the women was a sub-group who had attended both a co-educational and a single-sex secondary grammar (or technical

[1] Combining 'happy staff–pupil relationships', 'good atmosphere', 'good discipline' and 'mixed school happy'. The adverse comments combine the reverse of the above, together with 'sixth-form discontent'.

When these adverse and favourable comments for mixed and single-sex schools are opposed in a 2×2 table, the resulting Chi-square is significant well beyond the ·01 level for girls and beyond the ·025 level for boys.

or comprehensive) school. The comments of this group are important and objectivity of presentation is attained by quoting *all* those which compare the two types of school. First are given those remarks which were in favour of co-education, commencing with several which compared the formality of the girls' school with the informality of the mixed:

'Very happy—mixed; rather unhappy (single-sex). Grammar school tended to be less happy because it was more formal (not due to work).'

'Happy in the single-sex school, but very happy in the co-ed. school where there were no barriers between staff and pupils.'

'Happier in the co-ed. school. The atmosphere was better; not so many petty rules.'

'A very friendly atmosphere in the co-ed. school between all pupils and teachers and pupils.'

'The atmosphere of the school was happier when the school was mixed in my fifth year.'

'In single-sex schools in ... and ... I found the discipline unnecessarily severe and girls class-conscious in the extreme.'

'Happy, mixed; very unhappy, single-sex. Because of lack of organization in school, teaching methods and staff, and stupid attitude towards boys.'

Another woman remarks favourably on the presence of boys—or unfavourably on their absence:

'I preferred the co-ed. school and was far happier than in an all-girl community.'

Of the remainder some merely said they were happier at the mixed school while others gave a variety of reasons:

'Happy on an average. But period spent in co-ed. type was exceptionally happy.'

'Happy in the single-sex, very happy in the co-ed.'

'I liked the work and I liked the companionship of the girls.'(Co-ed. school.)

One woman preferred her girls' school:

'Happier at the single-sex school as [i.e. than] at co-ed. I disliked the headmaster.'

MALE EX-PUPILS

When we compare the comments of the two groups of male ex-pupils (Table 3.1), the most marked difference is in the greater variability of the happiness of boys in boys' schools. One seventh of them were happier in the upper than the lower school; in the mixed schools this proportion was less than one-fourteenth. If the categories of pupil–staff relations, atmosphere, discipline and 'mixed school happy' are combined there is a trend in favour of the mixed school, in line with—but emphasizing—the slight trend shown in the *estimates* of happiness by Figure 2.1. Almost one-third of the boys from mixed schools comment favourably, but only one-fifth of those from boys' schools; again, while about one in eighteen from the mixed schools comment adversely in these sections, the proportion from the boys' schools is one in ten.

Male ex-pupils who attended both types

As with the women, the comments of the sub-group of men, 73 in number, who had experienced both types of school, are especially valuable and *all* those that compare the mixed and single-sex school are given here. The favourable ones concentrate mostly on social relations with the girls and the good 'atmosphere', e.g.:

'The attitude of the whole school (mixed) was different. At the first school (co-ed.—happy) we were still willing to learn. At the second school (single-sex—jogging along) there were not any females.'

'It was only towards the later stages of co-ed. school life that I realized how happy school could be.'

'Although the amount of work done in the co-ed. was not as great as in the single-sex school I think the feeling of looking on the girls as companions in work had a good effect on me and influenced greatly my later dealings and friendships with girls or women.'

'First year at the grammar school (single-sex) was terrible due to the change. Last year at grammar school (single-sex) was tense due to failure at "O" levels. Two years at the comprehensive were great, due perhaps to the ability to assert oneself more fully intellectually.'

'A pleasant atmosphere, especially in the co-ed. school.'

'At the mixed school the tutors seemed personally interested in you as an adult—this was, to some extent, true of my first school (single-sex) but less so.'

[Happy co-ed.; very unhappy single-sex] 'Complete change of atmosphere in single-sex school, unable to re-orientate myself. Lost in the artificial segregation I think.'

There were also a few comments which were either unfavourable or less favourable to the co-educational school:

'First school snobbish co-ed.—poor district. Second school single-sex not snobbish—Borough. Also my father died.'

'I gained greatly from the experience I had in the single-sex school and this stood me in good stead for my 2 years in a co-ed. school.'

'Life at the co-ed. school was made unhappy by a headmaster who should never have had a co-ed. school—he obviously wasn't in agreement with both sides mingling freely together.'

'Very happy applies to single-sex as I was in the sixth and staff–pupil relationship was very good. Happy in co-ed.'

A few critical comments written by men who had attended only one type of grammar school are given in the next section because of their general interest:

Jogging along 'I was only an average scholar and did not really feel connected to the school.' (Co-ed.)

Jogging along 'Seemed an aimless existence because you were merely trophy hunting ("O" levels) with no incentive.' (Co-ed.)

Rather unhappy 'Bullying rife in the school, especially felt in the first three forms, imposed by the 4th, 5th and 6th forms.' (Boys' school)

Jogging along 'The public school is not ideal for the artistic temperament.' (Boys' school)

The comments are informative but the estimates given in the previous chapter are a more reliable guide to the comparative happiness of these men when they were pupils in school. The next results to be considered are those from the 'Both schools' survey, where *all* the pupils who took part had actually attended both a co-educational and a single-sex secondary school (excluding secondary modern).

The 'Both schools' survey

FEMALE EX-PUPILS

Each student in the 'Both schools' survey was requested to make a comment on his or her happiness at the co-educational school and

another about the single-sex school attended. The comments of the
female ex-pupils are classified in Table 3.2, and the totals show at

TABLE 3.2 *Female ex-pupils' comments on happiness*
'*Both schools*' *survey*

Categories of comments, classified according to *estimate*	About co-ed. schools	About girls' schools
FAVOURABLE ESTIMATES ON HAPPINESS*		
Atmosphere: pleasant, free, good school spirit	242	99
(but impersonal, tense, insecure)		(25)*
good because no boys		9
tradition good	3	9
(but overawed first school)	(5)	
good facilities		17
(but not school conscious)		(4)
Staff: friendly	144	67
(but unfriendly)	(6)	(14)
Head good	6	8
(but head feared, bad)	(1)	(7)
discipline good	34	25
(but discipline lax)	(7)	(4)
(but discipline too strict)	(4)	(17)
Pupils: friendly	127	150
(but unfriendly, catty, cliques)	(12)	(26)
(but prefects officious)		(3)
good social life	73	17
(but poor social life)		(9)
good societies	32	12
(but unhealthy attitude to boys)		(5)
boy–girl mixing	115	—
friends from junior school	8	
(but difficulties of settling in)	(25)	(10)
		[*continued*]

To secure objectivity the free responses are classified according to
whether the students underlined a favourable or unfavourable *estimate*.
If the estimate and comment differed in this respect the comment is
classified in brackets, e.g. a student might underline 'happy' and then
comment 'but the atmosphere was too impersonal'; this comment is
placed *in brackets* in the 'favourable' section under 'atmosphere'. Comments made after a 'jogging along' estimate are placed in the 'unfavourable' section. In the *totals* for 'unfavourable' are included those category
totals in brackets in the 'favourable' section, and vice versa.

TABLE 3.2 *(continued) Female ex-pupils' comments on happiness*
'Both schools' survey

Categories of comments, classified according to *estimate*	About co-ed. schools	About girls' schools
FAVOURABLE ESTIMATES ON HAPPINESS		
Work: good standard	17	81
(but poor standard, narrow)	(11)	(2)
enjoyable, education for life	110	2
(but unsuccessful, boring)	(4)	(1)
good boy–girl rivalry, discussion	29	
(but examinations bad, pressure)	(4)	(9)
First school, therefore enjoyed		30
Pleasant surroundings	19	
Sixth especially happy	24	15
Small school liked	19	16
(but disliked)	(3)	
Girls' school better—less self-conscious		7
Girls' school compares unfavourably		(13)
Others	41	19
UNFAVOURABLE ESTIMATES ON HAPPINESS		
Atmosphere: poor school spirit	9	10
(but good tradition, pleasant)		(2)
overawed—first school	3	8
convent school		5
unpleasant, impersonal, tense, insecure		69
poor facilities		7

[continued]

once that the comments give the same picture as the estimates except that the tendencies are more accentuated.

Whereas the students gave 86 per cent of favourable remarks about their co-educational schools, the percentage dropped to 51 for their girls' schools. It made very little difference whether the co-educational school was attended first or last, and the percentage of favourable comments was only a little lower for the girls' schools attended last, compared with those attended first. Sometimes a favourable *estimate* (and perhaps main comment) would be accompanied by a less important unfavourable qualifying clause, usually prefaced by 'but', e.g: 'I loved the school but the building was in a

TABLE 3.2 (*continued*) *Female ex-pupils' comments on happiness*
'*Both schools*' survey

Categories of comments, classified according to *estimate*	About co-ed. schools	About girls' schools
UNFAVOURABLE ESTIMATES ON HAPPINESS		
Staff: unfriendly	10	46
head feared, poor	3	16
discipline too strict	1	32
Pupils: unfriendly, catty, cliques	11	62
(but friendly)	(3)	(13)
wanted boys		4
poor social life		11
unhealthy attitude to boys		9
Work: poor standard	6	
(though good standard)		(5)
examinations bad effect, pressure	2	21
narrow, boring	8	24
unsuccessful	2	2
(but rivalry good)	(1)	
(but enjoyed)	(2)	(7)
Large school: disliked		7
Small school: disliked	3	
Difficult change, settling down	11	17
But co-ed. better		29
Others	15	7
FAVOURABLE	1049 86·3%	610 53·3%
UNFAVOURABLE	166 13·7%	535 46·7%
Totals	1215	1145

shocking state.' Such qualifying clauses are classified in the 'favourable estimates' section but placed in brackets.

As the overall results for the first and last schools are so close together for women, they will be merged for appraisal except where there is any noteworthy divergence. Much of the co-educational advantage is to be found under the heading 'atmosphere', which attracts (on the favourable side) one-fifth of their total comments, and almost no unfavourable ones, while the girls' schools receive far fewer favourable comments under the same heading, and about as many unfavourable as favourable. Other appreciable advantages to the co-educational schools are to be found under the headings 'friendly' and 'unfriendly' staff, and also under 'good social life' and 'good societies'. Under the last two headings the co-educational schools received 105 favourable comments compared with 29 for the girls' schools. Naturally the girls' schools had no counterpart to the 115 comments favouring the mixing of the sexes as in co-educational schools, the nearest being 7 comments favouring girls' schools because the absence of boys makes the girls feel less self-conscious. Perhaps the most dramatic differences are in the 'work' section, where 81 said the girls' schools reached a good standard and only 17 the co-educational schools; on the other hand while only 2 ex-pupils said their girls' schools had enjoyable lessons and educated for life, the co-educational schools received praise in 110 comments for the same topics. As, however, the borderline between these categories is sometimes ill-defined, and the classification subjective, a broad impression is better than these apparently precise numbers. A sound interpretation would be that the ex-pupils of girls' schools tended to stress the good standard of work rather than enjoyment in work, while when reporting on their co-educational schools they stressed the enjoyable nature of the lessons rather than their good standard, but these two qualities will often go hand in hand; it is partly a question of which quality is dominant in the memory of the ex-pupils. In the 'unfavourable' section girls' schools received 21 complaints of overpressure, as against 2 about mixed schools, and 22 complaints about 'narrowness' as against 8 for the mixed.

Though both the co-educational and girls' schools received many comments praising the friendliness of the pupils (127 and 150), the latter had also 62 about unfriendly pupils, compared with 11 from the mixed schools. On the specific point about which kind of school was preferred, including such phrases as 'wanted boys' or 'good because no boys', the co-educational school received an overall total of 46 direct preferences (without including the 115 comments which found boy–girl mixing beneficial), against 18 for the girls' schools. A not insignificant number of ex-pupils found the sixth forms of both types of school to be especially happy.

The usual reminder is given to readers that though an earnest attempt was made to make this classification as objective as possible it must be inferior in this respect to the *estimates* of happiness given by the ex-pupils. As implied at the beginning of the chapter, this is a price which is worth paying for the additional depth, interpretation and colour which the comments give. They also have a watch-dog role as detectors of ambiguities and hidden difficulties in the questions. In these results, however, estimates and comments tell a similar story, except that the latter give an increased emphasis to the unfavourable aspects of girls' schools.

This next section gives a selection of the comments; in each section the favourable ones are given first. *Under each sub-category the proportion of quoted comments to the total for that sub-category is the same for co-educational and single-sex schools, but the proportion quoted is smaller for the larger categories* to avoid overburdening the chapter with quotations. Many of the small sub-categories must necessarily be omitted.

School atmosphere

First let us take that elusive quality said by pupils, staff and even visitors to be the 'atmosphere' of a school, remembering that all the students quoted had attended both co-educational and girls' schools.[1] They speak of their co-educational schools in such terms as the following:

Very happy 'There was an atmosphere in the school of unity. All activities were mixed . . . everyone got on well with each other.'

Very happy 'There were plenty of activities to join in, a friendly atmosphere throughout the school, behaviour on the whole was very good. I just enjoyed going to school.'

Very happy 'Because the social life of the school created a warm atmosphere and made the school a main part of my life, which made the work too more interesting.'

Very happy 'A generally happy atmosphere, an attempt on the part of pupil and teacher alike to make one feel "at home" when new. Also strong element of cheerful competition between sexes.'

Very happy 'The atmosphere was open and friendly with lively discussions in lessons and I used to look forward to going to school every day.'

Very happy 'Happy atmosphere—good teachers and headmaster —friendly children.'

Very happy 'Good young friendly teachers. Enjoyable curriculum. Pleasant surroundings and atmosphere. Active social life connected with school. Variety of school societies and activities.'

[1] Atmosphere is here amalgamated with 'good school spirit'.

Very happy 'The school had happy atmosphere, the staff were co-operative and friendly. The sixth formers were treated well. Many activities.'

The comments on the atmosphere of the girls' schools are much fewer; examples are:

Very happy 'The form was small and so we were all very good friends, we were the top form and on friendly terms with the staff.'

Very happy 'I had a great deal of friends and I boarded so I was with them all the time just like a family.'

Very happy 'It was a small, warm, happy friendly school.'

As there were only a negligible number of criticisms of the atmosphere of the co-educational schools, and these consisted partly of non-typical comments such as being overawed by one's first secondary school, no single comment is as representative as one would like, but the following is quoted:

Rather unhappy 'The atmosphere of the school was hostile.' (In a second co-educational school she was much happier.)

More characteristic of their kind are the quotations from those who criticized the girls' schools:

Rather unhappy 'I hated the petty narrow-mindedness of the women teachers. Most were frustrated old spinsters who wanted us to become the same.'

Rather unhappy 'I found the influence of a rather dictatorial spinster headmistress fermented the atmosphere of the whole school making the staff and pupils tense all the time.'

Rather unhappy 'I found that everyone was narrow-minded and that although I had my own circle of friends I was glad to leave.'

Rather unhappy 'There was a strained feeling among the pupils and the staff. Each trying to out-do the other over trivial things.'

Jogging along 'Rather morbid atmosphere. I had little interest in work.'

Rather unhappy 'The discipline was very strict. Even as a third-year sixth I was marched everywhere and due to the fact that the headmistress was very strict she terrified everyone and the atmosphere was very tense and awful.'

Rather unhappy 'I found the majority of girls giggly over boys and the staff were quarrelsome and catty often in front of the girls. The atmosphere was very wrong.'

Jogging along 'Exam. pressure from school, competitiveness of school. Happy home life, spiteful atmosphere at school—everybody for herself.'

Readers need to be aware that the above strictures present only the pupils' side of the story, and the staffs of girls' schools might argue that a certain amount of discipline is healthy for growing adolescents, even though they sometimes resent it. On the other hand the pupils whose estimates fall into this category seem to have had an experience which goes beyond this and certainly most of them classed themselves as rather unhappy at school—a state of affairs which is without question undesirable. The protagonists of mixed schools would point out that far fewer of the same ex-pupils said they were unhappy at their mixed schools, and though their opponents might reply that the pupils might well be happier because discipline was too lax, the balance of the argument in this sector, after reading the comments and considering the findings of the whole research, would seem to lie with the co-educational schools.

Staff and discipline

The next major category is 'staff', including 'discipline'. Here the co-educational school had 184 favourable references and the girls' schools 100. A twentieth of each total yields a sufficiently representative sample of comments about each type of school, commencing with the co-educational. Readers will notice that the word 'atmosphere' still occurs frequently, and in general this is a marked feature of the comments on the co-educational schools.

Very happy 'There was a happy atmosphere surrounding the school and good pupil–staff and pupil–pupil relationship on the whole.'

Very happy 'A generally happy atmosphere, an attempt on the part of pupil and teacher alike to make one feel "at home" when new.'

Very happy 'The school had a happy atmosphere, the staff more co-operative and friendly.'

Fairly happy 'Happy atmosphere in this fairly new school between staff and pupils, and vice versa. Treated like an equal rather than a pupil.' (Co-ed. school first)

Fairly happy 'General feeling of belonging—sense of team work —meeting people more on a social level.'(Am.)[1]

[1] The comments of pupils from 'amalgamated' schools are distinguished by (Am.).

44

Very happy 'There was a very pleasant atmosphere and the teachers treated you as adults not as children.'

Very happy 'Free and easy atmosphere. Pleasant staff. Able to have varied conversations with both the girls and the boys.'

Fairly happy 'Good-looking maths, physics and P.E. teachers (male, of course). Young history teacher near my age when in sixth form—good parties.'

Very happy 'Communal atmosphere. Very big school—awe inspiring, many out-of-school activities.' (Here we have a not so usual positive attitude to the very large school)

Though some of the comments on the girls' schools are almost identical there are also differences of which a glimpse is given here:

Very happy 'We were good friends and on good terms with the staff. The attitude of staff to pupils was more personal and our school had a character of its own.' (Am. later)

Very happy 'The staff were all very friendly and everyone knew everyone.' (Am. later)

Very happy 'Good headmistress who was respected.'

Fairly happy 'Nice atmosphere. Well disciplined. There could have been more freedom.' (Am. later)

Very happy 'Girls were catered for and not put second to the interests of the boys. There was lots to do and a greater feeling of a community.'

Three of the comments are about schools which were later amalgamated with boys' schools; one notes also the references to 'well-disciplined' and the complaint that sometimes the interests of the girls are subordinated to those of the boys in a co-educational school. These points were brought to the readers' attention in the first volume of this work.

On the unfavourable side the students made 33 adverse comments about the staff or discipline of their co-educational schools and 135 about their girls' schools. The former are a mixed but amusing collection, of which three are quoted:

Very unhappy 'My father sacked the husband of the mistress who took two subjects and made my life pure hell.'

Rather unhappy 'Disrespect of women teachers by the boys.'

Jogging along 'Because I was in a single-sex school for 6 years and my year in upper sixth when two single-sex schools joined under new headship. Most problems were hardly dealt with, never

45

reviewed, no unity amongst staff—two staffs joined together, each favouring former positions. As school captain I found only three members of staff helpful.' (Am.)

The same proportion of comments is quoted about the girls' schools:

Jogging along 'Most of the staff were old unmarried women and weren't in touch with our generation.'

Jogging along 'I did not like the stiff formal relationship between the staff and pupils.'

Rather unhappy 'At first I tried to like the school and got on quite well, but as time progressed the pettiness of the rules and aloofness of the staff got me more and more irritated.'

Rather unhappy 'Unpleasant headmistress.'

Rather unhappy 'I disliked the atmosphere created by staff of middle-aged spinsters.'

Jogging along 'I didn't like boarding, didn't like so many females, didn't like the snobbery and rigid discipline of the place.'

Jogging along 'At the time it wasn't bad, but when I look back now I don't know how I could have stood it for five years.'

Very unhappy 'It was run by narrow-minded nuns.'

Rather unhappy 'I arrived in time to be thrown into a gigantic pre-G.C.E.-pushing campaign in a vast anonymous building with a vast anonymous staff and collection of girls.'

Rather unhappy 'Far too strict and impersonal.'

Fairly happy 'The dominance of the headmistress tended to make life a little unpleasant.'

Rather unhappy 'The atmosphere was extremely authoritarian.'

Very unhappy '. . . didn't get on with teachers who made life unpleasant, also discipline far too strict.'

Pupil relationships

In the consideration of the section on pupil relationship there is a logical amalgamation of the sub-categories 'friendly pupils', 'good social life' and 'good societies', producing 235 comments favourable to the co-educational schools and 192 for the girls' schools, after omitting from present consideration the '115 plus' comments

46

welcoming the presence of boys. Examples of those praising the co-educational schools are:

Fairly happy 'The first year was very difficult—I found the boys most uncouth and they thought me peculiar. The second year we understood each other and I was extremely happy.'

Very happy 'Got on well with fellow students, more social life, few school rules and restrictions.'

Very happy 'I found a happier and a more easy-going relationship between the pupils themselves and the teacher–pupil relationship.'

Very happy 'There were plenty of activities to join in, a friendly atmosphere throughout the school, behaviour on the whole was very good. I just enjoyed going to school.'

Very happy 'Because there was a good friendly atmosphere between pupils and I did pretty well academically.'

Very happy 'Very pleasant relationship existed between staff and pupils in almost every case.'

In this category the girls' schools are not at such a disadvantage (apart from the postponed sub-category of boy–girl mixing), and typical favourable remarks were:

Fairly happy 'I found it easy to make friends and became less timid because I could talk freely to the girls.'

Very happy 'I had a lot of friends at this school and my work improved beyond recognition. I gained places of responsibility.'

Fairly happy 'There was a happy spirit among members of classes.'

Very happy 'Most people were very friendly to each other and there was no unpleasantness.'

Fairly happy 'The girls were very friendly when I first went there and welcomed me in the school and this impression has always remained.'

By no means all the students had happy experiences at school, and although those who complained were a minority, their remarks can sharpen our insight into conditions that create difficulties.
Criticisms of the co-educational schools were:

Jogging along 'I felt an outsider a lot of the time as many of the pupils had known each other from their infant school days. Also I felt bored.'

47

Rather unhappy 'I was made unhappy by other girls being jealous of me going out with a popular boy. Except for that I was very happy.' (Am.)

Jogging along 'Suddenly confronted with half a class of boys—took time to fit in properly.'

The following are typical of the unfavourable comments about pupil relationships in the girls' schools. The first complaint is common to both girls' and co-educational schools:

Rather unhappy 'Entered at 17 in 6th form with girls who had been in the school for 10 years, was never really accepted.'

Rather unhappy 'Girls tended to be jealous and catty—I was smaller than the rest and got the butt of everything.'

Jogging along 'I felt rather insignificant and never seemed to excel in any field. Also the social side of school life left much to be desired, one never felt an integral part of the school.'

Very unhappy 'I had to leave because I was unhappy. This was partly because I was too timid, weak and sensitive. They called me a snob but it was really their inverted snobbery and I took it to heart. I was surprised that they were so affectionate when I left.'

Rather unhappy 'I found the girls tended to be rather catty and unfriendly. They all split up into small groups very soon and it just happened that I was the one who was left out.'

Rather unhappy 'Something awful happened to girls when they were altogether—spiteful, etc.'

Very unhappy 'I didn't like the all-female staff of teachers, nor did I like the all-female pupils.'

A few quotations are added from the 115 remarks about the benefits of boy–girl mixing:

Very happy 'I then felt more comfortable with members of the opposite sex and gained more confidence in their presence in out-of-school hours.'

Very happy 'Appreciated the view of the opposite sex and the stimulus it gave in work and socially.'

Very happy 'Being small it was a close community. Boys and girls were at ease together and this diminished adolescent shyness of the opposite sex.'

Very happy 'I prefer to be in mixed, rather than one-sexed, company. This situation seems right to me, it is more like real life.'

Very happy 'I found the early years of secondary education spent in a co-ed. were interesting and exciting. I enjoyed the many different activities in which both sexes took part.'

Work

The last major group of comments to be examined is that devoted to academic work. Here the co-educated have an advantage only because of the large number of ex-pupils of these schools who said they *enjoyed* their school work, and regarded it as an education for life. As mentioned previously, it is interesting that the comments on the girls' schools emphasize the good standard of work, with very little about enjoyment of it, while those on the co-educational schools have a smaller number on the good standard and a much larger number on the enjoyment. Though this general analysis holds good it should not be exaggerated because the enjoyment comments quite often imply a good standard, and the comments which emphasize the good standard sometimes imply enjoyment:

Very happy 'Friendly atmosphere. School completely united. Gentle rivalry between girls and boys stimulated work.'

Very happy 'Strong element of cheerful competition between the sexes.'

Very happy 'I felt secure in a natural surrounding and worked happily, feeling that I was benefiting from the full life this gave me.'

Very happy 'Good, young, friendly teachers. Enjoyable curriculum . . .'

Very happy 'Modern buildings. Rural area quite close to the sea. Was able to acquire good educational standard.'

Very happy 'I enjoyed school life. The mixing of boys and girls made it more enjoyable. Our outlook on life became broader. The staff were good teachers.' (Am.)

Fairly happy 'Most teachers good. Standard improved especially in subjects I liked. Probably liked it better because achieved better results.'

The following comments were about the girls' schools:

Fairly happy 'Worked hard; no distractions from opposite sex.'

Very happy 'There was not the embarrassment resulting from

49

mistakes in lessons etc. which would have been present with boys attending.'

Fairly happy 'I made friends fairly easily and work never troubled me unduly, I enjoyed it as a contrast to strict home.'

Fairly happy 'Able to concentrate on work without boys fighting or making a row.'

Fairly happy 'I enjoyed school work and out-of-school activities.'

Now we examine the *unfavourable* comments on work, taking first as usual those about the co-educational schools. There were 37 of these in all, compared with 59 about the girls' schools, giving a ratio of roughly 3 to 5. Here we see the other side of the coin:

Fairly happy 'Although I enjoyed life in general more at the co-educational school, there was not the same working atmosphere there and I realized that my work was suffering.'

Rather unhappy 'I was studying science and I had the impression that it was wrong for a girl to do science subjects for "A" level G.C.E.' (Co-ed. last two years)

Fairly happy 'The atmosphere in the classroom was sometimes disturbed by the boys fooling about. Didn't seem to get on with the lessons as in a single-sex school.' (Co-ed. first year only)

The unfavourable comments on the work in the girls' schools are more often about strain, examinations and narrowness of outlook, e.g.:

Jogging along 'Finicky school rules, anxiety about exams.'

Fairly happy 'Pressure of work brought tension.' (Girls' school first five years)

Rather unhappy 'I spent two years in (1) and these were rather unpleasant; the work was hard and had little relief.'

Fairly happy 'Many of the lessons were uninteresting.'

Jogging along 'I had a limited circle of friends. There was little stimulus to work (I was in a third stream). Few after-school activities—bar games as in lunch hours.'

Direct comparisons

Perhaps the most interesting section is the one which follows, where ex-pupils have, without being requested to do so, compared the two types of school they attended. As the total yield of such quotations would have overburdened the chapter and to have given a selection would not have been sufficiently objective, recourse was had to publishing *all* those direct comparison quotations which appeared in the first twenty colleges, as coded, the others being unseen. First are given the comments based on the students' co-educational schools:

ABOUT CO-EDUCATIONAL SCHOOLS

Atmosphere

Very happy (Co-ed. first) 'The atmosphere was much easier, the pupil teacher relationship was friendlier. You didn't feel awkward when you met boys of your own age.'

Fairly happy (Co-ed. last) 'But atmosphere tended to be far freer than in single-sex school.'

Very happy (Co-ed. last) 'The whole atmosphere of the school was completely different from that in the single-sex school, probably because the headmaster's study was accessible if we had a problem—it was not a Mount Olympus as in the single-sex school.'

Fairly happy 'Enjoyed the work. Atmosphere more liberal in co-ed. school. Wider curriculum.' (Am.)

Staff–pupil relationships

Very happy (Co-ed. last) 'More life in general than single-sex school. More easy-going.'

Fairly happy (Co-ed. last) 'The atmosphere seemed a lot easier between members of staff, and staff and pupils. The discipline was not so strict and petty.'

Very happy (Co-ed. last) 'People much more friendly both pupils and teachers—atmosphere much more relaxed.'

Very happy (Co-ed. last) 'There was a much happier atmosphere among the children and also the staff. The staff seemed more helpful.'

Very happy (Co-ed. last) 'More freedom than in single-sex school. Better relations with the staff who taught me.' (Am.)

Very happy (Co-ed. last) 'Good atmosphere, the pupils and staff more friendly. It was *so* different to my previous school.' (Which was girls' boarding)

51

Happiness in school: (b) the free responses

Very happy (Co-ed. last) 'Because although being teased by male section after having been at girls' school the acceptance of you as a person was genuine, also easy relations with all staff. Enjoyed male company.'

Very happy (Co-ed. last) 'The whole atmosphere was happier. There was more friendly contact between staff and pupils. The rules were less rigid.'

Fairly happy (Co-ed. last) 'I found it difficult to become used to the different atmosphere around and people were not so friendly.'

Very unhappy (Co-ed. last) 'Very unhappy to begin with because of change from strict high school. Things improved in sixth form.'

Pupil relationships

Very happy (Co-ed. last) 'I felt it easier to talk to men and boys after my school became co-ed. than before. As a single-sex school I got used to mixing with girls only and felt shy when I had to speak to boys out of school.' (Am.)

Very happy (Co-ed. last) 'I felt that I fitted in better.'

Very happy (Co-ed. first) 'The classroom atmosphere was more relaxed, not so dictatorial. The inter-pupil relationship was more easy-going, not clique forming.'

Very happy (Co-ed. last) 'Healthier, more social atmosphere.' (Am.)

Fairly happy (Co-ed. first) 'The fact that it was a co-ed. school I think made the staff more broad-minded and our social life was more varied.'

Very happy (Co-ed. last) 'Boys and girls mixed easily. Previously the only conversation was about boys.' (Co-ed. boarder)

Fairly happy (Co-ed. last) 'We amalgamated at the beginning of the 5th year—the boys were a rather bad addition—we were much happier without them.' (Am.)

Fairly happy (Co-ed. last) 'Opportunities for viewpoints from opposite sex. A more natural relationship with opposite sex. Advantage of mixed staff.' (Co-ed. boarder)

Fairly happy (Co-ed. first) 'I found that the boys in my co-ed. school tended to be immature and foolish and that as a result the girls had a difficult time.'

ABOUT GIRLS' SCHOOLS

Next are given the direct-comparison comments which are based on the girls' schools:

Atmosphere

Jogging along (Single-sex last) 'I went into the girls' school from the free atmosphere of a co-ed. and found it difficult to adjust. Also, most of the girls had by that time made their friends.'

Very happy (Single-sex last) 'Happy friendly atmosphere. Girls more passive. School quieter than co-ed.'

Rather unhappy (Single-sex last) 'It was a big change to go to a single-sex school after a co-ed. I found it easy to adapt to this, but the whole atmosphere was entirely different.'

Rather unhappy 'I always wanted to return to my co-ed. school.'

Staff–pupil relationship

Fairly happy (Single-sex first) 'The school was all right, although I found the rules much stricter, and the headmistress was one to be feared, not a friend.'

Rather unhappy (Single-sex last) 'After the co-ed. I felt somewhat inhibited and frustrated in a single-sex school.'

Very happy (Single-sex last) 'More individual attention, nicer company, better discipline.'

Rather unhappy (Single-sex last) 'It seemed old-fashioned and narrow after my co-ed. school.'

Fairly happy (Single-sex first) 'Security amongst own sex. Staff very understanding with girls.'

Pupil relationships

Jogging along (Single-sex last) 'Very good friendships but school itself not as happy.'

Fairly happy (Single-sex last) 'In comparison with the previous school (co-ed.) greater tendency to group together—not such a free or pleasant atmosphere: influence of more male staff would have perhaps eased a certain amount of ill-feeling between girls.'

Very happy (Single-sex first) 'Lessons uncomplicated though perhaps not as light-hearted. Much wastage of time when boys present except when offering a different side in discussion.'

Happiness in school: (b) the free responses

Very happy (Single-sex first) 'I was popular in my form, always near the top of the class (brains not being looked down upon in this school). The school was interested in developing whatever talents one had and did not concentrate solely on sport.'

MALE EX-PUPILS

The comments made by the male ex-pupils are presented in Table 3.3, divided into 'favourable' and 'unfavourable' sections according to the *estimates* students gave in answer to this item.

As with the estimates by far the greater number of free responses or comments were favourable with reference to the co-educational schools, but those about boys' schools were approximately equally divided between favourable and unfavourable. Judging by the totals in the different categories, the happiness of the pupils depended much more on personal relationships than on academic work or any other factor, though one presumes that if the standard of work had been clearly unsatisfactory there would have been more pronouncements under this heading. In most major categories the co-educational schools got roughly twice as many favourable mentions as the boys' schools, e.g. 'pleasant atmosphere', 'friendly staff', 'enjoyable socially', and, not so marked a difference, 'friendly pupils'. There is one favourable category on the co-educational side—the mixing of the sexes, with 39 direct mentions, to which the boys' school has no reply. Only in the section labelled 'work' is there a major sub-heading ('good standard') where the boys' schools, at first glance, come off best, though even this is dubious if we look more closely, as under two similar sub-headings, 'enjoyable work' and 'successful in work' the co-educational schools receive 30 mentions without anything to balance it on the boys' school side.

The unfavourable comments are scattered in small numbers throughout the range of categories, with those about the boys' schools being more than three times as numerous as those about the co-educational schools. The largest categories are the 24 mentions of 'poor atmosphere' in boys' schools, 12 of unfriendly staff, 12 of too strict discipline, 10 of unfriendly pupils, and 9 of bullying. Worthy of mention in the light of present trends are the 11 complaints that over-long travel prevented the writers from being happy at school.

Some direct comparisons are given but they are curtailed more rigorously than for the women, where the need for illustration was stronger. To preserve impartiality these comments are selected in proportion to the 'favourable' and 'unfavourable' totals for the two types of school in Table 3.3, using a factor of 30. They are too few for classification.

TABLE 3.3 *Male ex-pupils' comments on happiness*

'*Both schools*' *survey*

Categories of comments, classified according to *estimate*		About co-ed. schools	About boys' schools
FAVOURABLE ESTIMATES*			
Atmosphere:	pleasant	55	25
	(though poor, unpleasant)		(4)
	good school spirit	18	3
	(but disliked being first school)		(3)
	(but disliked mixed sexes)	(2)	—
Facilities:	good	2	12
	(but poorer)		(1)
Staff:	friendly	48	22
	(except women)	(3)	
	(but some not)	(2)	(1)
	head good	5	
	(but head poor)	(2)	
	discipline good	15	4
	(but too lax)	(4)	(1)
	(but too strict)	(1)	(1)
Pupils:	friendly	58	36
	(but unfriendly or bullying)	(3)	(4)
	enjoyable socially	19	10
	good societies	5	
	mixing both sexes	39	
	(but shy because girls)	(1)	
Work:	good standard	12	16
	(but narrow or poor)	(4)	(1)
	enjoyable	18	
	(though travel nuisance)		(2)
	successful in	12	
	(unsuccessful, boring)	(1)	(1)
Pleasant surroundings		6	
Though first year strange		6	
Mixed school happier		3	(1)
Boys' school happier			4
Sixth especially happy		7	8
First secondary—enjoyed			6
Others		20	11

TABLE 3.3 (*continued*) *Male ex-pupils' comments on happiness*

Categories of comments, classified according to *estimate*		About co-ed. schools	About boys' schools
UNFAVOURABLE ESTIMATES*			
Atmosphere:	poor	1	24
	not school conscious	0	1
	(but facilities good)		(2)
Staff:	unfriendly	2	12
	(but friendly)		(2)
	discipline too strict	1	12
	discipline too lax	2	2
Pupils:	unfriendly	2	10
	(but friendly)	(1)	(5)
	bullying	1	9
	snobbish		2
	disliked mixed sexes	1	
	wanted mixed sexes		3
	poor socially		2
Work:	poor standard, boring	3	11
	(but good)		(1)
	narrow	1	6
Sports, etc. over-worshipped			2
Travel:	too far	4	5
Disliked school			3
Mixed school happier			11
Others		6	10
FAVOURABLE		349	167
		88·1%	53·5%
UNFAVOURABLE		47	145
		11·9%	46·5%
Totals		396	312

* Unfavourable includes all comments accompanied by a 'jogging along' estimate or worse, and all comments in brackets in the 'favourable' section. Vice versa for favourable comments.

About co-educational schools

Very happy 'The presence of the opposite sex aided one's social maturity as well as adding colour to the school surroundings.'

Very happy 'The staff–pupil relationship was excellent. They did not set themselves on a pedestal they were easily approachable.'

Very happy 'It was such a change from the single-sex school that I began to enjoy school. Before I had been in a bit of a rut.'

Very happy 'Having been at a very severe and old-fashioned boys' boarding school, the opportunity of working in relative freedom, and mixing with girls, and at the same time being a day-boy, made life much happier.'

Fairly happy 'Previous to single-sex grammar school I had been at a co-ed. secondary modern school. I was glad to return to the freer atmosphere of the co-ed. school system.'

Very happy 'Very friendly atmosphere—a body of people rather than a factory—good staff–pupil relationship.'

Very happy 'We were treated as grown-up in a combined community preparing for later life which would be shared between the sexes.'

Fairly happy 'Lessons seemed to become less stern and more beneficial.'

Fairly happy 'I had friends, the atmosphere of the school was free, and staff was interested in one as people. First years were not treated as an unfortunate necessity.'

Fairly happy 'Seemed to get on well with the other pupils; had a bit more security as older brother also there. There always seemed something to look forward to.'

Very happy 'Excellent preparation in social life, informal atmosphere, high standard of teaching, many great friends in both sexes, wide choice of subjects, excellent headmaster.'

Very happy 'A very happy atmosphere pervaded the school, social life was full and varied and in general there was a good relationship with staff.'

Comments unfavourable to the co-educational schools are few when kept to the same proportion.

Rather unhappy 'Masters not liking the change, new head, lack of school discipline.' (Am.)

Rather unhappy 'Distance involved in travelling, too many female teachers, dislike of mixing with girls.'

About boys' schools

Fairly happy 'Close unit of friends. Also lack of girls was not missed as it had not been experienced.'

Very happy 'The relationship between boys and boys, and boys and staff was excellent.'

Very happy 'School life ran freely and making lasting friends was very easy.'

Very happy 'You always have much more fun with people of the same sex and age groups.'

Fairly happy 'There was a tremendous atmosphere in the school and harmony.'

Very happy 'The school had a friendly, pleasant, personal atmosphere.'

The other side of the coin is to be seen in the following:

Very unhappy 'An unfriendly and unco-operative staff who ran the school in an almost military fashion, led by the headmaster.'

Rather unhappy 'General attitude of fear towards authority (military type staff) and rebellion.'

Rather unhappy 'Didn't like the single sex idea. Games, house-master, C.C.F. Boarders were highly *privileged*! One of the masters was a homosexual. Proved.' (Boarding) [This is only what the young man wrote, and the writer cannot vouch for its truth]

Rather unhappy 'Hated the change from co-ed. to single-sex— apathetic attitude of pupils—homosexuality in sixth form rife— indifferent teachers.' [Comment as previously]

Rather unhappy 'A lot of bullying, prefects tended to be little Hitlers enjoying power, corporal punishment.'

It is difficult to ensure that such a collection of quotations, even when selected in the correct general proportions, are sufficiently characteristic. Undoubtedly co-educational pupils tend towards praise because of the pleasant 'atmosphere', friendly staff–student relationships, and the presence of the opposite sex, while boys from boys' schools like the friendship and the boy–master relationship when at its best. Whenever co-educational schools are criticized there is a tendency for this to be centred on lack of firm enough discipline, with an occasional comment expressing a preference for the company of the male sex alone. Criticism of boys' schools centres on severity of discipline and the abuses that go with it; the mention of homosexuality is usually in connection with boarding schools and is only occasional.

The Schools project

Though the free responses of the pupils about their happiness at school have been obtained and classified their inclusion would add little that is new to what has already been written. The 'Check' questionnaire did not invite free responses as the time available was inadequate.

4

School atmosphere

The atmosphere of a school is something difficult to define but powerfully felt. Perhaps the word which comes nearest is 'tone'; this, however, seems to have slight overtones of orderliness maintained by the staff, though not with much difficulty. A 'pleasant atmosphere' or 'good atmosphere' seems to go a step further and imply that staff and pupils are a happy co-operative community working and playing together. No such community is without its blemishes—the disliked member of staff, the difficult pupils, the awkward situations that arise from day to day—but the pleasantness of the atmosphere makes them small in significance and quickly forgotten, with no sense of harshness or injustice lingering afterwards. Such a state is obtained only by a finely balanced poise between the discipline that is too consciously imposed and if increased degenerates too easily into authoritarian harshness, and the undue permissiveness or lack of leadership which fails to secure willing pupil co-operation and causes the school to decline quickly into a state of indiscipline.

A good atmosphere is the hallmark of a good school. A poor one may be the result of staff severity or of lack of leadership and control, though occasionally the nature of the neighbourhood may make the task one for strong angels rather than mere mortals. What then do our ex-pupils and pupils say about the atmosphere in their co-educational and single-sex grammar schools? The results of the surveys will be presented in the same order as in the two previous chapters.

The Second College survey

Almost 2,000 students who were training to be teachers were asked, 'Do you think the school atmosphere was Very pleasant/Pleasant/ Neutral/Rather unpleasant/Very unpleasant?' There was no provision for comment, because the questionnaire was already long. The results are given in Table 4.1.

Few pupils in either kind of school found the atmosphere to be 'rather unpleasant' or worse. Both men and women from co-

TABLE 4.1 *School atmosphere*

Second College survey

Estimates of school atmosphere	Replies from male ex-pupils of				Replies from female ex-pupils of			
	Co-educational schools		Boys' schools		Co-educational schools		Girls' schools	
	N	%	N	%	N	%	N	%
Very pleasant	95	27·2	114	19·5	135	33·2	94	14·7
Pleasant	175	50·1	324	55·2	224	55·1	365	57·0
Neutral	67	19·2	114	19·5	42	10·3	140	21·9
Rather unpleasant	10	2·9	33	5·6	5	1·2	37	5·8
Very unpleasant	2	0·6	1	0·2	1	0·2	4	0·6
Totals	349	100	586	100	407	100	640	100

NOTE: The differences between the men's estimates for co-educational schools and boys' schools are statistically significant at ·025 level.

The differences between the women's estimates for co-educational schools and girls' schools are statistically significant well beyond the ·001 level.

educational schools considered it to be more pleasant than did those from single-sex schools, the difference between the two women's groups being much greater than that between the men's groups. Just over one in a hundred of the co-educated women judged the school atmosphere to be 'rather unpleasant', whereas the proportion for women from girls' schools was one in seventeen. It is, however, on the positive side that the chief difference lies; whereas one-third of the girls from mixed schools assessed the school atmosphere as 'very pleasant' only one-seventh of those from girls' schools were as enthusiastic. Whereas a tenth of the co-educated girls evaluated the atmosphere as 'neutral', more than a fifth of the opposite group registered the same assessment. It must be understood that one is here merely reporting results and that these can have various interpretations. Those women who are teaching in girls' schools and are devoted to their profession may understandably feel hurt and misjudged when they read these figures, but unnecessarily so for several reasons. First, because research may reveal other aspects in which girls' schools are superior; second, because we are dealing with averages and there are certainly good girls' schools and poor mixed schools as well as vice versa; third, because the nature of the results may be due mostly to the fact hat a mixed staff and mixed pupils in themselves produce a better atmosphere—and it may be that no woman teaching in a girls' school could prevent this difference arising.

The difference between the co-educated men and those from boys' schools is to be found mostly in the 'very pleasant' and 'pleasant' categories, the former group having nearly 8 per cent more estimating 'very pleasant', though they had 5 per cent fewer estimating 'pleasant'. Rather fewer of those from co-educational schools judged they were rather unhappy or worse than did those from boys' schools.

Let us now look at the estimates of those students in the Second College survey who attended both types of school. Although there were more than 70 women in the group data is available for only 30 owing to lack of clarity in the instructions, but as their special experience is important their results are given in Table 4.2.

TABLE 4.2 *School atmosphere (women): Ex-pupils with experience of both types*

Second College survey

Estimates of ex-pupils who had attended both types	Replies from female ex-pupils about their:	
	Co-educational schools	Girls' schools
	N	N
Very pleasant	15	6
Pleasant	11	7
Neutral	3	11
Rather unpleasant	0	2
Very unpleasant	1	2
Totals	30*	28

NOTE: The difference between the two groups is statistically significant by the Wilcoxon Sign-Rank test for matched pairs.
* Two students each gave estimates for two co-educational schools.

This small group of women thought the atmosphere of their co-educational schools pleasanter than that of their girls' schools, a difference which is statistically significant. It should be noticed that the difference is considerable and, although the numbers are small it is in the same direction as that seen in the large parent sample. The men's sample was too small to be quoted.

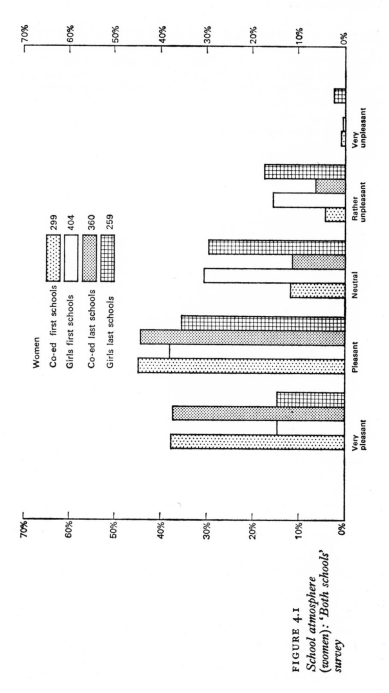

FIGURE 4.1
*School atmosphere
(women): 'Both schools'
survey*

63

The 'Both schools' survey

The next survey to be examined is the 'Both schools' survey (Figure 4.1). Readers will recollect that in order to make sure that the results were not swayed unduly by the order in which the schools were attended (especially as 58 per cent of the women attended a co-educational school last), this influence was removed by classifying the results into ex-pupils who attended a co-educational school first and those who attended a single-sex school first, and similarly for last schools.

Estimates

FEMALE EX-PUPILS

Rather surprisingly the order in which the schools were attended appeared to have little or no influence on the ex-pupils' estimates on the pleasantness of the atmosphere, either in co-educational or girls' schools. Though the estimates for first and last schools of the same type were necessarily given by different sets of people, it is a reasonable presumption that if the influence of the order of the schools attended were strong this would show itself in the results as indeed it does with some items.

The difference in the opinion of the female ex-pupils about the atmosphere in their co-educational compared with their girls' schools is convincingly large; some 37 in every hundred said that the atmosphere in their co-educational school was 'very pleasant' while only 15 in every hundred thought the same about their girls' schools. At the other end of the scale—perhaps the more important end—whereas 1 woman in 18 reported the atmosphere was 'rather unpleasant' or worse at her co-educational school, the corresponding figure for girls' schools was 1 in 6. The analysis increases in significance when it is remembered that it was the same group of women who had attended both types of school.

MALE EX-PUPILS

Through no fault of the researchers the sample of male ex-pupils was much smaller than that of the females, but their results are important because of their experience in both types of school (Figure 4.2).

In Figure 4.2 the influence of the order in which the school were attended is apparent in the estimates for both co-educational and boys' schools. On this occasion the difference between the co-educated men and those from boys' schools is, unexpectedly, greater than that found between the corresponding groups

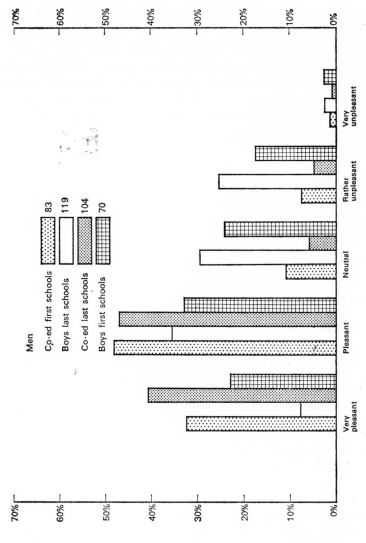

FIGURE 4.2
*School atmosphere
(men): 'Both schools'
survey*

65

of women. Whereas 1 in 3 of the men estimated that the atmosphere of their co-educational schools was 'very pleasant', the figure for the boys' schools was 1 in 8, and while 1 in 14 of them recorded a verdict of 'rather unpleasant' or worse for the co-educational schools, this was the estimate of 1 in 4 of them for their boys' schools. This is a greater difference than that obtained in the other surveys, and its size may be due to the nature of the sample; as all the students had experience of both types of school they were able to compare them, and any change in the atmosphere from one school to the other would be brought sharply to their attention.

Free responses

Though full analyses have been made of the free responses to this question they are not treated in detail because they resemble the answers to the question on happiness; instead, a concise account will be given using the adjectives that constantly recur in the free responses, but illustrating sometimes with direct quotation.

FEMALE EX-PUPILS

Co-educational schools

When writing about the atmosphere of their co-educational schools the women repeatedly brought up three themes. The first clings to the word atmosphere, describing it as 'friendly, happy, relaxed, informal, like a family', or uses the word 'community'. The second is good teacher–pupil relationships, 'friendly, with a spirit of tolerance, the staff enjoying teaching'. Third is 'normal boy–girl relationships'. Other adjectives often used are 'enjoyable, co-operative, balanced, broadness of view, security, humour' and even occasionally 'exciting' and 'enthusiastic'. A few examples are given:

Very pleasant 'The school ran smoothly and was friendly in atmosphere because of this. The atmosphere of co-operation was pervasive. There was no antagonism between staff and pupils.'

Very pleasant 'Discipline was observed by all but not drilled into you. We were not aware we were under rules and regulations.'

Very pleasant 'Teachers and pupils worked together as a team, not against each other, usually. Everyone very friendly.'

Very pleasant 'Boys and girls were learning side by side, as a family almost. This was considered to be perfectly natural and from this stemmed the very pleasant atmosphere.'

Pleasant 'The pupils were treated as far as possible as adults and were given a great deal of freedom which seemed to give a sense of self-discipline.'

Very pleasant 'An all-female community leads to bad feeling arising. Men seem to introduce a practical, logical element which keeps things in perspective.'

Lesser but still important themes are identified as 'individual attention, good discipline, more freedom, co-operation' and 'work enjoyable and interesting', and 'good, lively, enjoyable social life', and 'head good'.

To conclude this section on comments favourable to co-education two quotations are used, one of which is evidently deeply felt:

Very pleasant 'The atmosphere—marvellous school spirit and unity.'

The other discerningly puts its finger on a key quality in a good school:

Pleasant 'Staff seemed to trust pupils, delegate authority and listen to opinions.'

The comments unfavourable to the co-educational schools were few and scattered. Fifteen ex-pupils commented on a poor headmaster, nine on a too-lax discipline, and nine on the school being too impersonal, compared with 175 who praised the atmosphere and 145 who referred to the good pupil–teacher relationship. Mentioned several times were dislike of a large school and dislike of rough lower social class pupils in a comprehensive school.

Girls' schools

The free responses about the girls' schools were more favourable than unfavourable, but, as would be expected from the estimates, the unfavourable aspect was markedly more prominent than in the case of the co-educational schools.

The three chief favourable themes have a strong resemblance to those about the co-educational schools: the friendly, happy, community atmosphere; good pupil–teacher relationship, and good pupil–pupil relationship, but each of these has quite a strong reverse side: strained, tense atmosphere; poor pupil–teacher relationship, and bad pupil–pupil relations ('catty, bickering, spiteful, bitchy'). Less frequently mentioned favourable themes are good discipline and organization, good headmistress, small school, good tradition (13 mentions) and social and extra-curricular life, but all these except good tradition are accompanied by about the

67

same number of opposite responses. Examples of favourable comments are:

Very pleasant 'The teachers and pupils worked with one another in unison—the teachers were highly respected and yet never officious.'

Very pleasant 'Very helpful approach to children's social development—also old with plenty of tradition.'

Very pleasant 'Whole school (apart from odd one or two) was willing to help in all out-of-school activities and there was an air of happiness all the time.'

Very pleasant 'Cultured atmosphere. Fee paying—uniformed etc. Therefore girls of same social status.'

Very pleasant 'It was a community, each working for the good of the whole body.'

Pleasant 'Long established tradition fostered by excellent headmistress.'

The nature of the criticisms is illustrated by the following:

Rather unpleasant 'The small rules and regulations made it difficult to relax, particularly after the co-ed. school.'

Neutral 'Life just went on. Nobody really "fought" but nobody was really friendly. Nobody bothered—it was just a place we attended.'

Rather unhappy 'Tendency for an all-female community to become extremely spiteful and callous.'

Rather unhappy 'Fear was the key word in all discipline.'

Rather unhappy 'The emphasis was on learning for exams, not on preparation for society. It was run on similar lines to a prison, I imagine.'

Rather unhappy 'An unhealthy attitude towards and preoccupation with the opposite sex. They were sex mad and frequently coarse. When I first went there this revolted me.'

MALE EX-PUPILS

Co-educational schools
The reasons given by the male ex-pupils for their high estimates of the pleasantness of the atmosphere in their co-educational schools do not differ fundamentally from those given by the women. Added

to the three main themes of friendly family atmosphere, good pupil–teacher relationship and normal social environment (presence of girls) are a few new descriptive words like 'comradeship' and 'genial', with a little more emphasis on 'co-operation', but the similarity is marked. This can be seen in the illustrations:

Very pleasant 'Everything seemed natural, relaxed, complete. The staff and pupil morale was very high indeed.'

Very pleasant 'Pupils and teachers mixed on the same level and pupils admired the teachers for this.'

Pleasant 'Co-operation between boys, girls and teachers.' (Am.)

Very pleasant 'The different sexes treated each other with respect and there was a pleasing atmosphere of co-operation.'

Pleasant 'General ease and relaxed atmosphere. No continual hounding.'

Again, like the women's, the men's comments adverse to co-education were few and widely scattered, the biggest contributions being four complaints about over-lax discipline and three about harsh or restrictive discipline. Prominent, on this small scale, were complaints about 'amalgamated' schools; for example:

Rather unhappy 'Many of the students thought that with the school being twice as big they could do less work and break more rules and get away with it. They did.' (Am.)

Neutral 'There seemed to be some conflict on ideas of punishment between the old members of the staff of the Boys' Grammar School and the members of the staff of the Girls' High School.' (Am.)

Boys' schools

For the boys' schools the principal favourable themes were reduced to two, namely 'friendly community' and 'good pupil–teacher relations', but the latter was opposed by an equal number of comments which complained about the poor pupil–teacher relations and the harsh, restrictive and autocratic discipline. The remainder of the comments, both favourable and unfavourable, were again very diverse in content, the most numerous class being nine protests about bullying. Typical comments were:

FAVOURABLE

Pleasant 'We were all "mates" or comrades. There was plenty of brotherhood which I haven't experienced since.'

Pleasant 'Perhaps just the communal growing up of all the lads together.'

Pleasant 'Everyone knew their place. Prefects were respected and addressed as "Sir". A great deal of tradition was present in the school. It is obviously very old.'

Pleasant 'The headmaster really had the right idea and brought the tone of the school to a high state from nothing.'

Pleasant 'The staff, even if they were a little strict, always made sure that the pupils knew where they stood.'

UNFAVOURABLE

Very unhappy 'Autocratic discipline allowing no freedom of movement or thought. All pupils were finally of the same type.' (Boarding)

Rather unhappy 'I was scared stiff; glad to get home. Staff seemed hard, demanding and bossy.'

Rather unhappy 'There always appeared to be violence of one sort or another in the school.'

Neutral 'Rather unhealthy attitude towards sex.'

Rather unhappy 'Life was so formal that school resembled the army.'

Very unhappy 'A boy of 10 is likely to be affected by very harsh treatment. I've never forgotten this and it seems to have shown itself in stronger forms than it perhaps ought.' (Boarding)

The next set of results to be presented are those from the Schools project, where an attempt was made to tap the experience of some 2,000 boys and girls in grammar schools.

The Schools project

In the Schools project the question on atmosphere was not included in the 1964 administration, but was given in 1966. The results are in Tables 4.3 and 4.4.

The gap shown in Tables 4.3 and 4.4 between the co-educational school estimates and those of the single-sex schools is much narrower than in the previous surveys. This trend is consistent for all questions common to these enquiries. The differences are, however, all in favour of the co-educational schools, as before, except for the two groups of girls aged 13 plus, where there is virtual equality. (In the following section the girls aged 13 plus in

TABLE 4.3 *Pleasantness of school atmosphere*

Schools project (girls aged 13 plus and 17 plus)

| | Replies from girls aged 13 plus in | | | | Replies from girls aged 17 plus in | | | |
| | Co-educational schools | | Girls' schools | | Co-educational schools | | Girls' schools | |
	N	%	N	%	N	%	N	%
Very pleasant	34	15·8	40	18·8	20	17·4	11	9·2
Pleasant	131	60·9	119	55·9	76	66·1	71	59·2
Neutral	43	20·0	44	20·6	17	14·8	28	23·3
Rather unpleasant	6	2·8	9	4·2	2	1·7	10	8·3
Very unpleasant	1	0·5	1	0·5	0	0	0	0
Totals	215	100	213	100	115	100	120	100

NOTE: At the age of 13 there is virtually no difference between the groups. The co-educated girls aged 17 find the atmosphere more pleasant (statistically significant at the ·025 level).

TABLE 4.4 *Pleasantness of school atmosphere*

Schools project (boys aged 13 plus and 17 plus)

| | Replies from boys aged 13 plus in | | | | Replies from boys aged 17 plus in | | | |
| | Co-educational schools | | Boys' schools | | Co-educational schools | | Boys' schools | |
	N	%	N	%	N	%	N	%
Very pleasant	29	12·9	16	7·4	17	12·8	15	10·9
Pleasant	117	52·0	117	54·4	95	71·4	92	67·2
Neutral	65	28·9	60	27·9	18	13·5	21	15·3
Rather unpleasant	13	5·8	19	8·8	3	2·3	9	6·6
Very unpleasant	1	0·4	3	1·4	0	0	0	0
Totals	225	100	215	100	133	100	137	100

NOTE: The difference at age 13 is almost statistically significant.

the much larger 'Check' sample, attending the same schools as those of the Schools project, yielded a statistically significant difference in favour of co-education, though even this difference was smaller than previously.) The advantage of the co-educational schools in the group of boys aged 13 plus, while fairly substantial, was not quite statistically significant. Only in one case did the differences reach this level, that in favour of the co-educated girls aged 17 plus, where it was significant beyond the ·025 probability.

The 'Check' sample

Over 1,100 girls aged 13 in grammar schools answered the 'Check' questionnaire, including the question on atmosphere. The results are in Table 4.5.

TABLE 4.5 *Pleasantness of school atmosphere*

'Check' sample

Estimates of school atmosphere	Replies from girls aged 13 plus in			
	Co-educational schools		Girls' schools	
	N	%	N	%
Very pleasant	91	20·3	92	13·7
Pleasant	255	56·8	373	55·5
Neutral	94	20·9	186	27·6
Rather unpleasant	7	1·6	21	3·1
Very unpleasant	2	0·4	1	0·1
Totals	449	100	673	100

NOTE: The difference between the samples from co-educational and girls' schools is significant beyond the ·01 level.

In this sample the girls from the co-educational schools gave more favourable estimates for their school atmosphere than did those from girls' schools. The difference is not as large as that found in the ex-pupil surveys, particularly in those where the ex-pupils had attended both types of school. The reason for the narrowing of the gap may be the difference in age or the schoolgirls' lack of experience of the other type of school. There was no time in this instance for pupils to write free responses.

Conclusion

In all groups to which this question was put, the co-educational schools were found to have a pleasanter atmosphere, except in one case where there was equality. This does not mean that in all co-educational schools the atmosphere is better than that in all single-sex schools, because other powerful forces affect the situation, such as the quality of the head and staff, the nature of the school recruitment area, and to a lesser extent the type of buildings. Hence there are co-educational schools with a good atmosphere and others with a bad one, and similarly for single-sex schools. We can say, however, that a school being co-educational increases the likelihood that pupils and ex-pupils will find the atmosphere pleasant. As we saw at the beginning of this chapter, this is not the only criterion which should be used for judging the success of a school, but it is an important one.

5

Inter-pupil relationship

One of the powerful forces determining whether pupils are happy
at school and whether the school atmosphere is pleasant is the
relationship between the pupils themselves, which this chapter
begins to explore. As the Second College survey contained nothing
directly on this topic the first research to be examined is in the
'Both schools' survey. The central question was 'Within your co-
educational/single-sex school did you find it easy or difficult to
make friends?' Provision was made also for a free response.

The making of friends

'BOTH SCHOOLS' SURVEY

Female ex-pupils

The results of the girls are treated first (Table 5.1).

TABLE 5.1 *The making of friends*
Both schools' survey (women)

	Replies about first school attended				Replies about last school attended			
	Co-educa-tional		Girls'		Co-educa-tional		Girls'	
	N	%	N	%	N	%	N	%
Very easy	126	42·0	111	27·4	163	45·3	85	32·7
Fairly easy	95	31·8	155	38·3	119	33·1	89	34·2
Neither easy nor difficult	51	17·1	74	18·3	43	11·9	41	15·1
A little difficult	22	7·4	56	13·8	28	7·8	37	14·8
Very difficult	5	1·7	9	2·2	7	1·9	8	3·2
Totals	299	100	405	100	360	100	260	100

NOTE: The difference between the first co-educational and first girls'
schools is significant beyond the ·001 level and for last schools beyond
the ·01 level.

The results in Table 5.1 show that these 620 women were strongly of the opinion that it was easier to make friends in the co-educational than in the girls' school. If the 'first schools' had not been separated from the 'last schools' it might have been thought that this hidden variable could have caused the difference, but the same result is obtained when co-educational schools which were attended first are opposed to girls' schools attended first, and similarly for 'last schools'. Moreover, the 'order of school' effect seems to be less strong than expected, at least for this topic.

The comments are not as interesting in their distinction between the two types of school as they have often been with other topics; their treatment is therefore curtailed, and 'first' and 'last' schools are taken together.

Easily the most numerous statements about the co-educational schools were those which came rather loosely under the heading 'school atmosphere conducive to easy natural relationship' (67). A long way behind came 'organization of school helped to foster friendship' (25), 'easy natural relationship between boys and girls' (19), 'process aided by common interests, such as sports' (16), 'all friends together from primary school' (14), 'the pleasantness of heterosexual groups in the upper school' (12) and 'compared favourably with girls' schools' (11). Rather apart from the rest were the responses 'always found it easy to make friends' (21).

By far the most serious difficulty encountered in making friends was 'entering school late' (33), with the somewhat related 'pupils in cliques and difficult to join' (14), while some girls, coming from a girls' school, had to overcome a shyness with boys (18). There remained a group which admitted that personally they had difficulty in making friends (18). A few illustrations give a little more light:

Fairly easy 'At first I found it difficult but once I had overcome my shyness about boys I seemed to flourish.'

Fairly easy 'It was difficult where the groups were tightly knit— a new person was considered queer.'

Very easy 'To share a form room and have mixed lessons inevitably ensures easier conversation with the opposite sex.'

Very easy 'Not as petty as single-sex schools.'

Fairly easy 'Easier with boys than girls.'

Very easy 'Pupils in a co-educational school are more friendly towards each other than in a single-sex school where groups tend to form who dislike each other.'

75

Fairly easy 'I think because boys and girls were together getting in with the girls was better—they tended to be less "catty" than those in the single-sex school.'

Very easy 'At first one gets romantic ideas towards the boys but this soon evaporates as the newness of the idea of a co-educational school wears off and you are soon all good friends.'

Very easy 'The girls were very friendly when I first went there and through them I got to know the boys and lost the shyness of them I had acquired at single-sex schools.'

Very easy 'After having been to about 14 schools I found when I first went to the co-ed. at the age of 13 I made friends far easier than in any other school.'

The suspicion which people (even children) have at first of those who are somewhat different is shown by:

A little difficult 'I spoke with a different accent coming from 8 years in Hertfordshire and the children (Lancs.) would laugh at first. After a while I made friends with some children.'

A little difficult 'I was an English girl in a Scottish school.'

Fairly easy 'I did not [make friends] at first because I went from England to Wales and the pupils seemed to resent my nationality. Later I found it easier.'

Pupils who move from one part of the country, therefore, may have to contend with difficulties arising from accent and nationality, as well as those arising from being a latecomer trying to join rings of already established friends, and girls could be made very unhappy in this way.

The same types of comments were made about the girls' schools, but as would be expected from the estimates the proportion of those favourable was reduced. The most numerous group came, as before, under the general heading 'school atmosphere conducive to easy natural relationship' (29), and 15 under the heading 'tie over from primary school', while 12 said friendship was easy 'because they were all new together'. As with the co-educational schools, for some ex-pupils friendships grew out of common interests (10), and there were 10 students who always found making friends easy.

The principal comments about the difficulties in their girls' schools, as in their co-educational schools, were that it was difficult to make friends if one entered the school late (24) and that it was hard to break into the established cliques of girls (35), but the latter is here more prominent. Eleven women confessed to having personal difficulties in making friends. Minor factors mentioned were social class bias (3) and that the girls discriminated against people who were not identical to themselves (10). The comments ranged from such remarks as:

A little difficult 'There tended to be "cliques" of friends that were difficult to enter. I spent a very bewildering and uneasy few years in this school'

to the ex-pupil who found it 'very easy' and wrote, 'It seemed to be an unwritten rule that it was everyone's duty to make all welcome.' In spite of the estimates and the proportion of comments in favour of the co-educational schools, there were one or two informative and slightly amusing comments showing an influence in the opposite direction; for example:

Very easy 'Because there were no boys to distract them—firmer and more secure friendships were made with girls.'

Very easy 'Girls together and boys together is the best situation in a school where you are rubbing shoulders for the main part of your life. Hatred arises in a co-ed. school if one girl is favoured by a particularly charming young male.'

Interesting comments are the following, for different reasons:

Very difficult 'Very easy at first, then gradually as the atmosphere got me down and the other people conformed to the desired "image" very very difficult. I eventually had no friends at all. Some days the only people who spoke to me were the teachers.'

A little difficult 'This was partly due to the influence of my father who allowed me no opinions or ideas of my own. At school I found difficulty in communication.'

Male ex-pupils

The 172 male ex-pupils were in this instance of very similar mind to the women. They considered it had been much easier to make friends in their co-educational than in their boys' schools. As the order in which the schools were attended had a powerful influence in the boys' schools and a slight one in the co-educational, it being easier in schools attended last, this variable was held constant, but in both first and last schools the co-educational schools had a highly significant advantage (Table 5.2).

From this Table one can see that, whereas almost half of the men said that it had been very easy to make friends in their co-educational schools, only a quarter said the same for their boys' schools. At the other end of the scale the numbers finding it

Inter-pupil relationship

TABLE 5.2 *The making of friends*

'*Both schools*' *survey (men)*

Estimates of ease or difficulty in making friends at school	Replies about first school attended				Replies about last school attended			
	Co-educational		Boys'		Co-educational		Boys'	
	N	%	N	%	N	%	N	%
Very easy	37	44·6	28	23·5	51	49·0	21	30·0
Fairly easy	30	36·2	31	26·1	35	33·7	26	37·1
Neither easy nor difficult	9	10·8	33	27·7	13	12·5	16	22·9
A little difficult	5	6·0	25	21·0	3	2·9	5	7·1
Very difficult	2	2·4	2	1·7	2	1·9	2	2·9
Totals	83	100	119	100	104	100	70	100

NOTE: The difference between the first co-educational and first boys' schools is significant beyond the ·001 level and for last schools beyond the ·05 level.

'fairly difficult', or worse, to make friends, were three times as numerous for the boys' schools as for the co-educational.

The free responses of the men were inevitably less numerous than those of the women, numbering only 89 about the co-educational schools and 67 about the boys' schools. When classified they split into many small categories, the only sizeable group being that which said the school atmosphere in the co-educational school was conducive to easy natural relationship (18), apart from those in both schools who maintained that they personally always found it easy to make friends. The next most important groups, favourable or unfavourable, were those who found friends through common interests (12 in the boys' schools), and those who found difficulty because of cliques or gangs (8 in the boys' schools and 2 in the co-educational). Five comments said it was easier to make friends in the co-educational school, with none saying the opposite. These low numbers are not of course reliable, but are given because we are more concerned with the total effect of all the research than with any small portion in itself. Nothing new would be added by quoting from the free responses, so they are omitted.

Before passing on to the next attempt to explore (in an admittedly superficial way) the relationship between pupils, it should be said that this question on making friends would have been improved if it had been accompanied by a simple definition of what was meant, i.e. making close friends or just friends in general. The lack of greater precision, however, presumably had the same effect on the two groups and was not serious enough to invalidate the findings, though interpretation of these is a little more difficult. In any case the findings do not depend on the one question, but on a number that are related. The one to be considered next was asked in the Schools project.

The friendliness of pupils

THE SCHOOLS AND 'CHECK' QUESTIONNAIRES

These questionnaires included the question, 'Do you find other pupils, in general, Very friendly/Friendly/Indifferent/Unfriendly/Very unfriendly?' Respondents were asked to comment on the estimate they chose. The results of the girls are taken first.

Girls' estimates

This questionnaire was administered in 1966 only, in 36 grammar schools to girls aged 13 plus and 17 plus. The results are not tabulated because they show a clear equality at 17 plus and only the slenderest of advantages to the girls' schools at 13 plus, far below statistical significance.[1] Of some 335 pupils of both ages, there were merely two in each type of school who found their fellow pupils to be unfriendly or very unfriendly.

In the 'Check' survey (1,122 girls) the superiority of the co-educational schools which has been reported for happiness and atmosphere was not continued, the result of the Schools project for 'friendship' being repeated, and the difference again being far from statistical significance. Nearly 4 in 10 girls of both types thought their fellow-pupils 'very friendly', and more than half thought them 'friendly'; the only difference was that 1.4 per cent more of the pupils in girls' schools estimated 'friendly', leaving none in the 'unfriendly' or 'very unfriendly' categories, in which the co-educational schools had 1.5 per cent. This is one of the few occasions where the gap in favour of the co-educational schools, which always narrows in the Schools and related 'Check' surveys, closes and moves minimally in the opposite direction.

Boys' estimates (*Schools project, 1966*)

The boys' results were similarly inconclusive. At age 13 plus the boys' schools had a slight advantage which could have been a

[1] Chi-square = 1·284 for 3 degrees of freedom.

chance effect,[1] and at age 17 plus the co-educational schools had a bigger advantage which was nearer to statistical significance.[2] This question was not included in the 1964 testing. Discussion is postponed until the picture can be seen as a whole.

Pupils were given the opportunity to comment in the Schools project question, but as the comments add nothing to our knowledge they are not used.

Spitefulness

'BOTH SCHOOLS' QUESTIONNAIRES

The female ex-pupils of the 'Both schools' survey were asked two other questions which are related to 'the friendliness of pupils'. One of these was, 'Do you think that the girls in your form, judged

FIGURE 5.1 *Spitefulness (girls): 'Both schools' survey*

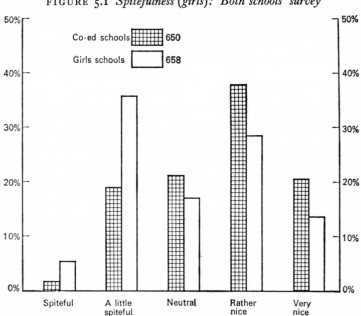

as a whole, were 'Spiteful/A little spiteful/Neutral/Rather nice/ Very nice?' They were also asked to comment on their estimates, which are given in Figure 5.1. As there are no clear social class differences these classes are merged, and similarly for first and

[1] Chi-square = 4·012 for 3 degrees of freedom.
[2] Chi-square = 5·278 for 3 degrees of freedom.

last schools, the difference between last schools (highly significant) being only a little less than that between first schools.

The figures speak for themselves, the respondents estimating twice the amount of 'spitefulness' in their girls' schools as in their co-educational, but most of it not extreme. The free responses are not sufficiently interesting to tabulate, but the principal aspects are summarized. For both the co-educational and girls' schools the proportion of comments complaining of spitefulness was as expected from the estimates. Apparently there are conflicting forces at work. On the one hand the girls tend to refrain from spitefulness in front of boys because boys laugh at them; on the other, girls are sometimes spiteful in a mixed school when they quarrel over a boy-friend, though several free responses mention this in girls' schools also. One of the themes was that a certain amount of spitefulness was to be expected in all-girl groups; some of the individuals confessed to indulging in it themselves! One said that girls are spiteful at heart! A theme which appeared only about the girls' schools (merely three mentions) was 'the malicious teasing of individuals' including 'ganging up on one girl' in a boarding school. Only a few quotations are given:

Co-educational schools

'Some were spiteful but the boys in the class laughed at them, so they were not spiteful in public.'

'Boys were present and would have laughed had the usual spitefulness present among girls been shown.'

'*Very nice* because of the presence of boys. All-girls breeds spitefulness—but a mixture breeds thoughtfulness.'

'When I had a boy-friend before my other girl-friends they were very spiteful towards me but when they had their own boy-friends there was little or no friction.'

A little spiteful 'This was because we had always been together and a spiteful atmosphere had prevailed in the girls' school.' (Am.)

'Any girls getting together in a group are a little spiteful so it cannot be avoided at times when one-sex lessons take place, e.g. gym, or domestic science.'

' "Cat-sessions" between the girls fighting over "best" friends.'

Girls' schools

'Some girls could be very spiteful indeed. I found this only seemed to happen in all-girls schools.'

'Most girls tend to be spiteful if they have to work or live together all the time. It is one of the chief interests.'

'A defect such as wearing national health glasses or being fat—was made fun of often in a very spiteful way. Even I took part in this type of teasing of people.'

'There was a definite split—the big "nobs" and the underdogs.' (Boarding)

'Particularly about other girls' boy-friends.'

'No cattiness because no boys were present.'

We pass on to the second question which was about quarrelling.

Quarrelling

This question was, 'Did the other girls in your form quarrel Very often/Fairly often/Sometimes/Seldom/Never?' The results closely resemble those obtained from the question on spitefulness, as will be seen in Table 5.3.

TABLE 5.3 *Quarrelling* (*girls*)

'*Both schools*' *survey*

Estimates of frequency of quarrelling	Replies about schools attended			
	Co-educational		Girls'	
	N	%	N	%
Very often	10	1·5	37	5·6
Fairly often	61	9·3	148	22·4
Sometimes	324	49·7	333	50·2
Seldom	233	35·7	135	20·4
Never	25	3·8	9	1·4
Totals	653	100	662	100

NOTE: The difference between the co-educational and girls' schools is statistically significant beyond the ·001 level. This is also true if 'first' and 'last' schools are taken separately.

In Table 5.3 well over a quarter of the respondents estimated that quarrels occurred 'often' or 'very often' in their girls' school, and an eighth in their co-educational school. In both cases a large group estimated 'seldom' or 'never', being over 70 per cent about the co-educational schools and 44 per cent about the girls' schools. It could be argued that this difference might be caused by the smallness of the number of girls in co-educational classes, there being, as it were, only half a class to quarrel with, as the girls would rarely quarrel with the boys. If this argument has any force—and the effect is problematic—it would seem to admit that mixed classes result in less quarrelling, thus producing a better atmosphere. This does not, of itself, ensure that mixed classes are better —many other factors would need to be examined before such a pronouncement could be made.

6

Bullying and related aspects

The central theme of this chapter is bullying by boys, and similar behaviour—usually less physical—by girls. Such conduct results in the weaker pupils having a miserable time, particularly in a boarding school, from which the unfortunate boys and girls have no escape, day or night; schools in which this conduct is rife can scarcely be called good schools. It was therefore thought useful to investigate whether the presence of girls in a school toned down such conduct on the part of the boys, and similarly for the influence of boys on girls, in comparison with conduct in single-sex schools. A variable which necessarily has great influence is the age of the pupils, and another might be parental occupational class. Variation between individuals, between heads of schools and between staffs, whether within single-sex or mixed schools, will be countered by the use of a large enough number of pupils and of schools.

The question on bullying was first asked in the 'Both schools' survey, and the nature of the topic makes it perhaps more relevant than usual to remind readers that these ex-pupils were all intending teachers and are not representative of all types of pupil. This, however, should not vitiate the comparison between the two types of school. On this occasion the boys are taken first.

Male ex-pupils

BULLYING

The male ex-pupils were asked, with reference to their co-educational school and later to their boys' school, 'Would you say bullying by boys occurred, Very frequently/Frequently/Not so frequently/Infrequently/Not at all?' For each school they were asked to make a comment. The results are in Figure 6.1

There is no doubt about the result: whereas almost half of these ex-pupils of boys' schools estimated that bullying in them was 'frequent' or 'very frequent', this was reduced to little more than one-fifth when they estimated for their co-educational schools.

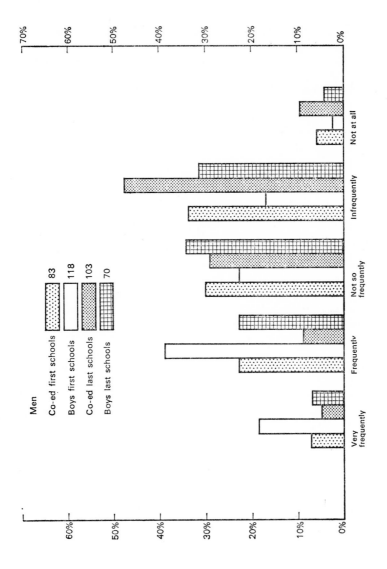

FIGURE 6.1
Incidence of
bullying (boys):
'Both schools'
survey

Considering first and last schools, the difference between the co-educational and boys' schools is noticeably not as great for last schools as for first, though still of statistical significance, and there is not as much change from co-educational schools attended first to those attended last as there is in the case of the boys' schools; yet in both cases bullying decreases in the senior school. This could, of course, be interpreted to signify that the seniors are big enough to look after themselves and are likely to be the bullies rather than the bullied. This factor would certainly have an influence in spite of the question asking in effect whether the respondents knew about any bullying in general. The free responses in Table 6.1 are especially interesting.

The free responses paint the same picture as the estimates while adding interpretative detail. Additional points of interest are the frequent prevention of bullying, in both types of school, by staff, prefects and pupils themselves, and the stronger support in co-educational schools for the reply that bullying was not a feature of the school because of the friendly atmosphere and the pervading sense of comradeship. In the co-educational school we see opposing forces caused by the presence of girls—bullying to show off in front of them, and restraint because they were there. Rather more space than in recent chapters will be devoted to quotations, as these are illustrative of important differences between boys' and co-educational schools. To preserve objectivity the proportion of favourable to unfavourable quotations given is the same as that in the estimates, considering 'very frequently' and 'frequently' as unfavourable, and 'infrequently' and 'not at all' as favourable.

Co-educational schools

FAVOURABLE 'The school's friendly atmosphere was generally reflected in the attitude of the boys to one another.'

'I found that because of the presence of girls they had much better things to do in their break times.'

'Not at all. This was mainly due to the presence of girls.'

'If at all when girls were not present, which was rare.'

'There was very little of this done due to the strict control of prefects, and if necessary the formation of gangs to sort bullies out either in school or out of school.'

'Mainly any bullying was by a small percentage of prefects. The girls would scorn any boy whom they heard was a bully. This seemed to be a very effective deterrent.'

TABLE 6.1 *Free responses about bullying (boys)*
'*Both schools*' survey

Estimate	Categories of comments	Co-educational school	Boys' school
Very frequently and Frequently	by individuals (e.g. to assert masculinity)	13	16
	by group	7	5
	to juniors	7	17
	among juniors	5	6
	to own age group	1	
	not restricted by school/staff	2	4
	resisted by group of boys	3	4
	result of environment	1	3
	through traditional rituals		5
	very frequently and frequently		9
	more at single-sex than co-ed.		4
Total		39	73
Not so frequently	by individuals (to assert masculinity)		5
	by individuals—to impress	13	
	by individuals—to impress girls	2	
	by group	1	2
	resisted by boys	3	4
	controlled by staff/prefects	12	5
	restrained by presence of girls	7	
	result of friendly atmosphere	8	
	through traditional fagging		3
	more in single-sex than co-ed.		4
	less in single-sex than co-ed.		1
	more in juniors than seniors		3
	seniors bullying juniors		6
	not so frequently		9
Total		46	42
Infrequently or Not at all	controlled by staff (including through prefects)	23	14
	not a feature of the school	14	3
	seniors asserting position	6	4
	mainly in lower forms		4
	only through traditional rituals	3	
	restrained by presence of girls	13	
	occasionally (impress girls)	7	
	controlled by sense of maturity	6	
	pervading sense of comradeship	4	
	none except out of school	2	
	bullying exceptional trait of particular year	1	
	infrequently		16
Totals		79	41

UNFAVOURABLE 'I think that boys from rough homes were the bullies and went in gangs. But every day there was a fight or a quarrel.'

'The secondary modern boys would bully weaker first years excessively. Otherwise there was little bullying.'

'An air of bravado often overcame some in the presence of girls and [they] wanted to show off. These, however, were disliked by both sexes.'

Boys' schools
Here the same ratio of quotations (1 in 13) is used as for the co-educational schools.

FAVOURABLE 'Quite a few fights, but a sense of fairness prevailed—an older boy who bullied was disliked by his own age group.'

'The bullying was natural as it always is with boys. But it was not excessive.'

'Boys took it out on themselves during organized games, etc; it was difficult to fight due to prefects.'

UNFAVOURABLE 'You were put in the coal-hole and thumped. The coal-hole was some steps leading to the boiler-house.'

'Frequently. Intimidation was always occurring but seldom was physical force used. The senior boys used the juniors for their own needs—despicable.' (Boarding)

'A kind of outlet for built-up tensions in the classroom—and this was *real* bullying.'

'With no girls around there were no niceties to watch or manners to consider.'

'This was the dominant feature of the school social life.'

The 'direct comparison' technique is now used again, whereby *all* free responses which compare the two types of school are quoted.

Direct Comparisons
FAVOURABLE TO CO-EDUCATION 'There was no fagging of the first years and bullying was punished severely. Far more normal relationship with newcomers was established.'

'There was more bullying than in the co-ed. school.'

'Family atmosphere curbed this. Mixed school had calming effect. Head very strict on this behaviour.'

'From a prefect's point of view I had to stop far less fights here than at my other school.'

'Frequently [in boys' school] that is compared with my other school. Gang warfare at one time was quite a problem and the bullying of individuals quite common.'

'I never recall any large amount of bullying as I experienced it in a single-sex school.'

'Bullying was kept in check by the prefects and it decreased when the school went co-educational.'

'More bullying than at co-ed. school.'

'More bullying than in co-ed. school. There seemed to be a hard core of "teds". Roughness and toughness were admired among boys far more than in co-ed. establishment.'

FAVOURABLE TO BOYS' SCHOOLS 'The older boys when I was younger and the school co-ed., seemed to be more aggressive than we were when I was older and the school single-sex.'

'That bullying which occurred was caused by the notorious dinner queue which older and bigger boys pushed into. Apart from this for practical reasons there was very little superficial bullying as in my mixed school where it was done for fun.'

'This practice seemed to die out after the division of the school. Young boys went readily to see staff so it did not pay to bully.'

'To younger pupils from adolescents. Not as much as co-educational school, less showing off.'

'There was less bullying than in the co-ed. school.'

PREFECTS OFFICIOUS

Pupils were asked to answer another item which sometimes could be related to bullying, namely, 'Do you agree or disagree with the following statement about your co-educational school? "The prefects were officious." Agree strongly/Agree/Doubtful/Disagree/Disagree strongly.' The same question was asked about the girls' schools. It is likely that the wording of the statement suggests agreement, and this tendency would be reinforced by the position of 'Agree strongly' at the start of the continuum, but this matters little as the study is primarily concerned with comparing single-sex and co-educational schools, and the effect would be much the same for each group. The data from the estimates are in Table 6.2; there was no opportunity for free responses.

TABLE 6.2 *Prefects officious (boys)*

'Both schools' survey

Estimates about prefects officious	Replies about first school attended				Replies about last school attended			
	Co-ed.		Boys'		Co-ed.		Boys'	
	N	%	N	%	N	%	N	%
Agree strongly	9	11·0	37	31·6	7	6·9	8	11·3
Agree	29	35·3	38	32·5	18	17·8	26	36·6
Doubtful	14	17·1	31	26·5	22	21·8	12	16·9
Disagree	24	29·3	9	7·7	39	38·6	22	31·0
Disagree strongly	6	7·3	2	1·7	15	14·9	3	4·2
Totals	82	100	117	100	101	100	71	100

NOTE: The difference between the first co-educational schools and the first boys' schools is significant beyond the ·001 level and that between last schools is significant beyond the ·025 level.

Table 6.2 shows in this instance the great effect of the order in which the schools were attended, the seniors of the schools naturally finding the prefects less officious than when they themselves were juniors. Some of the seniors would of course have been prefects themselves and would be eager to decry any charge of officiousness. Because of this big difference between first and last schools the main comparison between co-educational and boys' schools takes first and last separately, and finds the difference to be statistically highly significant for first schools and significant for last schools. (As more of the students finished in co-educational schools the process of combining first and last schools could sometimes produce an invalid result.)

Some 64 per cent of the students agreed that when they were in their boys' schools as juniors their prefects were officious (combining 'agree strongly' with 'agree'); the corresponding percentage for co-educational schools was 46, almost all of the difference being on 'agree strongly'. When the schools compared are those in which students finished last the relevant percentages are 48 and 25. Unfortunately there was not sufficient time at the researchers' disposal to allow them to ask the students for free responses to this question; this lack of data will become evident during the discussion section.

Female ex-pupils

BULLYING ('Both schools' survey)

The women ex-students in the 'Both schools' sample also answered the question on bullying, the wording being: 'In your co-educational school would you say bullying of girls by girls occurred, Not at all/Infrequently/Not so frequently/Frequently/Very frequently?' with the phrase 'single-sex school' substituted for 'co-educational' in the relevant section. The verdict of the students can be seen in Table 6.3.

TABLE 6.3 *Bullying of girls*

'Both schools' survey

Estimates about bullying of girls	Replies about first school attended				Replies about last school attended			
	Co-educational		Girls'		Co-educational		Girls'	
	N	%	N	%	N	%	N	%
Not at all	85	30·9	62	16·5	137	41·5	42	17·5
Infrequently	124	45·1	151	40·3	147	44·6	113	47·1
Not so frequently	51	18·5	83	22·1	28	8·5	43	17·9
Frequently	14	5·1	70	18·7	16	4·8	40	16·7
Very frequently	1	0·4	9	2·4	2	0·6	2	0·8
Totals	275	100	375	100	330	100	240	100

NOTE: The differences between co-educational and girls' schools both for first schools and last schools are statistically significant beyond the ·001 level.

Perhaps the most important feature of Table 6.3 is that in schools attended first, some 1 in 5 of the students thought that bullying was 'frequent' or 'very frequent' in their girls' schools and 1 in 18 in their co-educational schools: in schools attended last the corresponding figures are approximately 1 in 6 and, again, about 1 in 18, both differences being statistically highly significant.

The free responses to this question were not analysed for the women, as they would tend to be duplicates of the replies to the next question on 'made life unpleasant'. Because of its near relationship to bullying this question is here taken before the one on the officiousness of prefects. It was not put to the boys.

'MADE LIFE UNPLEASANT'

The wording of the question was, 'In your co-educational school would you say that a group or groups of the girls "made life unpleasant" for some girls (or girl), Very frequently/Frequently/Not so frequently/Infrequently/Not at all?' The students' estimates are given in Table 6.4.

TABLE 6.4 *Making life unpleasant (girls)*

'*Both schools*' survey

Estimates about making life unpleasant	Replies about first school attended				Replies about last school attended			
	Co-educational		Girls'		Co-educational		Girls'	
	N	%	N	%	N	%	N	%
Very frequently	9	3·1	20	5·0	6	1·7	12	4·7
Frequently	34	11·6	105	26·0	39	11·0	51	19·9
Not so frequently	68	23·3	114	28·3	58	16·3	66	25·8
Infrequently	140	48·0	128	31·8	171	48·2	94	36·7
Not at all	41	14·0	36	8·9	81	22·8	33	12·9
Totals	292	100	403	100	355	100	256	100

NOTE: The differences between co-educational and girls' schools for first and last school are significant well beyond the ·001 level.

In Table 6.4 we see that there was some improvement from 'first' to 'last' school for both the co-educational and the girls' schools. The principal feature, however, is the decidedly lower estimates of the incidence of 'making life unpleasant' for co-educational schools compared with girls' schools, a difference which is highly significant statistically. More insight into these differences is obtained by the study of the free responses (Table 6.5).

In Table 6.5 the comments from ex-pupils who had been seniors in a school (last schools) were amalgamated with those who had been juniors in the same type of school, because there was (surprisingly) insufficient difference between the replies about 'first' and 'last' schools to justify their separate treatment. The data fully confirm the trends in the two previous tables of estimates —that these ex-pupils state that there was less unpleasantness

TABLE 6.5 *Girls 'made life unpleasant' (free responses)*
'Both schools' survey

Estimate	Comment	Co-educational schools	Girls' schools
Not at all	not at all (non-specific)	48	31
and	infrequently (non-specific)	134	58
Infrequently	because of friendly atmosphere, close contact	27	19
	because other girls would stop it	6	5
	only petty things; just quarrels	21	15
	groups kept to themselves	3	5
	occasional sending to Coventry		3
	because no boys present		2
	jealousy over boy	14	3
	presence of boys prevented it	14	
	more than in co-ed. school		2
	jealousy over exam. results	2	
	One girl 'picked on' because different	30	22
	mostly in lower school	13	15
	between groups	8	8
	by 'bossy', by boy-mad girls, by boy haters	1	4
	others	8	11
Totals		329	203
Not so	not so frequently, only normal	32	33
frequently	petty arguments	7	4
	presence of boys and boys as peacemakers	6	
	competition for boys	9	3
	more than in co-ed. school		3
	one girl 'picked on' because different	26	26
	because of boredom		3
	jealousy, changing friends, etc.	3	
	ridicule of dress, hair, etc.		2
	occasional sending to Coventry		6
	occasionally in lower or middle school	8	17
	only in lower streams		2
	between groups	4	15
	one spiteful or dominating girl	2	2
	by boy-mad girls	1	
	by trouble-makers, rebels	7	
	others	2	8
Totals		107	124

[*continued*]

TABLE 6.5 (*continued*) *Girls 'made life unpleasant' (free responses)*
'*Both schools*' *survey*

Estimate	Comment	Co-educational schools	Girls' schools
Frequently	frequently	13	15
and	very frequently	3	2
Very	petty arguments	3	7
frequently	one girl 'picked on' because		
	different	26	60
	jealousy over boys	8	3
	because boys not present		3
	attitude of some groups to boys	1	1
	more than in co-ed. school, all		
	girls		6
	in lower forms, less in higher	6	9
	mostly in higher forms	4	
	by groups, cliques against		
	others	3	20
	between groups		10
	by boy-crazy girls		1
	by rough girls	3	
	by 'catty' girls		6
	others	4	6
Totals		74	149

between girls in their co-educational than in their girls' schools. Table 6.5 endeavours to summarize the responses; apart from the influence of the type of school the salient features were the unhappy lot of the girls who were 'picked on because they were different', and the double role of boys, who caused jealousy in both co-educational and girls' schools and also acted as peacemakers and as a restraining influence in the former. The quotations from these comments are in proportion to the numbers in each category (1 in 20), except that the middle ('not so frequently') category is omitted as adding very little to the illustration, and the number from the combined 'not at all' and 'infrequently' categories is halved to avoid over-loading the chapter. This last category is taken first. All the quotations relate to the 'made life unpleasant' question.

'*Not at all*' *and* '*infrequently*'

CO-EDUCATIONAL SCHOOLS 'Always tried to be helpful and friendly towards the minority of girls who kept to themselves, and did not interact between the groups. Felt sorry for them.'

'If this happened the boys usually made life so unpleasant for the offensive group that they stopped.'

'They found it might lead to scorn from the boys which they did not wish to incite.'

'After exam results had come out girls could make one girl's life a misery if she had a higher result than them.'

'Often a rise was taken out of some girls because they spoke without accents.'

'They had other people to talk to and about when boys were there and found it a waste of time to quarrel between themselves.'

'The girls tended to be too bothered with making the boys behave!'

'Arguments and disagreements usually settled by discussion—often boys present.'

'Can't remember this happening. Most groups were mixed in sex.'

GIRLS' SCHOOLS 'Quarrels would be of short duration—probably between girls who were friends.'

'A little friction with girls in the 5th year, probably over boys, with whom there was no organized contact.'

'This hardly ever happened, because the school was small and everybody knew everybody else.'

'This happened once or twice, and after we had tasted it, and its after-effects, it never happened again.'

'Nearly all were friendly, not much time for unpleasantness.'

'Tended to be more numerous in the lowest streams.'

'Frequently' and 'Very frequently'

CO-EDUCATIONAL SCHOOLS 'Some sets were worse than others—frequently arose if a girl was dated by a boy who was liked by someone else.'

Often a group would gang up on a girl. Once some girls went to the extent of attacking one girl (sticking pins in her).'

'Mixing of all social classes with a high proportion of working class. Often the working-class girls would pick on the middle-class ones.'

'Some girls were rather mean to one girl because she was less well off than them and rather unattractive.'

GIRLS' SCHOOLS 'A large antagonistic group of sex-obsessed atheists dominated the 6th form.'

'Especially "Rolls Royce" cliques. Anyone slightly different was picked on.'

'There is always a set in a single-sex school, in my opinion, which makes life unpleasant for another.'

'One group of second years terrorized the 1st, 2nd and 3rd years—even fighting!'

'Girls when together are often spiteful and tend to make life unpleasant for a girl who finds it difficult to make friends.'

'Groups of girls made life difficult for girls with rich fathers, good accents, shy girls, clever girls or girls who were "favourites".'

'My own case is a good example. As I was "different" in my speech, etc., I was "ragged" most viciously for the first year. I never believed girls could be so spiteful and unfeeling.'

Direct comparisons

FAVOURABLE TO CO-EDUCATION 'This occurs in a group of children, but not so much in a co-ed. school.'

'This fact was reversed in a single-sex school.' ('Not at all', co-educational school.)

'Can't remember any specific instances. Not nearly as likely as in my single-sex school.'

'A decided lack of spitefulness compared to my single-sex school. I was, however, younger then.'

'It was more obvious in an all-girls school.'

'This often happens among girls and more so in single-sex school than co-educational.'

'Life made unpleasant for single girls by groups—far more than in co-ed.'

'This seemed to occur much more in a single-sex school.'

'There is not the same sense of "fair play" as in school with mixed staff.'

'It happened more than in the co-ed.'

'Much more than in co-educational school.'

'In any girls' society quarrels and backbiting take place but not so frequently in the co-ed. because it was frowned upon by the boys.'

'Just before I left this happened infrequently but just after the change [to co-ed.] and before it was very frequent.' (Am.)

'I have seen one or two cases of this in lower forms. The effects do not seem as great as in a single-sex school.'

'There tended to be more grouping together of girls in individual forms and some girls were left out.'

'More often than previously [i.e. than at the co-educational school].'

'This happened sometimes. I think it is natural in a single-sex community.'

'Seemed to happen more frequently than in the co-educational school.'

'The girls generally seemed to be more aggressive to one another as regards boy-friends.'

'In my opinion it is inadvisable to segregate girls from boys. Both contribute towards growing up. To avoid excessive unpleasantness I recommend mixed school.'

'Sometimes life was made unpleasant for single girls, sometimes little groups from within the class, far more than in the co-educational school.'

'There seemed to be more "ganging up" when the school split up than before it did.'

FAVOURABLE TO GIRLS' SCHOOLS 'Boys were more likely to make life unpleasant for a girl who was quieter and not so friendly.'

'Probably because there was no rivalry for the opposite sex in the single-sex school.' ('Not so frequently')

It is surprising that these direct comparisons are so one-sided, and it is therefore more important than usual that they should be considered against the background of the more dependable estimates, which, though favourable to co-educational schools, are less severe in their criticism of girls' schools. Peculiarly enough, the one comment unfavourable to co-educational schools is quite uncharacteristic of this research, in that the presence of boys is usually welcomed by the girls and judged by them as toning down the 'cattiness' which the quiet girl might find hard to bear.

The section is concluded with a special look at the comments the girls made about the influence of boys. Against the background of welcome in the co-educational school may be discerned both favourable and unfavourable influences. On the one hand the boys act as the peacemakers and their presence inhibits the catty remarks which the girls admit to occur in their absence. On the other hand there is jealousy about boy-friends, which in turn is a cause of 'cattiness'. The balance evidently tips over heavily on the 'less cattiness' side. Here the quotations are not selected according to the total number of each type, but merely to illustrate each theme.

In the co-educational schools whatever cattiness occurred appeared usually to be about boys, e.g. one young woman writes that the girls 'made life unpleasant' for another girl 'not so frequently', but it was 'generally due to competition for boys and jealousy'. Another estimated 'infrequently' but 'generally over boy-friend snatching'. Similar is 'infrequently: this only happened when two girls liked the same boy or vice-versa', and 'if some girls hadn't a boy-friend they would make fun'. There was, however, a reverse influence: 'Girls would not do this often because they realized that the boys would think them nasty and stupid to do such a thing.' Again, 'The girls were on the whole friendly. We did not want the boys to consider the remark about girls being "catty" was true.'

In the remarks about their girls' schools the women reach virtually a consensus of opinion—that girls will have a strong tendency to 'cattiness' and similar conduct if boys are not present, e.g. 'Girls when together are often spiteful and tend to make life unpleasant for the girl who finds it difficult to make friends'; 'Girls on their own are much more inclined to be spiteful and clan against other girls.' Another woman puts it more humorously: 'I think this may have happened because of boredom with female company.'

We might think that the girls' schools, with no boys present, would be free from jealousy about them, but the girls provide plenty of evidence that this is not the case. This is shown by the frequency of remarks such as, 'Trouble over boys, feuds in classroom'; 'Girls tended to do this when they had nothing else to occupy their time and when some girls had a boy-friend they all liked.' Of related interest are, 'A hard core of boy-mad individuals made life unpleasant for the others', 'There was a definite element of spiteful girls and these were usually boy-mad girls', and 'One group kept spreading rumours indiscriminately, mostly about boys.'

The last question to be considered in this section on girls is about prefects and their attitude to the other pupils.

PREFECTS OFFICIOUS

The same question was put to the girls as was put to the boys: 'Do you agree or disagree with the following statement about your co-educational school? "The prefects were officious." Agree strongly/ Agree/Doubtful,' etc. The phrase 'girls' school' was substituted for 'co-educational school' in the parallel questionnaire. The estimates are in Table 6.6; no free responses were requested because of time limitations.

TABLE 6.6 *Prefects officious (girls)*

'*Both schools' survey*

Estimates of ex-pupils about prefects' officiousness	Replies about first school attended				Replies about last school attended			
	Co-educational		Girls'		Co-educational		Girls'	
	N	%	N	%	N	%	N	%
Agree strongly	12	4·1	67	16·7	13	3·7	31	12·1
Agree	77	26·1	131	32·6	54	15·4	71	27·7
Doubtful	70	23·7	93	23·1	108	30·9	60	23·4
Disagree	116	39·3	97	24·1	134	38·3	80	31·3
Disagree strongly	20	6·8	14	3·5	41	11·7	14	5·5
Totals	295	100	402	100	350	100	256	100

NOTE: The differences between the co-educational and girls' schools both for 'first' and 'last' schools are statistically significant beyond ·001 level.

As with the previous results presented in this chapter, Table 6.6 gives a more favourable result for co-educational than for girls' schools and this is true whether the school was attended as a junior or as a senior, though the seniors of both types of school (some of whom would have been prefects themselves) are less inclined than the juniors to criticize the prefects as being officious. We see that whereas 30 per cent of the women agree about the officiousness of the prefects in their co-educational school when they were juniors, this rises to almost half for those who were juniors at girls' schools. The corresponding figures for seniors are 19 and 30 per cent. This is not reported as a criticism of the working or organization of girls' schools, but merely as something that is recorded by responsible ex-pupils and which might arise simply through the one-sex nature of the schools. It could be argued that the prefects would appear to be more officious in single-sex schools because of the tighter control that these schools seem to entail compared with co-educational schools, and even that the 'consumers' would naturally consider the prefects to be more officious than they really were.

Comment

It cannot be said too often that the co-education/single-sex variable is not the only one which affects pupils' attitudes about such questions as those discussed in this chapter. There is in consequence a wide range of pupil attitude and tone within schools of each kind. The views expressed, though not usually those of the *best* pupils academically, are those of good academic pupils who are obviously endeavouring to give carefully considered judgments and who are able through their experience to compare co-educational and single-sex schools. It is likely that the views of the less academically minded pupils might be more extreme in both types of school.

7

Life in school I

Under the heading 'Life in school' are gathered together a number of inquiries which seek to probe, even if somewhat superficially, various aspects of day-to-day life in co-educational as opposed to single-sex grammar schools. Some questions, such as those on pupil happiness and school atmosphere, are regarded as sufficiently important to merit treatment independently of the others, while the present ones, though not without their own importance, need not be analysed so intensively. It is not pretended that all the important questions have been included, merely that an effort has been made to examine some claims and counter-claims that have been hurled between the contending groups. The first of the inquiries to be reported was concerned with the narrowness of the education.

Narrowness of education

In the 'Both schools' inquiry students were asked whether they agreed or disagreed with the following statement about first their co-educational and then their single-sex school: 'The education I got was extremely narrow. Agree strongly/Agree/Doubtful/ Disagree/Disagree strongly.' No provision was made for free responses. The results of the women are taken first.

FEMALE EX-PUPILS

A mere scanning of Figure 7.1 reveals that, as is usual in this survey, the women's replies are decidedly more favourable about their co-educational schools than about their girls' schools.

For both types of school, the women who attended a particular type last thought the education provided in it was rather less narrow than did those for whom this type was their first secondary school. The difference between co-educational and girls' schools, however, is only a little less for 'last schools' than for 'first schools'; in both cases the education provided in the girls' schools was considered to be narrower. Those who disagreed or disagreed strongly

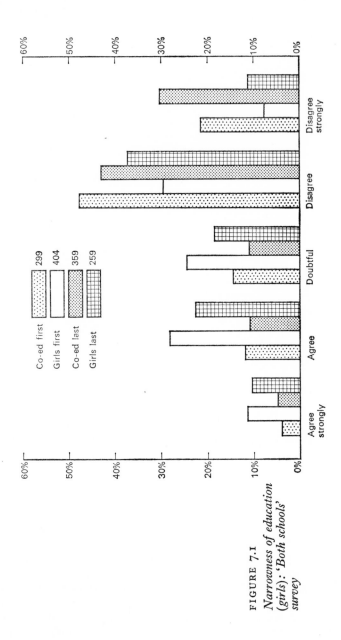

FIGURE 7.1
Narrowness of education (girls): 'Both schools' survey

that the education was narrow in co-educational schools were 70 per cent (first schools) and 73 per cent (last schools), and for girls' schools 35 per cent and 48 per cent. To report these results is one thing, but to interpret them is another. The wording of the statement tended to suggest that it was true; this would increase somewhat the affirmative response, but would presumably have a similar weight for both opposing groups. There is some evidence from the free responses made to other items that the view taken of 'education' was something more than academic instruction. At the same time the students also appear to think that the girls' schools place more emphasis on examination success, at the expense of other matters, than do the co-educational schools.

MALE EX-PUPILS

The results for male ex-pupils are in Table 7.1.

TABLE 7.1 *Narrowness of education (boys)*

'*Both schools*' *survey*

Estimates of narrowness of education	Replies about first schools				Replies about last schools			
	Co-educational		Boys'		Co-educational		Boys'	
	N	%	N	%	N	%	N	%
Agree strongly	5	6·0	17	14·3	4	3·8	2	2·8
Agree	14	16·9	38	32·0	16	15·4	17	23·9
Doubtful	12	14·5	18	15·1	18	17·3	12	16·9
Disagree	35	42·1	40	33·6	42	40·4	26	36·7
Disagree strongly	17	20·5	6	5·0	24	23·1	14	19·7
Totals	83	100	119	100	104	100	71	100

NOTE: The difference between co-educational and boys' schools is statistically highly significant for first schools but not significant for last schools, though the difference is in the same direction.

Here again the co-educational schools are considered to provide the less narrow education, but though the difference between the 'first school' groups is statistically highly significant, that between the 'last school' groups is not significant. Approaching half those students who attended boys' schools first agreed or agreed strongly that the education provided in them was narrow, as opposed to almost a quarter of those who attended co-educational schools first. Even for those in the 'last schools' groups the difference was in the same direction, the corresponding percentages being 27 and 19.

This question was not considered to be quite suitable for asking in schools, but the Schools project questionnaire contained a related question on 'preparation for the adult world'; the results from this are, however, placed more appropriately in Chapter 16.

A part of school life which can help to prevent the education from being too narrow is out-of-class activities, such as debating societies, drama groups and various societies catering for hobbies. The next section of the chapter has a somewhat cursory look at this area.

Out-of-school activities

In the 'Both schools' survey the ex-pupils were asked, 'Do you agree or disagree with the following statements about your co-educational school? There were enjoyable out-of-school activities (other than games).' The same question was asked about their single-sex school, and the ex-pupils could choose between the categories of the usual five-point scale, beginning 'agree strongly'. The women's estimates are summarized in Table 7.2.

These female ex-pupils evidently thought their co-educational

TABLE 7.2 *'Were enjoyable out-of-school activities'* (*female ex-pupils*)

'*Both schools*' *survey*

| | Replies about first school attended | | | | Replies about last school attended | | | |
| | Co-educa-tional | | Girls' | | Co-educa-tional | | Girls' | |
	N	%	N	%	N	%	N	%
Agree strongly	82	27·6	23	5·7	123	34·2	34	13·1
Agree	107	36·0	94	23·3	151	41·9	89	34·4
Doubtful	44	14·8	106	26·3	41	11·4	47	18·2
Disagree	48	16·2	114	28·3	36	10·0	49	18·9
Disagree strongly	16	5·4	66	16·4	9	2·5	40	15·4
Totals	297	100	403	100	360	100	259	100

NOTE: The difference between co-educational and girls' schools was statistically highly significant (beyond ·001 level for both first and last schools).

schools were better at providing enjoyable out-of-school activities than were their girls' schools, both in the schools attended as juniors and those attended as seniors. Possible interpretations are that the girls' schools did not provide enough out-of-school activities or that they were not as enjoyable as in the co-educational schools. As there were no free responses we do not know what was in the minds of the students when they gave their estimates. An analysis of the results according to the occupational class of the fathers of the respondents produced no discernible association, but analysis by first and last schools gave a more favourable result for last schools, whether they were co-educational or girls' schools.

The results for male ex-pupils yield the same direction of difference, but the amount is smaller, that between first schools (i.e. those attended as juniors) being statistically significant but that between last schools being far from significant, so that this advantage for co-educational schools attended as seniors is not reliable. As in the case of the females the male ex-pupils gave more favourable estimates of the out-of-school activities when they were seniors in the school—both co-educational and boys' schools— than did ex-pupils who were junior pupils.

Look forward to coming to school

The next item to be considered comes from the Schools project (1966) and was, 'I look forward to coming to school each day. Agree strongly/Agree/Doubtful/Disagree/Disagree strongly.' The estimates of girls aged 13 plus and 17 plus are in Table 7.3.

TABLE 7.3 *'Look forward to coming to school' (girls' estimates)*

Schools project

	Replies of 13-plus girls				Replies of 17-plus girls			
	Co-educational schools		Girls' schools		Co-educational schools		Girls' schools	
	N	%	N	%	N	%	N	%
Agree strongly	14	6·5	16	7·6	6	5·3	2	1·7
Agree	73	34·0	70	33·2	49	43·0	39	32·5
Doubtful	71	33·0	52	24·6	25	21·9	34	28·3
Disagree	41	19·1	50	23·7	30	26·3	35	29·2
Disagree strongly	16	7·4	23	10·9	4	3·5	10	8·3
Totals	215	100	211	100	114	100	120	100

Here the girls from the co-educational schools look forward to coming to school each day rather more than do those from girls' schools, especially the seniors, but neither the difference between the senior groups nor that between the junior groups is statistically significant, though the former approaches it. Support, however, is given to the finding by the direction of the differences being common to both seniors and juniors, and by this direction being the same as that found in most of these inquiries. Incidentally, the differences between the distributions are to be seen more clearly in the two 'disagree' categories than on the positive side.

The pupils' comments about 'looking forward to coming to school' were much more responsible than might have been expected. Though they show only a few differences between co-educational and girls' schools they are given a fairly full treatment

TABLE 7.4 *'Look forward to coming to school' (girls' responses)*
Schools project, 1966

Estimate	Comment	Co-educational schools	Girls' schools
Agree and	*School*		
Agree	like school very much	16	3
strongly	fun, interesting, enjoyable, love it	15	15
	friendly atmosphere, happy	10	6
	like usually, on the whole	9	18
	Pupils		
	to meet friends	16	24
	to meet boy-friend	1	
	to meet boy-friend nearby		1
	because mixed	1	
	Teachers and teaching		
	nice, kind, helpful	6	2
	if lessons interesting that day	11	5
	one particular teacher		1
	enjoy lessons	5	3
	lessons useful	1	3
	Activities		
	various, enjoyable, exciting, games	2	6
	Others		
	bored at home, better than home	13	6
	except in rain, getting up early	6	1
	unhappy at home		1
	other single mentions	5	3
Totals		117	98

[*continued*]

TABLE 7.4 *(continued)* '*Look forward to coming to school*' *(girls'* *responses)*
Schools project, 1966

Estimate	Comment	Co-educational schools	Girls' schools
Doubtful	doubtful in general	6	5
	depends which teacher, lessons, that day	30	21
	sometimes	10	3
	depends on mood, health, weather	5	6
	depends whether test, homework done	2	3
	dislike getting up early	3	2
	like meeting friends	3	
	all right when get there	5	11
	too much routine, monotonous		3
	others	9	5
Totals		73	59
Disagree and Disagree strongly	*School*		
	hate school	3	3
	dislike school	15	25
	dislike but necessary		2
	but don't hate it	3	5
	but enjoy when get there	3	6
	Teachers and teaching		
	boring	6	6
	depends what day, teacher	9	4
	dislike teacher attitudes	1	5
	pressure too great, too difficult	2	3
	depends homework done		1
	not tests or exams	1	
	Activities		
	prefer leisure activities, home	3	8
	Personal		
	don't like getting up, too early	16	13
	get very tired		4
	depends on mood		2
	Work		
	rather be working	2	1
	Others	3	4
Totals		67	92

because they also have value as a documentation of one aspect of life in school (Table 7.4).

The analysis of the girls' free responses provides good support for the verdict of their estimates. From the 329 girls in co-educational and 331 in girls' schools there came 258 and 249 comments respectively. Of these, 118 favourable comments were from the co-educational and 98 from the girls' schools, and 67 unfavourable comments from the co-educational and 92 from the girls' schools. An analysis which separated the girls aged 13 plus from the 17-year-olds showed that at age 17 plus the co-educated girls looked forward to going to school appreciably more than the 17 plus girls from girls' schools, while at age 13 plus the co-educated girls had decidedly fewer *adverse* comments than did the girls from girls' schools. The difference between the distributions from co-educational and girls' schools is not quite statistically significant at the ·05 level for either the 17-year-old or 13-year-old group. In Table 7·5 these results are presented in numerical form.

TABLE 7.5 *'Look forward to coming to school'. Breakdown of free responses by age of pupil and type of school (girls)*
Schools project

	Favourable				Unfavourable				Doubtful				Totals		
	17+		13+		17+		13+		17+		13+		17+	13+	
	N	%	N	%	N	%	N	%	N	%	N	%	N	N	%
Co-ed. schools	50	51	68	42	31	32	36	23	17	17	56	35	98	160	100
Girls' schools	33	36	65	42	35	38	57	36	24	26	35	22	92	157	100

NOTE: The difference between the co-educational and girls' schools distributions is not significant in either case (13 plus and 17 plus).

If we compare the responses from the two types of school in the detailed Table (7.4), the emphasis is clearly on the similarity of the causes of 'looking forward to coming to school', and the same applies to the negative side; in other words, the underlying basis of human nature asserts itself, whatever the type of school. Some girls do not like getting up early to go to school and this force is not removed or neutralized by either type of school. This therefore 'waters down' any difference caused by the school type. A few of the differences, however, are worthy of mention. In the favourable section ('agree', etc.) there are sixteen mentions under 'like very much' for co-educational schools compared with three for the girls' schools, an imbalance not removed by the results given in the other sub-sections of the 'school' category. On the other hand, in the returns from girls' schools there was greater emphasis on going to school 'to meet friends'. In the unfavourable section the most important difference is between the twenty-seven girls from the girls' schools who disliked going to school as against the fifteen from co-educational schools. One of the most prominent replies, from both types of school, is understandably 'depends on the day, or the teacher', but it is a little surprising to find so many pupils complaining about having to get up early!

The differences in detail reported above are not substantial enough to stand by themselves, but their general trend agrees with the findings in the rest of the research.

A few interesting or amusing quotations are selected to illustrate the text, taking those from co-educational schools first. A few of the co-educated girls look forward to going to school each day because they will meet a boy-friend:

'Because my boy-friend goes to the same school.'

'Because we are in a mixed school!!!!' (sic)

Some of the comments are so enthusiastic they are refreshing to read:

'I would stay at school always if I could.'

'School is always happy because of sports, drama etc.'

Then there is a hint that it is not quite done to admit openly that you enjoy school:

'I pretend not to but I enjoy it all the same.'

Occasionally one comes across an unexpected or droll reason:

'I only like a few subjects, but I like the uniform.'

The negative reasons cover a wide range:

'The lessons are dry and I hate getting up.'

'The thought of getting up in the morning is painful.'

'The thought of hard work gets me down.'

'Sometimes I feel queer when I come to school.'

'My mother misses me strongly so I dislike leaving her.'

'Who'd look forward to it?'

The girls from girls' schools give similar reasons, including even the boy-friends:

'To see the boys from the boys' school down the road.'

There is also the same sprinkling of enthusiastic comments:

'School days are really the happiest days of my life.'

'There are usually exciting things to do.'

Again we have the somewhat unexpected reasons, such as the girl who looks forward to coming to school because, 'Sometimes I am very unhappy at home.' Those who dislike school express themselves more forcibly than those from the co-educational schools:

'School stinks.'

'As I have said before, I *hate* school.'

'School's a drag.'

'All I look forward to in school is the dinner and home time.'

'I don't like school and the teachers are like a lot of old maids.'

'I dislike school and the attitude of teachers.'

'I am always tired and the thought of school is awful.'

The general trend of these results was again confirmed in the 'Check' survey, with 1,122 pupils aged 13 plus. The tabulated data may be consulted in Table A.11. Although a rather greater percentage of co-educated girls say they look forward to coming to school each day than do those from girls' schools, and rather fewer disagree with the statement, the difference between the distributions is not quite statistically significant.

The estimates made by the boys in answer to the same question are in Table 7.6.

The estimates of the boys resemble those of the girls in that the co-educated boys look forward to coming to school rather more than do those from boys' schools, but they differ in that the result for the boys aged 13 plus is almost statistically significant, while on the other hand there is a near equality between the two senior groups.

The free responses made by the boys (Table A.12) support the estimates. Although there were 538 of these they produce rather small numbers when divided into the numerous sub-sections, and it is therefore safer and more illuminating to consider the effect of the tabulated results as a whole rather than to consider individual sub-sections. This overview is also made necessary by the subjective element which enters into some parts of the classifying process.

The table indicates that the co-educated boys score rather more heavily in the more important items of the favourable section, such as 'like school much' and 'like school usually', and correspondingly score lower than boys from boys' schools on the unfavourable side, as in 'hate it, depressing, dread it', 'dislike school', and 'too boring'.

The comments from the co-educated boys are perhaps a little more humorous than those of the girls, varying from 'school days

TABLE 7.6 *'Look forward to coming to school'* (*boys' estimates*)
School project (1966)

	Replies of 13-plus boys				Replies of 17-plus boys			
	Co-educational schools		Boys' schools		Co-educational schools		Boys' schools	
	N	%	N	%	N	%	N	%
Agree strongly	9	4·0	6	2·8	6	4·5	5	3·7
Agree	62	27·8	52	24·1	51	38·8	48	35·9
Doubtful	67	30·0	60	27·8	32	24·2	46	34·3
Disagree	69	31·0	67	31·0	32	24·2	27	20·1
Disagree strongly	16	7·2	31	14·3	11	8·3	8	6·0
Totals	223	100	216	100	132	100	134	100

are the happiest days of your life!' and 'I would be lost without school to go to', to 'I consider every school day as bringing me nearer to a Saturday', and 'would you enjoy going to prison?' One young man wrote, 'some days I do not like coming, so I don't.' Another is doubtful 'because it is like a tape-recorder, it keeps the same each week,' while another looks forward to school 'on Thursday, Friday and Tuesday'. Finally we have a somewhat precocious lad of thirteen saying, 'from a young boy I have always been fascinated by study.'

The comments from boys in boys' schools also have this touch of humour, though it is sometimes unconscious, beginning with the seventeen-year-old who hoped 'in a sense never to leave school, i.e. be a teacher'. Another who agreed that he looked forward to school added, 'but I don't jump for joy at the thought.' One boy turned the question round and asked the inquisitor, 'Do you like doing work—or forced labour?' Similar in opinion—though not in tone—is, 'I find the thought of school each day depresses me.' A boy more thoughtful in outlook wrote, 'Residual working-class distrust of education. Anyway I want to earn money.' Finally there are three comments which succinctly sum up the attitude of the discontented:

'To look forward to school is not normal.'

'Most of the teachers dislike me.'

'I hate masters and I hate school.'

Comment

The major part of the discussion is reserved for the concluding chapter, but here a few comments are necessary. For the themes of this chapter the comparison of co-educational and single-sex schools is advantageous to the former. In the Schools project and its ancillary research, the 'Check' questionnaire, this advantage is slight and occasionally disappears and a state of equality is reached, but in the 'Both schools' project, where the ex-students had experienced both types of school, the co-educational lead became considerable. The difference between these results occurs throughout the book and will be discussed later.

8

Life in school II

The subject of the previous chapter is continued in this, but the merging of the two chapters would have created one of unwieldy length. In addition this chapter describes research which used a slightly different technique. It was thought that some of the pupils and students might have been 'on their guard' and might have answered the more formal questions defensively, trying not to give a bad impression of themselves or betray their loyalty to their school. For example, if asked, 'Do you consider the atmosphere of the school is Very pleasant/Pleasant/Neutral/Rather unpleasant/Very unpleasant?' pupils might not have cared to admit the worst, or even have been afraid to admit it for fear of the answer being seen by school authorities. By giving them, however, a forced choice between adjectives of opposite meaning (with an intermediate neutral option) which could describe the school, this defensive barrier or the fear of discovery might be surmounted. In addition the words chosen might also get to the heart of any difference in the spirit of the school life in the two types of school community.

To this end respondents were asked, 'Which of the following words *best* fits your school life? Try to choose one of the first two alternatives, even if it doesn't fit exactly. Use "neither" only as a last resort.

Q.45. Lively/dull/neither
Q.46. Variety/monotony/neither
Q.47 Enthusiasm/apathy/neither
Q.48. Kindness/unpleasantness/neither
Q.49. Friendly individuals/cliques or gangs/neither'

These questions were asked of pupils aged 13 plus and 17 plus in the Schools project (1966 only) and of different pupils (girls only) aged 13 plus in the 'Check' questionnaire. To have presented all the results in tabular form would have overcrowded the book, hence no tables are given where the replies from co-educational and single-sex schools are approximately equivalent.

The girls' estimates are presented first. For girls aged 13 plus there was either little or no difference between the co-educated girls and those from girls' schools for all five items; there was equality for Lively/Dull, a slight advantage to girls' schools for Enthusiasm/Apathy, a very slight advantage to co-education for Variety/Monotony, and a slight advantage to co-education in the remaining two items. None of these differences even approached statistical significance.

A more positive result came from the 17-year-old girls. Though the Lively/Dull item again yielded equality, and the Friendly individuals/Cliques item was only slightly favourable to co-education, the better results in the other three items came from the co-educated pupils (Table 8.1).

TABLE 8.1 *Life in school (items 46, 47 and 48)*

Schools project (girls aged 17 plus)

		Replies about co-educational schools		Replies about girls' schools	
		N	%	N	%
Item 46	variety	84	73·7	81	67·5
	monotony	30	26·3	34	28·3
	neither	0	0	5	4·2
	Total	114	100	120	100
Item 47	enthusiasm	78	69·0	73	60·8
	apathy	21	18·6	37	30·9
	neither	14	12·4	10	8·3
	Total	113	100	120	100
Item 48	kindness	103	90·4	97	80·8
	unpleasantness	4	3·5	18	15·0
	neither	7	6·1	5	4·2
	Total	114	100	120	100

NOTE: The difference between the groups from co-educational and girls' schools is statistically highly significant for the kindness/unpleasantness item, approaching significance (Chi-square = 5·04 for 2 D.F.) for enthusiasm/apathy, and for variety/monotony yields a Chi-square of 3·264 for 2 D.F. with Yates's correction.

If we look at item 48 in the table we find that more co-educated girls than girls from girls' schools thought kindness was descriptive of their schools (even here 81 per cent applied this adjective to their girls' school). Correspondingly, fewer of the co-educated girls thought the word 'unpleasantness' characterized their schools. In item 47 appreciably fewer of the co-educated girls than of the girls from girls' schools considered that 'apathy' described their schools, and appreciably more selected 'enthusiasm' as the most suitable word. The advantage to the co-educated girls on Variety/Monotony is smaller and no further comment is made.

Four of these same questions were included in the 'Check' questionnaire, the respondents being all girls of the same age as those aged 13 plus in the Schools project, and in the same schools, but who were *not* included in the 1964 testing. The item on Kindness/Unpleasantness gave a very slight advantage to girls' schools and that on Variety/Monotony a very slight advantage in the opposite direction, neither difference being anywhere near to statistical significance. The question on Friendly individuals/Cliques produced a result which was favourable to the co-educational schools, but not quite statistically significant. When asked, however, whether they thought their schools were 'lively' or 'dull' a significantly larger number of the co-educated than of girls from girls' schools answered 'lively' and fewer answered 'dull' (Table 8.2).

It is not often in all this research that the difference between the

TABLE 8.2 (*a*) *Lively/Dull*, (*b*) *Friendly individuals/Cliques*

'*Check*' *project* (*girls aged 13 plus*)

	Replies about co-educational schools		Replies about girls' schools	
	N	%	N	%
lively	384	86·5	526	78·6
dull	32	7·2	83	12·4
neither	28	6·3	60	9·0
Total	444	100	669	100
friendly individuals	279	63·0	389	58·6
cliques or gangs	135	30·5	242	36·4
neither	29	6·5	33	5·0
Total	443	100	664	100

NOTE: The Chi-square for lively/dull was 11·39 for 2 D.F., and for friendly/cliques 4·812 for 2 D.F.

two boys' groups is greater than that between the two girls' groups, but this is true of the result from their five items considered as a whole (Tables 8.3 and 8.4). We shall see, however, that one of these items does not conform to the general trend.

TABLE 8.3 *Life in school:* (*a*) *Lively*, (*b*) *Enthusiasm* (*boys*)

Schools project

	Replies from 13-plus boys				Replies from 17-plus boys			
	Co-educational schools		Boys' schools		Co-educational schools		Boys' schools	
	N	%	N	%	N	%	N	%
Lively	184	82·9	161	75·2	104	79·4	103	75·7
Dull	18	8·1	40	18·7	24	18·3	19	14·0
Neither	20	9·0	13	6·1	3	2·3	14	10·3
Totals	222	100	214	100	131	100	136	100
Enthusiasm	160	73·7	136	65·0	90	69·8	81	60·0
Apathy	31	14·3	39	18·7	35	27·1	34	25·2
Neither	26	12·0	34	16·3	4	3·1	20	14·8
Totals	217	100	209	100	129	100	135	100

NOTE: The 13-year-old and 17-year-old co-educated boys rated their schools as more lively (at ·01 and ·025 significance levels) than did those from boys' schools, and the 17-year-old co-educated boys also rated their schools as showing more enthusiasm. The same trend in the 13-year-olds falls short of statistical significance (Chi-square = 3·778 for 2 D.F.), but gains support from the other results.

The data in Tables 8.3 and 8.4 indicate that the 13-year-old co-educated boys believed their schools to be more lively and less dull, to have more variety and to be less monotonous, to show more kindness and less unpleasantness, and possibly to show more enthusiasm than the boys from boys' schools believed about their own schools. The 17-year-old co-educated boys similarly believed their schools to be more lively and more enthusiastic. For the Friendly individuals/Cliques item there was virtual equality for the two 17-year-old groups, and a very slight advantage, far from being statistically significant, to the 13-year-olds from boys' schools. The 17-year-old boys from boys' schools also had the slenderest of leads on the Variety/Monotony item, with equality for 'unpleasantness' versus 'unkindness'.

TABLE 8.4 *Life in school: (a) Variety (b) Kindness*

Schools project (boys 13 plus)

		Replies about co-educational schools		Replies about boys' schools	
		N	%	N	%
Item 46	Variety	177	80·8	152	71·0
	Monotony	32	14·6	52	24·3
	Neither	10	4·6	10	4·7
	Totals	219	100	214	100
Item 48	Kindness	158	72·5	124	59·1
	Unpleasantness	31	14·2	40	19·0
	Neither	29	13·3	46	21·9
	Totals	218	100	210	100

NOTE: The differences between the groups from co-educational and boys' schools are statistically significant at the ·05 and ·025 levels.

Comment

The results obtained from the slightly different technique used in this part of the research fit into the general picture which has emerged from the main approach. It would seem self-evident that co-educational schools would have more variety than single-sex schools in their social life and even in their classrooms (though what seems self-evident is not always true), but it is interesting to find evidence that this difference in atmosphere probably includes a greater liveliness, enthusiasm, kindness and friendliness between pupils in co-educational schools. In the twenty-four comparisons made in this section between co-educational and single-sex schools one would not expect, in view of all the forces involved, that every difference would be in favour of the co-educational schools, and we do find some of them becoming an equality, but only exceptionally does the difference swing slightly in the opposite direction. There are also distinct variations in atmosphere between schools of the same type; further research is therefore needed on different samples of schools. It would appear, none the less, that in this comparison the co-educational schools have a 'flying start' which may only be lost by the influence of such factors as a very bad head, unusually indifferent staff, or a very deprived catchment area.

Occupational Class

An interesting by-product of the results is a trend associated with occupational class, well defined in both boys' and girls' schools, less certain among co-educated girls and absent among this sample of co-educated boys (Table 8.5). The following section looks at this trend, departing for the moment from the main comparison between co-educational and single-sex schools.

TABLE 8.5 *Analysis by occupational class of items 45 to 49*
Schools project

	Replies from boys in boys' schools								Replies from girls in girls' schools							
	Boys aged 17 plus Class				Boys aged 13 plus Class				Girls aged 17 plus Class				Girls aged 13 plus Class			
	1 and 2		3, 4, 5		1 and 2		3, 4, 5		1 and 2		3, 4, 5		1 and 2		3, 4, 5	
	N	%	N	%	N	%	N	%	N	%	N	%	N	%	N	%
Lively	54	78·3	49	73·2	81	78·6	80	72·1	50	82·0	44	74·6	83	86·4	98	83·1
Dull	6	8·7	13	19·4	17	16·5	23	20·7	10	16·4	12	20·3	11	11·5	15	12·7
Neither	9	13·0	5	7·4	5	4·9	8	7·2	1	1·6	3	5·1	2	2·1	5	4·2
Total	69	100	67	100	103	100	111	100	61	100	59	100	96	100	118	100
Variety	50	72·5	43	65·2	77	74·0	75	68·2	42	68·8	39	66·1	75	78·2	90	77·6
Monotony	13	18·8	20	30·3	22	21·2	30	27·3	15	24·6	19	32·2	20	20·8	20	17·2
Neither	6	8·7	3	4·5	5	4·8	5	4·5	4	6·6	1	1·7	1	1·0	6	5·2
Total	69	100	66	100	104	100	110	100	61	100	59	100	96	100	116	100
Enthusiasm	43	62·3	38	57·5	71	68·9	65	61·3	38	62·3	35	59·3	75	79·0	82	72·9
Apathy	16	23·2	18	27·3	17	16·5	22	20·8	17	27·9	20	33·9	10	10·5	19	16·8
Neither	10	14·5	10	15·2	15	14·6	19	17·9	6	9·8	4	6·8	10	10·5	12	10·6
Total	69	100	66	100	103	100	106	100	61	100	59	100	95	100	113	100
Kindness	51	73·9	50	75·8	62	60·8	62	57·4	51	83·6	46	78·0	73	76·0	91	77·7
Unpleasantness	6	8·7	8	12·1	20	19·6	20	18·5	7	11·5	11	18·6	12	12·5	14	12·0
Neither	12	17·4	8	12·1	20	19·6	26	24·1	3	4·9	2	3·4	11	11·5	12	10·3
Total	69	100	66	100	102	100	108	100	61	100	59	100	96	100	117	100
Friendly individuals	50	71·4	42	64·6	79	75·9	73	67·6	33	54·1	25	42·4	54	56·3	70	59·4
Cliques or gangs	19	27·1	23	35·4	16	15·4	29	26·9	28	45·9	32	54·2	41	42·7	43	36·4
Neither	1	1·4	0	0	9	8·7	6	5·5	0	0	2	3·4	1	1·0	5	4·2
Total	70	100	65	100	104	100	108	100	61	100	59	100	96	100	118	100

In considering Table 8.5 let us follow the negative or less pleasant qualities, e.g. 'dull', 'monotony', in comparing the responses of those whose fathers were in occupational classes 1 and 2 (combined) with those whose fathers were in occupational classes 3, 4 and 5 (combined). If we look first at boys in boys' schools there are ten comparisons, in nine of which the proportion of occupational classes 3, 4 and 5 endorsing the less pleasant qualities is higher than the proportion for classes 1 and 2, the tenth difference in the opposite direction being the smallest of all. This trend is so steady that it would be surprising if it had occurred by chance, though none of the differences is individually statistically significant. When we turn to the girls in girls' schools we find that all five differences between the two occupational class groupings, at age 17 plus, are in the same direction; those for girls aged 13 plus in girls' schools, however, lack consistency. Intriguingly, the trend is less pronounced with the *co-educated* girls aged 13 plus and 17 plus taken as a whole; with the co-educated boys of the same ages the trend is absent. This possible difference in the atmosphere among boys in co-educational schools compared with those in boys' schools would again seem worthy of further research.

The causes of the trend are not clear and one can only theorize. It may be, for example, that the rather smaller proportion of pupils from occupational classes 3, 4 and 5 in these girls' and boys' grammar schools, compared with co-educational, leads to pupils from the lower occupational classes finding less enjoyment in school life. It may be that the co-educational schools are for some reason less snobbish. Whatever the reason, a somewhat greater proportion of pupils whose fathers are from occupational classes 3, 4 and 5 in the boys' and in the girls' schools (but not, in this sample, for girls aged 13 plus) may find school life, on the average, more dull, more monotonous, less enthusiastic, with more unpleasantness, and with more cliques, than their fellow-pupils from occupational classes 1 and 2 find it. Yet, though these items and the results obtained from them are related, they are not identical; for example, in the sample of boys from boys' schools the difference between the two groups is smallest for Unpleasantness/Kindness and greatest for Friendly individuals/Cliques. It should be emphasized that the analysis lacks statistical confirmation and that the theoretical explanation is merely an interesting speculation.

9

Unhappy pupils[1]

In order to obtain a more detailed insight into the significance of
the results from the large-scale Schools project a series of short
studies was made of all girls who said they were 'unhappy' or
'rather unhappy' at school and had been tested either at 15 years
of age in 1964 or at 13 years of age in 1966. It was thought that
such a study might also help to explain why in this particular
project there was a reduced advantage to the girls in co-educational
schools as against girls in girls' schools. Though full case-studies
could not be made there was much useful information available,
commencing with a detailed questionnaire on attitude to school,
teachers, school subjects, careers, marriage, etc., and ranging
through tests such as the High School Personality Questionnaire
(Cattell), the Mooney Problem Check List and Maudsley Personality Inventory, to teachers' ratings on the Bristol Adjustment
Guide[2] and heads' reports about school and home. Some of the
most valuable information came from the free responses of the
pupils themselves when they were invited to write down (anony-
mously and confidentially) the problems which were troubling
them most.

Of the original sample of 1,028 girls there were only 44 who
said they were 'unhappy' or 'rather unhappy' in school. This is a
small number but the analysis is not meant to stand independently
of the main studies—merely to illuminate them. As limitations of
space prevent the publication of the case-studies in full one has to
be content with an overall account, designed to illustrate the
differences between the 17 pupils from the co-educational schools
and the 27 from girls' schools, though other points arise which are
of general interest. The pupils assessed themselves on 'happiness'
as in Table 9.1, in answer to the question already given in Chapter
2 but here slightly modified, viz.: 'Was your life in school, viewed

[1] This chapter is based on the original full sample of 28 schools tested in
1964; and the 26 schools tested in 1966.
[2] Covering such aspects as, 'Withdrawn', 'Nervousness and Timidity',
'Hostility', 'Anxiety about adults'.

as a whole, Happy/Fairly happy/Jogging along/Rather unhappy/ Unhappy?'

TABLE 9.1 *Girls unhappy at school*

Schools project

| | Co-educated girls | | | Girls in girls' schools | | |
	13 plus	15 plus	Total	13 plus	15 plus	Total
Rather unhappy	6	10	16	7	9	16
Unhappy	0	1	1	5	6	11
Totals	6	11	17	12	15	27
Total sample	231	280	511	237	280	517

Of the 15-year-olds, three out of the eleven from the co-educated group stayed on at school till 17 plus. Two of the three became 'fairly happy' and the other said she was 'jogging along'. Six of the fifteen girls from girls' schools stayed on, of whom one was still 'unhappy', one 'rather unhappy', one 'jogging along', and one 'happy', while one was absent, and the sixth one could not be tested as the school had become co-educational. It should be borne in mind, of course, that chance variations in personality are a possible explanation of these differences, because of the smallness of the numbers.

In attempting to discover why these girls were unhappy or rather unhappy the first area to be explored was pupil–teacher relations, which produced Table 9.2.

TABLE 9.2 *Girls unhappy* at school, pupil–teacher relations*

| Teachers | Co-educated girls | | | Girls at girls' schools | | |
	13 plus	15 plus	Total	13 plus	15 plus	Total
Very friendly	0	0	0	1	0	1
Friendly	3	5	8	5	4	9
Neutral	1	6	7	5	6	11
Rather unfriendly	1	0	1	1	5	6
Very unfriendly	1	0	1	0	0	0
Total	6	11	17	12	15	27
Very helpful	0	1	1	1	0	1
Helpful	2	6	8	4	7	11
Neutral	2	4	6	5	7	12
Rather unhelpful	2	0	2	2	1	3
Very unhelpful	0	0	0	0	0	0
Total	6	11	17	12	15	27

* Includes 'rather unhappy'.

Though this handful of 'unhappy' girls assessed the teachers at the co-educational schools to be less unfriendly and more helpful than the teachers at the girls' schools, it would again be rash to draw any conclusions from this alone, especially as the difference falls short of statistical significance. We must also recognize that there may be other forces affecting pupils' attitudes in addition to those stemming from the co-educational and single-sex settings. Some school pupils, for example, can become unhappy because they haven't the ability to make a satisfactory job of the work demanded of them, and they dislike the constant failure as compared with the success of their fellow-pupils. Now it has already been demonstrated in the previous volume (Dale, 1969) that although an attempt had been made to equate the co-educated schools with the girls' schools there was a distinct (statistically significant) difference in intelligence levels for the full sample, the girls' schools having the superior average at both age levels. Some of this unhappiness, particularly in the co-educational grammar schools, might therefore have been due not to pupil–teacher relations, but to a less selective intake and consequent inability of those of relatively low intelligence to do the work. Although the only measure of intelligence available was the ten-item sub-scale in the High School Personality Questionnaire, this was much better than nothing, and it produced the results in Table 9.3 for the girls aged 15 plus.

TABLE 9.3 *Intelligence scores* of girls in unhappy categories*
(aged 15 plus)

Scores (maximum = 10)	Co-educated girls	Girls in girls' schools
10	1	1
9	4	5
8	0	4
7	0	4
6	4	1
5	1	0
4	1	0
Average	7·18	8·07

* Derived from the miniature scale in the High School Personality Questionnaire. If not high enough in reliability for individuals it suffices for this comparison of groups.

On this scale 7 would be a rather low score at age 15 plus for grammar school work, 6 is definitely low, 5 very low and 4 abysmal.

The girls' schools therefore have only 1 of their 15 unhappy pupils (aged 15 plus) who is clearly too low in score (i.e. below 7), while half of the unhappy co-educated girls are below the line. The 13-year-old girls had a similar distribution of scores (Table 9.4).

TABLE 9.4 *Intelligence scores of girls in unhappy categories*

(*aged 13-plus*)

Scores (maximum = 10)	Co-educated girls	Girls in girls' schools
10	0	1
9	1	1
8	0	5
7	3	2
6	2	3
5	0	0
4	0	0
Average	7·0	7·58

Reference to Tables 9.3 and 9.4 shows that the average score of the girls in girls' schools is in both cases greater than that of the girls in mixed schools. As was anticipated a greater proportion of these co-educated girls than of those in girls' schools could therefore have been unhappy because of their low ability in relation to the grammar school curriculum (cf. McCandless, 1956a and b; Sarason, 1960; Cowen, 1965). Let us then see what the girls themselves said when invited, by free response, to state their special problems (Tables 9.5 and 9.6, see pp. 129–30).

A notable difference about the free responses from the two samples of senior girls (Tables 9.5 and 9.6) is that whereas none of the co-educated girls say they dislike (or hate) school, three of the girls from girls' schools say they 'hate school', another complains that 'our teachers tend to be like icebergs', and another that 'the school atmosphere is rather unpleasant'. Whereas none of the group from girls' schools complain about the difficulty of the work (only one girl had the low intelligence test score of 6 (maximum 10)), with two worrying about passing examinations, such comments are more prevalent in the co-educational group, with its lower I.Q. level. Another pointer is that in the co-educated group, in spite of this lower intelligence level, there is no complaint about too much homework except from the girl who has to stay in to work for examinations, whereas in the group from girls' schools there are several complaints about too much homework and over-emphasis on examinations. It would be wrong, however, to place any reliance on this by itself; it should be viewed as part of the general picture. As the numbers are small it is of some interest to see whether the data obtained from the two groups of junior girls support a similar interpretation (Tables 9.7 and 9.8, see pp. 132–6).

In these tables there are strongly expressed statements showing dislike of school from seven of the pupils in girls' schools, while there is only one, or possibly two, from the co-educated group. Among the latter group it is—as was hypothesized from their lower intelligence level—the difficulty of the work which dominates their free responses. While this aspect is present among the group from girls' schools it seems less dominant.

As this appraisal is necessarily subjective a scheme was devised to obtain a more objective assessment. The free comments of the pupils both in the questionnaire and the Mooney Problem Check List were combined and assessed independently by another psychologist who did not know which groups were from girls' schools and which were from co-educational schools.[1] He was asked to classify the comments as in Table A.13, allocating a score of −2 for strongly unfavourable comments, −1 for adverse comments more moderate in tone, +1 for normal favourable comment and +2 for those enthusiastically favourable. A detailed description of each category is given as a footnote to the Tables. The resulting data confirm the subjective findings given above; by far the more important reasons for unhappiness among the 16 co-educational girls are 'out-of-school' or home difficulties (score − 33)[2] and work difficulties (− 20), with teachers' discipline almost the least important (−2), whereas the 25 girls from girls' schools placed general dislike of the school first (−32), with teachers' discipline second (−26),[3] work difficulties at almost the same level (−23), and out-of-school and home difficulties fourth (−19). In interpreting these figures observe that the two groups are unequal in size; the comparison may therefore be aided by the use of the averages, which are added to the table only to assist the reader.

These unhappy girls, as members of their main group, were

[1] One girl from each group failed to make any comments and had to be excluded from this section.

[2] The amount of unhappiness at home compared with that at school being statistically highly significant. The scores are the overall result after plus scores have been subtracted.

[3] A follow-up test after analyses of variance shows that the difference between the scores of the girls at co-educational schools and those at single-sex schools, for teachers' discipline and dislike of school combined, is statistically significant beyond the ·01 level.

given a number of psychological tests and were also rated for maladjustment by their teachers. Most of these data are presented in Tables A.14 to 18, partly for the benefit of those who would like to make a special study of this aspect, and partly to demonstrate the similarities as well as differences between the opposing groups. In view of the smallness of the numbers in each group, however, only large and consistent differences between the co-educated girls and those from girls' schools are mentioned here in the text. Apart from the slight but consistent advantage to the girls' schools in level of intelligence (which is a reflection of the situation in the main groups), and one other much larger trend, the emphasis in these additional tests is on similarity. This is so in ratings on maladjustment (Bristol, 15 plus), in scores on timidity, insecurity, and neuroticism, all of them being high. The greater anxiety score (in the H.S.P.Q. test) of the unhappy girls aged 15 plus in girls' schools, compared with those in co-educational schools, is not paralleled by the results of the younger (13 plus) unhappy girls in the same schools, who record merely the same high anxiety level as those in mixed schools. Similarly the greater number of *problems* recorded on the Mooney Problem Check List by the unhappy junior girls in girls' schools (than by the co-educated girls) is not present at the senior level, where the scores of both groups are again high.

The much larger—and consistent—trend is one of considerable interest. At both the junior and the senior level the unhappy girls from girls' schools record higher scores on extroversion than do those in co-educational schools. Only the difference between the 15-year-old groups of unhappy girls is statistically significant, but the finding receives some support from their main groups of relatively happy pupils, which show the same trend at both age levels, though here the differences are not statistically significant (yet near to it in the case of the 15-year-olds).[1] Incidentally these results are paralleled by the main groups of boys, where those from boys' schools also have the higher extroversion score, the difference between the 15-year-old groups being statistically significant.

Unless this difference is an artefact of some other variable which the research has failed to detect, the finding provides additional evidence for the argument set out previously that the co-educational and single-sex schools are communities with quite different atmospheres, which for years exert different psychological influences on children, and that the pupils are moulded into adults who

[1] The test for senior girls was the Maudsley Personality Inventory and for the juniors the High School Personality Questionnaire.

are psychologically not what they would have been if they had been educated in the opposite kind of school.

Unfortunately this test of extroversion–introversion was only a small part of a large project and the results have not been followed up. It has to be left to later research to determine first whether the difference in score is confirmed, and then whether it denotes that in this respect one type of school or the other gives a 'better' education. An interrelated question is whether the effect—if it exists—is present over a wide range of the extroversion–introversion scale—and whether the 'good' or 'bad' effects of the schooling vary with the temperament of the individual.

As such a test of personality is particularly sensitive to changes in administration it should be recorded that the same researcher administered the test to all the girls, and that no members of staff were present and no names of pupils appeared on the answer sheets. Pupils regarded the test as important but knew they would not be affected personally by the result. None the less it is not impossible that the difference in score might have been produced because of the contrast between the more friendly and less formal pupil–teacher relations of the co-educational school and the stricter discipline of the girls' school. The girls in the girls' schools might have been less ready to admit to tendencies which the school authorities (if they had read the answers) would perhaps have considered less desirable. On the other hand the unnatural deprivation of the company of the opposite sex might cause girls in girls' schools to become more out-going socially, but the difference between the two groups of girls is not large, and whether the higher extroversion is 'good' or 'bad' will be of little consequence for most of them. For some individuals, on the other hand, it could be important. One of the readers of the typescript—Dr Miller—made the interesting suggestion that there might be a greater tendency for extroverts to feel 'out of place' in a single-sex school than in a co-educational one.

This research was too wide in scope for the writer to be able to spend further efforts on this point. However, much of the above paragraph is theory which must be left to be examined by future research.

Discussion

To be unhappy, or merely 'rather unhappy', at school is, putting it mildly, a very undesirable fate for a child. Fortunately the proportion of such children in the grammar schools examined was very small, whether the schools were co-educational or single-sex, and the free responses of the pupils showed unmistakably that some of this unhappiness—especially in the co-educational schools —had its origin in the home, and was so deeply rooted that there was no escape from it wherever the pupil went. Other unhappiness probably stemmed from the temperament of the pupil herself, as many teacher readers must have been murmuring aloud for some time. Rarely is the teacher the villain of the piece, and even when she is it may often be because it is easier to arrive at a breaking point in friendly human relations in one type of school community than in another. We have seen that teachers and ex-pupils believe that the conduct of each sex of pupil is improved in the presence of the other, this opinion being almost unanimous in the case of the boys. The natural level of discipline in a co-educational school would therefore need to be less strict, with a consequent improvement in teacher–pupil relationships; in this atmosphere it would be less easy for pupil–teacher relationships to deteriorate to a point where lasting unhappiness was produced in a pupil.

In this Schools project, however, the results do not give as great an advantage to the co-educational schools as in the surveys involving ex-pupils and teachers. The reasons for this are examined in detail elsewhere, but this chapter has studied one of them through the case-studies of unhappy pupils. It was recognized at the outset of the research that 'happiness in school' is determined by many forces in addition to staff–pupil relationship, and it has been mentioned above that one of these forces is the home, and that this was the most powerful of the influences producing unhappiness in the co-educational schools examined, but not in the girls' schools, though it could by no means be ignored there. In the latter schools it was factors immediately connected with the schools which were dominant.

Unhappiness at school may also be caused by the attempts of pupils to cope with work which is above their level of intelligence, and this factor is much more prominent in the replies from girls in co-educational schools than in those from girls in girls' schools. In support of this it was shown that the intelligence scores of the co-educated unhappy girls were distributed lower in the scale than those of the unhappy girls in girls' schools. We also saw that the average intelligence score of the entire sample of co-educated girls was lower than that of their opposing group.[1]

The happiness of the pupils might not in itself be a guarantee that a school is good, yet it would be true to say that the *unhappiness* of an appreciable number of pupils, if produced by the school, would be a guarantee that the school was bad! In the

[1] The difference is statistically significant for both the 13-year-old and for the 15-year-old groups.

Schools project neither type of school had a large group of these pupils, and the difference between the schools in this respect was small.

The number of pupils providing the central data for the chapter is not as large as was desirable for reliability, but they are the extreme cases and are therefore important. The writer emphasizes again that the chapter is not meant to stand alone, and wherever possible the data have been linked with the data from the main sample of girls, comprising some thousand pupils.

TABLE 9.5 *Outlines of case-studies of unhappy girls*
Co-educated girls aged 15 plus in 1964

Pupil	Self assessment of happiness at school	Intelligence score	Pupil's free responses
1	Rather unhappy	10	None given.
2	Rather unhappy (1964) Fairly happy (1966)	9	'I am not developed enough for my age.' 'I do not like working indoors but I know that I have to. I would rather be out riding and with horses' (1964). 'I have to stay in every evening to work for exams. I worry if my boy-friend is going out with someone else. We have exams in two weeks and I can't settle down to work' (1966).
3	Rather unhappy	9	'My mother had a nervous breakdown last year and had to give up independent work. Now she misses this and doesn't eat anything. She seems to get terribly irritated with myself, father, etc.'
4	Rather unhappy (1964) Fairly happy (1966)	9	'Often ill at ease with friends, not knowing if they really like me (especially boys). I lack self-confidence. We [family] worry too much about friendship, money, everything' (1964). None given (1966).
5	Unhappy	9	None given.
6	Rather unhappy	6	'My parents expecting too much out of me in the way of schoolwork and therefore I'm afraid to fail because of my parents.'
7	Rather unhappy (1964) Jogging along (1966)	6	'School average marks not encouraging. Not allowed to go out except at weekends. Have to be in fairly early' (1964). 'Exams and not enough pocket money' (1966).
8	Rather unhappy	6	'Trying to find a suitable job in which I shall be happy. Worrying about exam results. Thinking about boys I like.'

[continued]

TABLE 9.5 (*continued*) *Outlines of case-studies of unhappy girls*
Co-educated girls aged 15 girls plus in 1964

Pupil	Self assessment of happiness at school	Intelligence score	Pupil's free responses
9	Rather unhappy	6	'I am very shy at doing things or talking in front of the people in class. Would very much like to have more self-confidence, and have a job.'
10	Rather unhappy	5	'Not being able to discuss matters with my parents; in matters of sex I just get embarrassed. Not being able to give up smoking.'
11	Rather unhappy	4	'What I am going to do when I leave. I'm not interested in the usual kind of job and I've no idea what to do if I don't find a job. I won't bring any money into the family and as our family is large we need more money.'

TABLE 9.6 *Outlines of case-studies of unhappy girls*
Girls in girls' schools aged 15 plus in 1964

Pupil	Self assessment of happiness at school	Intelligence score	Pupil's free responses
1	Rather unhappy	10	No special problem is given.
2	Unhappy (1964) Rather unhappy (1966)	9	'Lack of self-confidence' (1964). 'School atmosphere rather unpleasant. Getting into trouble with the teachers for no reason' (1966). 'Wondering if I'll ever get married' (1966).
3	Unhappy	9	'Want to earn money to buy myself the clothes my parents cannot afford. Am always quarrelling with my family. I can do nothing right.'
4	Rather unhappy	9	None given.
5	Rather unhappy	9	'Lack of self-confidence.'

[continued]

TABLE 9.6 *(continued)* Outlines of case-studies of unhappy girls
Girls in girls' schools aged 15 plus in 1964

Pupil	Self assessment of happiness at school	Intelligence score	Pupil's free responses
6	Rather unhappy (1964) Happy (1966)	9	'Wondering if I am really in love with a boy' (1964). 'Not liking to study; other things always seem more pleasant and I give in very easily. School simply trains you for exams' (1966).
7	Rather unhappy	8	'Problems at home—father—parents disliking my friends. Thinking too much about the opposite sex.'
8	Rather unhappy (1964) Absent (1966)	8	'Whether I will pass my G.C.E. and get a good job.'
9	Unhappy	8	'I hate school and wish I could earn my own money so as not to spend my parents'.'
10	Unhappy	8	'Passing exams before leaving school and getting a job.'
11	Unhappy (1964) Unhappy (1966)	7	'Not having enough money and not enough clothes' (1964). 'I hate school and have lost complete interest in it and I miss someone very much and I am constantly day-dreaming about her during lessons' (1966).
12	Rather unhappy (1964) Jogging along (1966)	7	'Homework takes so much time sometimes it is difficult to get enough sleep. Difficult to concentrate' (1964). 'Wishes to marry but *his* parents oppose' (1966). 'Too much stress on academic work.' 'Our teachers tend to be like icebergs.'
13	Unhappy	7	'Too much homework.'

[*continued*]

TABLE 9.6 (*continued*) *Outlines of case-studies of unhappy girls*
Girls in girls' schools aged 15 plus in 1964

Pupil	Self assessment of happiness at school	Intelligence score	Pupil's free responses
14	Rather unhappy	7	'I hate school and want to start work. At school you are treated much younger than you really are. I am always having arguments with my parents about boys I go out with.'
15	Rather unhappy	6	'School takes up too much of our time and we should have less homework. I don't seem to enjoy myself as much as others.'

TABLE 9.7 *Outlines of case-studies of unhappy girls*
Co-educated girls aged 13 plus in 1966

Pupil	Self assessment of happiness at school	Intelligence score	Pupil's free responses*
1	Rather unhappy	9	She is rather unhappy because, 'People leave me out of things.' The pressure of work worries her because, 'Homework takes too long. In the summer I want to get out in the sunshine.' Later, 'Everything is exams and I get very worried before exams.' 'I can't do as well in school as my parents expect me to do. People don't like me.' (Last two were special problems.)
2	Rather unhappy	7	'I find school dull and uninteresting especially the teachers.' The pressure of work worries her, 'Because it is too strict.'

[*continued*]

TABLE 9.7 (*continued*) *Outlines of case-studies of unhappy girls*
Co-educated girls aged 13 plus in 1966

Pupil	Self assessment of happiness at school	Intelligence score	Pupil's free responses
3	Rather unhappy	7	'I am not a really good pupil. I sometimes never understand the work we do.' The pressure of work worries her, 'Because we get too much homework.' 'The teachers pick on us for every little thing,' and 'I don't like school and some teachers.' 'If I want to get out somewhere special I do not have enough money. Too much homework, don't always understand it. Cannot stay out late at night.'
4	Rather unhappy	7	She disagrees strongly about looking forward to school each day because, 'I want to be a nice person when I grow up.' 'Not being good at French.'
5	Rather unhappy	6	Special problems: 'My father works hard for a good wage but the money does not seem to stretch as there are five of us and mum and dad never get any new clothes. I once went out with someone and worshipped him and when we parted it nearly killed me.' 'I dislike school because I am not clever and some of my friends look down on me.' Agrees the intense pressure of work worries her, 'Because I am not able to understand.' About looking forward to coming to school: 'My mother misses me strongly so I dislike leaving her.' The atmosphere is rather unpleasant, 'Because we have to be forced to come.'

[*continued*]

133

TABLE 9.7 (*continued*) *Outlines of case studies of unhappy girls*
Co-educated girls aged 13 plus in 1966

Pupil	Self assessment of happiness at school	Intelligence score	Pupil's free responses 1966
6	Rather unhappy	6	She is not worried by the pressure of work: 'I like working.' Most teachers 'Try to help us a lot.' She looks forward to coming to school each day, but she is rather unhappy, 'Because I am not liked by many girls.' 'You see all your friends at school.'

* The quotation marks indicate responses to separate questions. Responses volunteered as Special Problems in the Mooney Test are included.

TABLE 9.8 *Outlines of case-studies of unhappy girls*
Girls in girls' schools, aged 13 plus

Pupil	Self assessment of happiness at school	Intelligence score	Pupil's free responses 1966
1	Rather unhappy (1966) Rather unhappy (1964)	10	'I can't remember things and just cannot study. I also get mixed up.' 'Teachers expect rather a lot of you and they always ignore the ones who are not good enough.' 'The atmosphere is all right for working.'
2	Rather unhappy	9	'It's the teachers' attitude to work and Latin and doing homework that I hate. It takes so much of the evening up and is boring.' The pressure of work worries her: 'All work I hate and worry about unless I like it and people don't boss me too much.' She doesn't look forward to coming to school: 'The discipline and strictness of school is mainly the trouble.' 'There is often a feud between pupils and teachers.'

[*continued*]

Pupil	Self assessment of happiness at school	Intelligence score	Pupil's free responses 1966
3	Rather unhappy	8	'I was really excited when I heard I was coming to this school. Now I wish I had never heard of it. Not being able to keep up with the rest of the class. Afraid of dying and hoping there is no hell.' 'I don't seem to get along very well with either the teachers or my classmates—they seem to find me uninteresting.' Pressure of work worries her: 'Teachers expect more of you than you can do.' She disagrees strongly that she looks forward to coming to school: 'I *hate* school'.
4	Rather unhappy	8	'I cannot settle down well and I don't do homework well.' The teachers 'Do not express much emotion to either good or bad and keep themselves to their colleagues' (sic). 'No teachers in our school could take a joke.' Special problems: 'Parents separating. Skin rash since I was a child. Wanting to start work. I am fed up of school.'
5	Unhappy	8	'I find it difficult to get along with people at school.' Special problems: 'My future. Sex.'
6	Rather unhappy (1966) Rather unhappy (1964)	8	'I dislike most subjects. We get tests every week and I worry about them.' 'I hate school.' Special problems: 'I hate French and I just can't understand a word of it. Can't understand my new maths teacher.'
7	Unhappy (1966) Rather unhappy (1964)	8	'I feel I am disliked by many girls because I am poor.' 'Some teachers are too stern.' 'I just can't face school and friends.' Special problems: 'I am frightened about my mother and father having a

[*continued*]

135

Pupil	Self assessment of happiness at school	Intelligence score	Pupil's free responses 1966
			divorce. I have a terrible feeling that boys hate me and I'll never get married. I don't mean to swear but it just comes out and when people talk about dirty stories it makes me think.'
8	Unhappy	7	'I am not clever and you are at school for too long.' (But she is not worried by the pressure of work.)
9	Unhappy	7	'I think our school is unhappy because we are shut in too much. We aren't allowed out of school till we go home at night.' 'The teachers pile the work on us and they think it isn't much.' 'Our teachers are usually friendly, they like a joke as much as we do.' 'Our teachers are humorous but I still don't like school.' Special problems: 'Taking things too seriously. Sometimes lying without meaning to.'
10	Rather unhappy	6	'Teachers get annoyed, but sometimes can be pleasant.' (No special problems recorded.)
11	Rather unhappy	6	'There are too many rules to be obeyed.' 'Certain teachers can be very friendly but others are much too bad-tempered.' 'I hate school.' The atmosphere 'Is too serious and precise.' (No special problems.)
12	Unhappy	6	'I hate school and will be glad when I leave.' 'Teachers expect you to know too much, if you don't know they get mad.' 'A lot of teachers at our school are grumpy.' Special problems: 'Before German lessons I always get butterflies in my stomach.'

10

Out-of-school conduct

Most schools take an interest in the out-of-school conduct of their pupils, and many pupils agree that the intention is a good one. The debate is about where the line is to be drawn between parental rights and school demands, between the freedom of the pupil to do as he pleases after school hours, away from the school buildings, and the desire of the school to ensure that its pupils, in their contact with the world, should develop into good citizens and preserve untarnished the school image. The line is inevitably imprecise and is drawn in very different places by individual schools. It is naturally the extremes which attract attention, either undue interference or undue laxity. Though the main purpose of this chapter is to compare co-educational and single-sex schools, there is much that is of general interest, and more than a touch of humour.

This topic was examined in only the 'Both schools' enquiry, which included the question, 'Do you consider that the school's concern with the out-of-school conduct of pupils was, Excessive/Rather strict/Just right/Rather insufficient/Much too lax?' All the ex-pupils had attended at least one co-educational and one single-sex grammar school, and were therefore able to compare the two types. The estimates of the women are given in Table 10.1.

The salient features of Table 10.1 are, first, that whereas over half the estimates for the co-educational schools, both senior and junior, come into the 'just right' category, those for the girls' schools are only one third; second, that the remaining estimates for the co-educational schools are divided evenly above and below the 'just right' line, but those for the girls' schools are concentrated more in the 'rather strict' and 'excessive' categories which comprise over half the estimates. This concentration resulted in a reduction at the opposite end of the scale so that the proportion of those who thought the out-of-school control of the co-educational schools was rather insufficient was greater than in the case of the girls' schools. This finding (like that about the boys in the next section) is again in agreement with those found previously that discipline in single-sex schools is more severe; it also agrees with the theory

TABLE 10.1 *Out-of-school conduct of girls*

'*Both schools*' survey

Estimates of school's concern with out-of-school conduct of pupils	Replies about first school attended				Replies about last school attended			
	Co-educational		Girls'		Co-educational		Girls'	
	N	%	N	%	N	%	N	%
Excessive	7	2·4	66	16·5	10	2·9	40	15·7
Rather strict	62	21·2	142	35·6	73	21·0	103	40·4
Just right	155	53·1	145	36·3	179	51·2	82	32·1
Rather insufficient	56	19·2	37	9·3	76	21·8	26	10·2
Much too lax	12	4·1	9	2·3	11	3·1	4	1·6
Totals	292	100	399	100	349	100	255	100

NOTE: The differences between co-educational and girls' schools for both first and last schools are statistically significant beyond the ·001 level.

based on this, which ascribes the difference to the contrast between the psychological forces at work within the two school communities. It has been suggested that part of the difference between girls' and co-educational schools might be due to male teachers not noticing minor breaches of the code of conduct (as distinct from not wanting to notice); this, however, does not explain the stricter enforcement of this code in boys' schools.

The free responses under this heading have been classified. (Table A.9) and placed in *Appendix 2*. Their distribution in categories was as expected from the estimates. The examples quoted have been selected in equal proportions in the respective categories, from both girls' and co-educational schools, but the 'excessive interest' and 'much too lax' categories have been given double weighting to secure their adequate representation. As the distributions of the estimates for first and last schools were reasonably similar they were merged. The quotations about the co-educational schools the ex-pupils attended are as follows:

EXCESSIVE 'We were brought up before the senior master if we were known to be courting one of the boys out of school—even if we never saw them during the day—and given a lecture on "how to behave" so we wouldn't disgrace the name of the school.'

'It was thought wrong to mix with pupils from the Sec. Mod. school.'

RATHER STRICT 'The headmaster would frequently stop his car in the middle of a main street and reprimand his pupils for trivial misdemeanours.'

'The headmaster would not give his consent to any member of his school who wished to take art or pottery at night school.'

'The senior mistress fussed about uniform and eating lollipops in the street.'

JUST RIGHT 'Limited to caps and hats and common decency, especially on public transport.'

'Girls and boys were not allowed to associate with each other much straight out of school—when it was known they dated each other.'

'The only time the school went to extremes was when they tried to prevent the school members using a coffee bar—it had no effect.'

'They did not interfere so long as it did not affect school life.'

'Wished pupils to bring credit to the school.'

'Most noticeable on social occasions, polite, well mannered yet enjoyable to be with.'

RATHER INSUFFICIENT 'The women members of staff were more concerned than the men.'

'Behaviour on buses was dreadful at times but nothing was done about this.'

'The staff were concerned with some pupils' out-of-school conduct but I think they had given up hope with some and just ignored them.'

MUCH TOO LAX 'There appeared to be no concern for what happened to anyone out of school.'

'They never appeared to know what we did even though the 6th form as a whole went to the "pub".'

The comments about their girls' schools were:

EXCESSIVE 'They fussed to a ridiculous extent over outdated and silly attitudes, eating a sweet on the bus, etc.'

'If caught without a hat on for any reason you were forced to wear it in school for a day. No eating sweets on buses—no walking in groups, etc.'

139

'Half-terms, etc. were altered from the same time as the "boys' school" "to prevent unhealthy contacts" as our headmistress told us.'

'We weren't allowed to walk to school with a boy, brother or not.'

'Even told what kind of clothing to wear. In uniform we were not to speak to workers (in overalls) and such.'

'We were not even allowed to walk down certain streets or go shopping after school.'

RATHER STRICT 'Some of the staff carried this noseyness to extremes (older women).'

'One is bound to get some restriction with out-of-school conduct, but perhaps this is rather more so than the co-ed. school.'

'Had to wear hat all year round, no frilly petticoats. Other trivia.'

'You had to act "like ladies" at all times.'

JUST RIGHT 'The school was well known in the area. We ourselves wanted to help its public image.' (Boarding school)

'They were trying to educate us as people, not just encyclopaedias.' (Boarding school)

RATHER INSUFFICIENT 'The school had a bad name in the area owing to lack of interest from senior girls and staff.'

MUCH TOO LAX 'People went mad once they were let out.'

In both types of school the same problems appear, from boy–girl friendships and the use of coffee bars to wearing school hats and not eating sweets on buses! But there is a more rigorous control in the girls' schools—the school doing its best to produce well mannered young ladies and to protect them until they are old enough to protect themselves, and at the same time here and there overstepping the mark, or, as one girl puts it, insisting on out-of-date customs. The pupils express their annoyance at this, and occasionally add that the home itself resented interference. Which reminds one again of that wise French saying, 'Happy is the man who has not the faults of his virtues.' The quotation is so apt in this connection that no apology is made for using it twice. A laudable aim spelled out in too great detail and insisted on with vigilant supervision can rapidly become a cause of deteriorating pupil–teacher relationships, especially when many other equally laudable aims are added and just as zealously pursued, together with the inevitable age gap in customs and attitudes added to the brew. How long ago is it that girls' schools used to insist on girls wearing gloves when travelling to and from school, and how long did the schools persist with the uphill struggle?

Some women teachers in the co-educational schools evidently had the same virtues and the same faults, and there are at times complaints from them and even from some senior girls that the men teachers did not co-operate sufficiently in this control of out-of-school conduct. Perhaps men do not have the same sharp and vigilant eye of the female for the missing hat or the sucked sweet, or perhaps they just don't want to see. A third explanation that is sometimes put forward by women teachers—that the men are too lazy—is in the writer's *opinion* untenable, but being male he himself might be thought prejudiced. Be this as it may, the presence of men on the staff appears in this respect, as well as in others, to exert a moderating influence on the women. Whether this is good or bad is an additional question; there are women teachers in girls' schools who would claim that this influence is either wholly bad or at least that it goes too far. They would add that few young people like to be disciplined, but this is an inevitable part of the training of the younger generation by the older, and the writer is presenting only the views of the pupils and ignoring those of the teachers. In this there is much truth, but two points are made in reply. First, although these views are indeed those of ex-pupils, they are in fact adults and even intending teachers themselves, and looking back on their treatment they can view it more dispassionately; in their replies they show that they now realize more clearly that some of the discipline they then thought was unnecessary was, on mature reflection, justified. This makes their protests of course more reasonable, more balanced and more important. Second, if the result of a certain policy is that an appreciable proportion of the pupils become resentful and express these sentiments long afterwards, it seems as if it might be time to moderate this policy. The little lost on the swings might be gained on the roundabouts in the form of happier and closer teacher–pupil relationships.

Let it be emphasized that there will be many girls' schools where they have been gaining on the roundabouts for a very long time. The writer knows one such school well where a really great headmistress, now passed away, showed qualities of leadership, humanity and tolerance which made her loved and venerated by her pupils. The same qualities will be present in many other women teachers in girls' schools. This book, however, is concerned with average tendencies. The point that the writer is concerned to repeat is that whereas it has often been thought of relatively little moment whether a school is a co-educational or a girls' school, these are in fact very different institutions psychologically. This being so the decision whether to educate boys and girls apart or together is one of the most fundamental that can be asked in education. We have been a long time arriving at this truth, and having arrived there it now seems rather obvious.

The manner in which the estimates and comments about the ex-pupils' co-educational schools cluster closely around the mid-point suggests that there is on the whole satisfaction with most schools in the manner of their control of out-of-school conduct. Yet with the centre of gravity for the estimates situated in the 'just-right' category, it is easier for control in these schools to become 'rather insufficient' than it is the girls' schools, where the comparable centre of gravity is in the 'rather strict' category. The matter is put in proper perspective, however, by a comparison of the proportion of comments in the 'much too lax' category in the two types of school. For girls in girls' schools this was 4.4 per cent and for those in co-educational schools almost 6 per cent.

We now arrive at the male ex-pupils' comments about the control of both of their schools over the out-of-school conduct of pupils. First is presented the most reliable of the two measures—the estimates.

TABLE 10.2 *Out-of-school conduct of boys*
'*Both schools*' *survey*

Estimates of schools' concern with out-of-school conduct of pupils	Replies about first school attended				Replies about last school attended			
	Co-educational		Boys'		Co-educational		Boys'	
	N	%	N	%	N	%	N	%
Excessive	4	4·9	10	8·6	8	7·8	5	7·0
Rather strict	20	24·4	35	30·2	27	26·2	24	33·8
Just right	41	50·0	53	45·7	52	50·4	33	46·6
Rather insufficient	12	14·6	11	9·5	12	11·7	4	5·6
Much too lax	5	6·1	7	6·0	4	3·9	5	7·0
Totals	82	100	116	100	103	100	71	100

NOTE: The differences between the distributions for boys' schools and co-educational are not statistically significant, either for first or last schools.

In Table 10.2 there is little difference between the estimates about the schools attended as juniors and those about schools attended as seniors. Though in both junior and senior groups slightly more pupils thought the co-educational school's attitude was just right as compared with that of their boys' school, the difference is only some 4 per cent, with rather small numbers. Similarly, in both junior and senior groups slightly more boys thought their co-educational school had a 'rather insufficient' concern than their boys' school had, while a rather higher proportion of both age groups said their boys' schools were rather strict or excessively so, as opposed to their co-educational schools. If we combine the 'too strict' categories and compare them with the 'too lax' we find that 9 per cent more of the junior sample estimated their boys' schools to be too strict compared with their co-educational schools, and 7 per cent in the seniors, while 5 per cent more of the juniors and 3 per cent more of the seniors estimated the concern of their co-educational schools to be on the lax side. The differences are not great and are not statistically significant, but they agree with the previous findings on the differences between the two types of school in discipline, and with the theory which interprets this as a natural consequence of basic differences in the two kinds of community. When we are considering where the line *should* be drawn we must not forget, first that it may be right that the line is drawn in a different place for the different communities; second, that we are reviewing the experiences of the sufferers rather than those of the imposers; third, that these particular sufferers are in the process of becoming imposers, so that their views are likely to be a compromise between the two sides. This should be borne in mind when readers are considering the verdict of both boys and girls.

The reasons given by the boys for their estimates are not presented in a classified table partly because the number of responses was rather small for sub-division and partly because there was not much difference between the replies from co-educational and those from boys' schools. Those who thought control was excessive maintained that it infringed personal freedom and rights or complained about the narrow-mindedness of head or staff. Most boys who thought control 'rather strict' complained about interference in smaller matters such as the wearing of school caps, especially in middle and senior school, and resented this, but some accepted the strictness and felt it to be justified. Sometimes school tradition or school image was said to be the cause of the strictness, whether in itself the punishment was justifiable or not. Those who said the concern was just right acknowledged a need for control over such things as smoking, drinking, and bad behaviour. A number of boys, however, thought the oversight was rather insufficient because the pupils were drawn from a large area which it was impracticable to supervise.

Some of the more interesting comments are quoted, first from boys in co-educational schools. The first two quotations are from boys who thought the concern excessive.

Co-educational schools

EXCESSIVE 'In School two prefects had to sign a document that they wouldn't drink, etc., out of school hours even when we were over 18.'

'Deputy head (female) told a prefect not to walk with a girl on Sundays—it was his cousin. She was exceptionally narrow-minded.'

RATHER STRICT Those who thought the concern 'rather strict' included a minority who thought it was justified, but most felt it was unreasonable:

'No holding hands going down the road, no drinking, or smoking in school uniform.'

'All pupils had to wear hats. This (boys') consisted of the usual cap for 1–5 years, but a special beret was introduced for the 6th forms while I was there. Surely there is no need for hats after (say) the 3rd form.'

'It was rather strict but I think that it was justified as the reputation of the school with all its teachers and pupils was at stake, and its reputation for "job value".'

JUST RIGHT The 'just right' group included two more than usually thoughtful replies:

'Co-education was a new venture in the town's educational policy. Consequently the School had to strike the right balance between old narrow-minded attitudes, and the true spirit of co-education— this it did effectively.'

'The School should have a great concern for the pupils' conduct out of school. Child upbringing and education is a 24-hour business not to be undertaken only between 9.00 a.m. to 4.00 p.m.'

MUCH TOO LAX The few comments about laxness included:

'As soon as we were out of school we ceased to be influenced by it.'

'They were concerned about conduct if pupils were wearing school uniform, and then very much.'

Boys' schools

The comments from boys' schools reflect the rather greater strictness shown in the estimates; those who thought it excessive have a sharper tone:

EXCESSIVE 'If it occurred it was heavily punished irrespective of reason.'

'Teachers were known to actually hit pupils outside school hours!'

'Conduct outside the school was to be irreproachable, otherwise the pupil was punished by the head himself.'

'We were pulled up for the slightest thing, such as having a cap on slightly out of line.'

'We were not encouraged to mix with the girls' school next door, for example.'

RATHER STRICT As with the replies about co-educational schools, those who thought the boys' schools' concern was rather strict had a minority who said it was justified.

'The wearing of caps by 16–18-year-olds was rather ridiculous.'

'The school had an "image" to keep up in the North of England.'

'Rather strict in stupid ways, i.e. uniform, but not in ways of behaviour; many pupils were commuters, and warnings only existed for bad behaviour.'

JUST RIGHT Boys who thought the concern 'just right' consisted mainly of a group who wrote of the need to keep the good school 'image' and a group saying that the area the school drew from was too large for close control.

RATHER INSUFFICIENT There were few comments by boys who judged the control to be rather insufficient. One, rather illogically, wrote:

'No concern was shown at all which I think was a good thing.'

There were no comments from the few boys who thought the control to be 'much too lax'.

Little further analysis is needed on the comparison between boys in boys' and in co-educational schools except to mention that the distribution of comments supports the verdict of the estimates in indicating a much closer similarity between boys in boys' schools and those in co-educational schools than between the comparable groups of girls. The same difference is, however, present—the tendency of the single-sex school towards greater strictness of control, and the slightly greater bunching round the 'just right' category for the co-educational schools. The differences, however, are not regarded as statistically reliable.

Comment

As there has already been comment at the end of the various sections only a short note is added. In the matter of out-of-school conduct schools are in a difficult position because their legal right to interfere would appear to be uncertain; yet when pupils in school uniform behave badly the school itself receives the opprobrium of the public. The schools rightly endeavour to educate their pupils to become well-behaved citizens, but what exactly are their legal powers once the pupil sets his foot outside the school? It seems to the writer that schools may have understandably arrogated to themselves powers over out-of-school conduct which could be disputed, though on the whole these powers are exercised in a way which is useful to the community and good for the right social development of the pupils. In some cases, however, there is evidence of parents resenting the schools' attempt to push the boundaries of their claims into areas which the parents regard as their own. Who should decide the style of a girl's hair-ribbon—parent or teacher? In a time of changing fashions has the school the legal right to demand that a boy's hair be cut short? The parent may sign an agreement (does he always?) that he will provide a school hat or cap for his offspring, but has the school any legal—or even moral—right to compel the child to wear it *on the way to school*, against the wishes of both child and parent? These are delicate questions but it is perhaps time that they were asked, though wise guidance and wise oversight *in things that matter* are obviously of benefit to all concerned.

School preference

In the previous volume on the rival merits of co-educational and single-sex secondary schools, two of the chapters presented the views of teachers and the reasons for their preference. A decided majority of teachers in maintained day grammar schools considered that co-educational schools provided a better education and preferred them. Those who had taught in both types of school were strongly in favour of co-education, and teachers in co-educational schools were themselves almost unanimously in their favour. Opposition came mainly from those who had had no practical experience of these schools; in other words it is founded upon ignorance. This does not mean that the opponents are not sincere, but it is the writer's opinion that they often confuse effects caused by social class differences between co-educational and single-sex schools (and to some extent differences in status, type of staffing, and degree of selective entry) with differences caused by co-education.

In the present volume we pass on to consider whether co-educational or single-sex schools are preferred by pupils and ex-pupils, naturally placing most stress on the choice of those pupils who have attended at least one co-educational and one single-sex secondary school (excluding secondary modern). Fortunately we also have their reasons for this choice. Their preference, however, is not regarded as being in itself decisive, though its importance is clear. It is a tenable argument that junior and middle school pupils might prefer one school to another because in it they need not do much work and discipline is perhaps more lax than it should be. Against this the verdict of the teachers could be quoted, and it might also be pointed out that the senior pupils and responsible ex-pupils such as intending teachers would be unlikely to make this mistake in judgment. None the less the findings of this and the previous volume are best viewed as a whole, to see whether they result in a consistent picture in favour of one side or the other.

This chapter weighs up evidence on school preference which has been obtained from the ex-pupils of the First and Second College surveys, the 'Both schools' survey, and from two relatively small-scale inquiries among pupils in grammar schools. The results are first presented with a minimum of comment, then reviewed as a whole at the end of the chapter.

The First College survey

In the early days of this research work, in 1946 and 1947, a simple exploratory survey about attitude to co-education was made among ex-pupils of grammar schools who were training to be teachers. (A parallel survey was made at the same time among grammar school teachers.) As the questionnaire was administered in groups the percentage of completed forms was 100 per cent in most institutions, though in a few cases it was low. Institutions with low returns had results similar to those from institutions with high returns. Replies were obtained from seventeen University Departments of Education and (for comparison) four Colleges of Education, comprising in all 1,167 students. As mentioned in Chapter 1, these are not a representative cross-section of ex-grammar school students, but they represent one important type of pupil from both co-educational and single-sex schools, responsible in attitude, and with a deeper than average interest in educational problems. Students from University Departments of Education and those from Colleges of Education are considered separately, as are men and women. They were asked the question, 'Are you in favour of co-education in secondary schools?' and were given the opportunity of choosing between full co-education (Type A), co-education with mostly single-sex classes (Type B), dual schools (a girls' and a boys' school in one building under separate heads), undecided, and single-sex schools. Dual schools were called 'Co-educational, Type C', but were classed with single-sex in the analysis. Each respondent was requested to comment on the preference given.

The results from students in University Departments of Education are given first (Table 11.1); they reveal a change of opinion which few people suspected at that time.

The men's results show two principal trends: first, that a majority of the students preferred co-education, second, that the students educated in co-educational schools were more strongly in favour of these than were those educated in boys' schools. If we logically combine Types A and B (because Type B is much nearer to co-education than to single-sex schooling) and oppose it to Type C plus single-sex, the percentages as one goes down the table are 87 to 9, 59 to 29, 87 to 13, and 52 to 37, there being a majority in favour of co-education in all groups, but a more decisive one among ex-pupils of co-educational schools. The women's results are similar (Table 11.2).

TABLE 11.1 *Type of school preferred:* Male students*

First College survey

Type of student replying											
University Departments of Education	Type A		Type B		Type C		Single-sex		Undecided		Totals
	N	%	N	%	N	%	N	%	N	%	N	%
Co-educated men	98	74·3	17	12·9	6	4·5	6	4·5	5	3·8	132	100
Men from boys' schools	102	45·7	30	13·5	46	20·6	19	8·5	26	11·7	223	100
College of Education												
Co-educated men	47	74·6	8	12·7	3	4·8	5	7·9	0	0	63	100
Men from boys' schools	64	35·8	29	16·2	40	22·3	27	15·1	19	10·6	179	100

* Type C signifies only co-operation between boys' and girls' schools (in the same or adjoining buildings) for joint social activities, and should be counted as against co-education in the generally accepted meaning of the term. Type A is the normal co-educational school, Type B is a school for boys and girls organized in mostly single-sex classes (except perhaps in the Sixth).

TABLE 11.2 *Type of school preferred: Female students*

First College survey

Type of student replying	Type of secondary school preferred										
	Type A		Type B		Type C		Single-sex		Undecided		Totals
University Departments of Education	N	%	N	%	N	%	N	%	N	%	N	%
Co-educated women	144	90·6	8	5·0	5	3·1	0		2	1·3	159	100
Women from girls' schools	100	44·7	43	19·2	29	12·9	9	4·0	43	19·2	224	100
College of Education												
Co-educated women	42	100·0	0		0		0		0		42	100
Women from girls' schools	30	66·8	11	24·4	2	4·4	1	2·2	1	2·2	45	100

Here one sees the same preference for co-education in all groups and the same powerful influence of the type of school which the respondents themselves attended. Reading from top to bottom of the table, as for the men, the percentages in favour of co-education are 96 to 3, 64 to 17, 100 to 0, and 91 to 7, the last two groups being rather small. The female student teachers of this inquiry are still more favourably inclined to co-education than the men, a finding which will be supported by the results of other investigations described here.

The above findings might be opposed on the grounds that most of the ex-pupils had had experience only of the one type of school he or she had attended. This has been met by separating out those students who had attended both a co-educational and a single-sex secondary school, excluding secondary modern (Table 11.3). The numbers are small but should be considered in relation to other studies discussed later. As all groups had a big majority for co-education all male students are combined, and similarly for women.

TABLE 11.3 *Type of school preferred: Students who attended both types*

First College survey

	Type of secondary school preferred					
	Type A	Type B	Type C	Single-sex	Undecided	Totals
	N %	N %	N %	N %	N %	N %
Female students	31 64·6	11 22·9	3 6·2	1 2·1	2 4·2	48 100
Male students	33 63·4	7 13·5	3 5·8	5 9·6	4 7·7	52 100

Male and female students who had attended both a co-educational and a single-sex secondary school were heavily in favour of the co-educational school, the male by 77 to 15 per cent, and the female by 88 to 8 per cent, with a negligible number undecided. The numbers in the sample, however, were only 52 men and 48 women.

In their free responses the students set down reasons why they supported or opposed co-education in secondary schools. They could naturally have suppressed some reasons but there seems to be little cause for such an action, particularly as the questionnaires were anonymous. These free responses are classified in Table 11.4, where those from students who were educated in single-sex, mixed and both types of schools are combined because of their basic similarity. The sexes are given separately. In the classification procedure it was often necessary to place sections of a reply into two or even more categories, so that although there were 1,167 questionnaires returned, of which 59 had no comment, the remainder yielded 1,924 classified remarks. The numbers given are therefore more useful for studying the stress placed upon the various arguments than for comparing the preference for and against co-education, for which a comparison based on Tables 11.1, 11.2 and 11.3 is safer.

TABLE II.4 *Classified comments on co-education (full sample)*

First College survey

	Men	Women
For co-education		
preparation for adult life, training for social life	223	214
school societies and school social life	44	26
segregation is unnatural, healthier atmosphere	68	55
easy relations with other sex, more understanding, healthy sex attitude, less adolescent 'crushes', sex problems, emotional difficulties; sexes are complementary, co-operation learnt	324	315
competition and academic standards	33	68
broader outlook, different points of view and interests	61	78
better discipline, better behaviour	46	16
others	30	40
Totals	829	812
Against co-education		
different abilities, different interests, different rates of development of boys and girls	74	57
discipline difficulty	28	15
distraction by presence of the opposite sex	31	8
staff and head should be the same sex as pupils	24	3
others	32	11
Totals	189	94

From the data in Table 11.4 readers will see that those students in favour of co-education emphasize the social factors involved, indicated by such headings as 'preparation for adult life', 'training for social life', and 'easy relations with the other sex, more understanding'. Related to this but not identical with it is the idea that co-education is more natural and produces a healthier atmosphere. Though the academic side is a lesser factor it attracts an appreciable number of comments stressing the advantages of the broader outlook and the different points of view of the two sexes, and (for male students) the better behaviour of the boys.

The reasons given for opposing co-education are principally concerned with the different abilities, different interests and rates of development of boys and girls, while to a lesser extent there are some fears about distraction by the opposite sex and a few qualms about discipline. One cannot but feel that a section of the opposition did not put down their real fear—that it would be unhealthy and unwise for the two sexes to be in daily propinquity in a school building—though practical experience has shown these fears to be unfounded. It is a characteristic of all these researches that the arguments given for co-education are primarily social and those against co-education are concerned with instruction. The proof of the pudding, however, is in the eating, and as said before, no one has yet demonstrated that co-educated pupils reach a lower standard *because of* co-education than the single-sex educated pupils reach; the available evidence in fact points in the opposite direction (Dale, 1962a, 1962b and 1964).

In order to put a little flesh and blood on the bare bones of the statistics, some of the free responses are given in full, but the numbers for and against are not taken strictly according to the proportion found in the original voting, as this would not have illustrated the case against co-education sufficiently. This proportion, taking all students *who were not undecided*, is 73 to 27 for the men and 89 to 11 for the women.

Comments favourable to co-education[1] (*men*)

The type of education of each respondent is placed in brackets before his comment.

(Both schools) 'Since boys and girls have to mix with each other on leaving school, it strikes me as being ridiculous to segregate them when young. If they have mixed with the other sex in their school days they will have more experience of each other on going out into the world.

'In schools where only boys or girls are educated, there seems to be the opinion that it is wrong to associate with the other sex before reaching manhood or womanhood. This is nonsense and does a great deal of harm.

'The days spent in the co-educational grammar school were the happiest of my life. The atmosphere in the boys' grammar school which I attended later was far less pleasant and natural.'

(Co-educational school) 'It gives the child an opportunity of meeting and working with members of the opposite sex at an age approaching maturity, so letting them "gently" into normal adult life when it is essential for men and women to work together.

'More "colour" is added to school life for pupils and teachers,

---

[1] Occasionally favourable or unfavourable comments contain qualifying clauses which have the reverse significance, though the overall *estimate* by the student is as indicated in the text. When one respondent makes several points these are paragraphed.

since life can be a very monotonous thing when spent wholly with your own sex.

'It gives a child an opportunity of unconsciously observing the points in members of the opposite sex which later on will mean so much to him when selecting his mate.'

(Boys' boarding school) '(a) Less homosexuality— particularly in boarding schools. THIS IS A VERY SERIOUS POINT AND, I DO ASSURE YOU, IT IS NOT FRIVOLOUS [sic].
'(b) Much more natural attitude to members of the other sex.'

(Co-educational school) 'One aim of education is to enable children to develop as worthy citizens. This can only be achieved if the society of the school resembles society in general.

'In passing on the best of a heritage (or environment) it is essential to preserve a "model society" in the school. This cannot be done on a one-sex basis.

'A child cannot even begin to integrate its personality if it lives and learns in unnatural seclusion from the disturbing but moulding influences exerted by the other sex.

'Co-education will mean mixed staffs—and that *may* lead to the humanization of staffs and their return to the fold of sensible, broad and open-minded people. Teachers with "bees in their bonnets" and petty adherences to "do's and dont's" thrive on the one-sex staff—especially female!!'

(Boys' school) 'Greater opportunities for unusual class-room activities, e.g.—short historical plays with female characters.

'Equal intellectual opportunities for both sexes would lead to a more reasonable appreciation of woman's place in society and would end the deplorable "Back to the Kitchen" attitude which permeates modern society.

'The element of competition would be keener: neither sex would wish to "let the side down".

'The brute in the boys would be curbed by the refining influence of young ladies.'

(Boys' school) 'It is a more natural life and it approximates to conditions in every-day life.

'It does away with shyness and will take women off their pedestals.

'It is essential for plays, drama, dancing, etc.

'For an only child or two boys (or girls) in the same family it is their only chance to meet the opposite sex.

'Boys from co-ed. schools seem politer and more tolerant of women and old people than those from the other type.'

Comments favourable to co-education (women)

(Co-educational school) 'I think co-education helps children to develop a much more sensible outlook during adolescence: (I have heard it expressed this way—"Girls from a girls' school giggle if they see a boy get on a bus").

'It is good from the point of view of the work. I find that (in general) girls of 11–14 years are more industrious than boys of the same age and the boys in a mixed class just have to do some work to attain a good class position. Boys have a broader vision of a subject, can pick out salient features and tend to discard detail; average girls are more painstaking but tend to get "lost" in the detail and never view the subject as a whole. Surely each sex has something to learn of the other here? After the age of 15–16 years it is the girl who has to work harder than she might otherwise do to keep pace with the boys of the class (in general).

'The presence of the opposite sex in the class has no unsettling effect. It is taken as a matter of course when children have grown up in the system. I feel sure it is a better preparation for life after school when men and women work together in universities, offices, shops, etc.

'As regards Types B and C. To my mind, these types have little to recommend them which a unisexual school has not. In fact I would not class these types as "co-educational". As an experiment in the school I attended boys and girls were placed in separate classes one year on entering the school, and were mixed only on entering the Sixth form. I can only speak of the effect it had on the girls—they were by far the "silliest" section of the school and exhibited all those characteristics of adolescent girls which most people find so objectionable. (At any rate that was the opinion of we senior girls. I do not know what the staff thought of them.)'

(Co-educational school) 'School is part of life, in life there is no segregation of the sexes to such an extent, therefore there should not be a segregation of sexes in schools.

'In all-girl schools the main topic of conversation as far as one can gather seems to be males, whereas in co-educational schools, as the boys are there, girls seem to occupy their minds with other subjects to a greater extent.'

(Both schools) 'As I have had experience of both types of school I can state with personal knowledge on the subject that co-education is preferable. It gives a familiarity with the opposite sex and avoids any curiosity and emotional upset later in adolescence. It provides great opportunities for competition and rouses interest in subjects which might never be dealt with in schools of Type C. In social activities there is greater scope apart from the obvious advantages in school dramatics, etc.'

(Girls' school) 'Since, in their lives after school leaving age, boys and girls have to work together and spend their recreation periods in mixed company, then it is much better training for these adolescents to have experienced mixed company before they leave school. Furthermore, children from segregated schools who proceed to further education in mixed colleges waste valuable time settling down to working in mixed company, it is such a novelty for them that too much time is spent in the social life of the college, too little on the academic side.'

Comments unfavourable to co-education (men)
(Both schools—co-educational one year) 'The staff tend to be more heterogeneous than in a school of single-sex and from observation appear to be somewhat mutually antagonistic which is not in the interests of the pupils.

'Discipline must inevitably be a compromise between that suitable for boys and that for girls. At the adolescent stage a girl has far more respect for a woman teacher than she has for a man. Possibly something of the sort is true for boys also to a lesser extent.'

(Boys' school) 'The advantages—social life and joint activities— are in my opinion outweighed by the disturbances caused to both sets—boys and girls. It is far better that each should remain apart as long as possible—there will be plenty of time after leaving school for mixing. As may be seen I favour the monastic type of schooling. Surely co-education is far more difficult for the teacher!??'

(Boys' school) 'The difference in mode of reasoning, the male with his logic, the female with intuition, would not help the various teachers in forming their approach in teaching method. On the whole the average boy prefers segregated education.'

(Boys' school) 'Children appear to have a natural propensity for wasting time. Such wastage tends to be accentuated when the sexes are mixed.

'Judged by observations of Americans and Canadians, the co-educational system appears to have resulted in an exaggerated respect on the part of men for the so-called rights and privileges of women, while conversely women tend to treat men as "universal providers" to whom scant respect is due.'

(Boys' school) 'My secondary school life was spent in a boys' school. By nature I was shy and reserved. On coming up to university I find that my shyness persisted for some time before I became accustomed to mixed classes, tutorials, social activities, etc. There was a girls' school in close proximity to the boys' school but no mixed activities of any kind were allowed. I feel that this segregation was too rigid and severe. In some respects, apart from physical training and games, the needs and interests of boys and girls run apart and for this reason co-education of Type A is not desirable or advantageous.

'Education is preparation for life, and learning to know and respect each other's point of view should be a gradual process in an experience which can well begin in co-education in a school of Type C, where there is a joint social life and school society activities such as dancing, debates, play-producing, etc., where supervision in the nature of advice and guidance is maintained.'

(Boys' school) 'Boys and girls have widely different interests in many ways and in co-ed. schools there is a tendency for the different activities to clash.

'I have noticed a tendency where I was in classes, on occasions when girls were present, that very little work was actually done. A boy of 14 does not mind making a fool of himself before boys— but dreads the thought of doing so before girls.'

Comments unfavourable to co-education (women)

(Girls' school) 'Females become masculine, boys become effeminate.'

(Girls' school) 'Completely different treatment is required for boys and girls.

'Boys and girls distract each other in class.

'Girls are more physically mature than boys of same age although not necessarily more intelligent.

'Boys and girls have different interests and might require different curricula.'

(Girls' school) 'Having had teaching experience in Types A and C of co-educational schools, I find that in Type A interest flags largely because different approach is often necessary for subjects and children feel that they are not considered as individual boys and girls but rather as 'children'. In both A and C question of discipline is difficult for this must be treated differently and any apparent leniency to one sex is resented by the other.'

The Second College survey

The exploratory First College survey was followed in 1948-9 (supplemented in 1963-5) by the more detailed Second College survey, which included several questions on school preference. Among them was, 'If you attended a single-sex school would you have preferred it to have been a mixed school?' Students could answer Yes/No/or Undecided. Students who had attended a mixed school were asked if they would have preferred it to have been single-sex. No opportunity was given for free response because students confronted with an overlong questionnaire might have refused to complete it. The results (Tables 11.5 and 11.6) are similar to those of the earlier survey.

TABLE 11.5 '*If you attended a single-sex school would you have preferred it to have been a mixed school?*'

Second College survey

	Male ex-pupils		Female ex-pupils	
	N	%	N	%
Yes (preferred mixed school)	236	41·9	329	52·6
No (preferred single-sex school)	221	39·3	158	25·2
Undecided	106	18·8	139	22·2
Totals	563	100	626	100

TABLE 11.6 '*If you attended a mixed school would you have preferred it to have been single-sex?*'

Second College survey

	Male ex-pupils		Female ex-pupils	
	N	%	N	%
Yes (preferred single-sex school)	13	3·8	5	1·3
No (preferred mixed school)	311	90·9	382	95·7
Undecided	18	5·3	12	3·0
Totals	342	100	399	100

Table 11.5 shows that the men who were educated in boys' grammar schools were uncertain whether they would have preferred a co-educational or single-sex school, whereas a majority (53 per cent) of the ex-pupils of girls' schools (with 22 per cent undecided) would have preferred a mixed school. Table 11.6 gives the verdict of former pupils of co-educational schools and is more dramatic. In great contrast to the indecision of the boys from boys' schools and to some extent the girls from girls' schools, both boys and girls from co-educational schools are very decided in their preference for a co-educational school. As many as 91 per cent of the boys and almost 96 per cent of the girls would not have preferred their school to have been single-sex; only 13 boys in 342 and 5 girls in 399 wished that their school had been single-sex. Human nature and human temperaments being so varied one could scarcely expect to get a smaller number in the minority no matter what the question asked!

As with the First College survey the objection could be raised that most of the students of the Second College survey had attended only one type of school and could not therefore validly compare it with another type. This objection was again answered by taking the opinion of a separate sample of students who completed the questionnaire as part of the main sample, but whose results were kept apart; they were students who had attended both types of school.

TABLE 11.7 *School preference: Ex-pupils with experience of both co-educational and single-sex schools*

Second College survey

Type of school preferred	Males		Females	
	N	%	N	%
Single-sex very much	7	9·2	3	4·1
Single-sex a little	11	14·5	1	1·4
Neutral	10	13·2	11	15·1
Mixed a little	17	22·4	10	13·7
Mixed very much	31	40·7	48	65·7
Totals	76	100	73	100

NOTE: The preference for co-educational schools is statistically highly significant for both sexes (beyond the ·001 level).

Although the question which was asked was not identical to that used in the previous survey its significance is very close, sufficiently so for it to be said that the results are mutually supporting. In Table 11.7 some 63 per cent of the men who had experienced both co-educational and boys' schools preferred the co-educational as against 24 per cent preferring the boys' school. Of the women some 80 per cent preferred the co-educational while 6 per cent preferred the girls' school.

The 'Both schools' survey

The 'both schools' survey is the most important one because its sample is composed of a large number of men and women who had been pupils in at least one co-educational as well as at least one single-sex school, and because it is the most recent, the questionnaire being administered in 1965-6. One hundred and seventy-five male and 620 female students who were in Colleges of Education were asked. 'Which did you prefer, the mixed or the single-sex school?' They could choose from one of the following answers: 'Single-sex school much/Single-sex school a little/No preference/ Mixed school a little/Mixed school much.' Reasons for their choice were requested. The question was deliberately made specific to the schools the ex-pupils had attended, and equally deliberately the single-sex schools were given the advantage of the first two places in the list of options—these sometimes attracting extra votes by virtue of their position.

The results are important and will be given intensive treatment. The preferences of the ex-pupils are given in Figure 11.1, and because the order in which the schools were attended could be an important factor, 'last' co-educational schools are compared with 'last' girls' schools and similarly for men. (In this instance to compare 'first' schools in addition would be merely to duplicate the data, as those ex-pupils who attended a co-educational school first are in most instances those who attended a single-sex school last, and vice versa.)

Two trends are apparent in the Figure, first the dominant preference for the students' co-educational schools, second the important influence of the order in which the two (or more) schools were attended. The preference for the co-educational school is much more marked when this was the last school attended, both with males and females,[1] though even when it was attended first there is a decided preference for the co-educational school among the females[2] and a smaller one among the men.[3]

[1] and [2] All statistically highly significant.
[3] Not statistically significant.

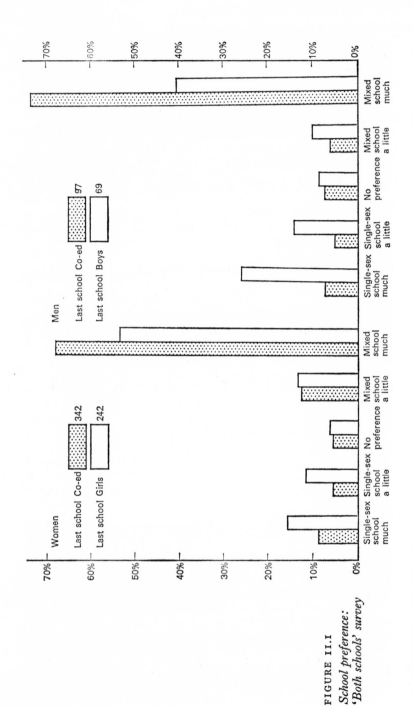

FIGURE 11.1
School preference:
'Both schools' survey

PLEASANTNESS OF POSITION

A hidden factor which might have affected the issue is the pleasant or unpleasant situation of the school, especially since there is a greater percentage of co-educational schools in sparsely populated areas. Accordingly the students were asked, 'Do you agree or disagree with the following statement about your co-educational school? Pleasant situation of school. Agree strongly/Agree/Doubtful/Disagree/Disagree strongly.' The same question was asked about the single-sex school. Though there was a difference in favour of the co-educational schools (which could even have been caused by a halo effect) it was much too small to have produced the large differences in school preference (cf. Table 2.3), and was statistically non-significant. The possibility was double-checked by comparing the school preferences which were based on co-educational schools in very pleasant positions (i.e. where ex-pupils 'agreed strongly' about the pleasantness) with those based on similar single-sex schools, thus neutralizing the influence of the pleasantness factor; the process was continued for other types of school situation and the sum total was taken for all cases where the situation of the two types of school was judged by the students to be similar in 'pleasantness', producing the data in Table 11.8.

TABLE 11.8 *School preference with pleasantness of position held constant*

'*Both schools*' *survey* (*women*)

Preferences of pupils matched on pleasantness of their co-educational and single-sex schools	Co-educational school last		Single-sex school last	
	N	%	N	%
Single-sex school much	10	7·2	8	10·8
Single-sex school a little	6	4·3	7	9·5
No preference	15	10·9	4	5·4
Mixed school a little	21	15·2	13	17·6
Mixed school much	86	62·4	42	56·7
Totals	138	100	74	100

NOTE: The differences between the proportion favouring the single-sex school and that favouring the co-educational is statistically very highly significant both for 'co-educational last' and 'single-sex last' categories.

The evidence shows that the preference for the co-educational school is overwhelmingly strong even when the pleasantness of school position is held constant. The assessment for the men was omitted because of their smaller numbers.

In case there are some readers who consider that the education of the intending teachers in Colleges of Education might have swayed their preference, even when choosing between schools actually attended as pupils, an examination was made of the preferences of the large group of students who said that their training as teachers had made no difference to their opinions about co-educational secondary schools. As an additional safeguard the ex-pupils were also matched as previously on their opinion of the pleasantness of the position of their co-educational school as compared with their single-sex school. Table 11.9 shows that the large co-educational advantage remains, both where the co-educational school was the last attended and where the single-sex school was the last; the influence of the order of schools can also be seen. Though the number in the sample has fallen drastically the interpretation has been made easier by the removal of three extraneous variables from the table.

TABLE 11.9 *School preference with position and College influence held constant*

'*Both schools*' *survey (women)*
'No change' on College influence

Position of school held constant by matching in pairs	School preference											
	Single-sex school much		Single-sex school a little		No preference		Mixed school a little		Mixed school much		Totals	
	N	%	N	%	N	%	N	%	N	%	N	%
Co-ed. last	7	10·3	3	4·4	10	14·7	13	19·1	35	51·5	68	100
Single-sex last	4	11·4	5	14·3	1	2·8	5	14·3	20	57·1	35	100

NOTE: The difference between the proportion favouring the single-sex school and that favouring the co-educational is statistically very highly significant both for 'co-educational last' and 'single-sex last' categories.

AMALGAMATED SCHOOLS

A factor which this research has shown to affect the comparison between co-educational and single-sex schools is whether the former is a school which has been created by the merging of two single-sex schools in the previous one or two years, termed here an 'amalgamated' school. An examination was therefore made of the influence of this factor on school preference, and it was found that both the men and the women[1] from amalgamated schools were less in favour of co-education than the rest of the sample who attended a co-educational school last (Table A.20). No change to this finding resulted when the 'pleasantness' of school position was kept constant for the amalgamated schools. (There was the possibility that most of this sub-sample had recently moved into pleasantly situated new buildings.) A broader analysis of the effects of 'amalgamation' is given in Chapter 20; here we move on to consider the free responses of the complete sample of the 'Both schools' survey.

FREE RESPONSES

The comments made by these responsible and interested adults about their preference for one or another of the two types of school they attended, are one of the most valuable pieces of evidence presented in this and the preceding volume, and they are given a full treatment. For those who do not wish to read the quotations a study of Tables 11.10 and 11.11 should suffice, but they will miss the human touch, the insight and the humour.

In the table the dominance of comments favourable to co-education was decided by the original school preference of the students. Except for its special importance, due to the double experience of the respondents, the table is similar to some given earlier. Co-education is favoured because of the natural relationship between the sexes, the educative effect of the presence of the opposite sex, the pleasant friendly relaxed atmosphere, the social life and school activities, the friendliness of staff–pupil relationships, the broad, balanced outlook on life, and the preparation for life in general. Also stressed, however, is that work is more enjoyable, lessons more interesting and more lively, with more discussions and more variety. There is greater freedom, less importance is attached to detail and there are fewer unnecessary rules.

It is difficult, from the table, to find something to say on the opposite side as the comments are so few and scattered, but the clearest feature is that the largest vote is in the 'work' category, where it approximately equals the co-educational vote. Apart from this the surprising feature is the amount of the difference between the two sides, especially as there is an appreciable variation among co-educational and among single-sex schools in academic standards, pleasantness of atmosphere, etc. That this sometimes leads to preference for the single-sex school is shown by the twenty-four students who found this atmosphere pleasant and friendly. Table 11.11 now presents the men's responses.

[1] Statistically significant for the women though not for the men.

TABLE 11.10 *School preference: free responses (women)*

'Both schools' survey — Preference

	Mixed much and a little	Single-sex much and a little
Pleasanter atmosphere and community spirit; happy atmosphere; friendly; natural; less tension; more relaxed; natural atmosphere; friendships	175	39
Natural relationship between the sexes; presence of boys educative	179	−1*
Prefers own sex; better attitude in single-sex		6
Staff—friendly, helpful; better staff-pupil relations	65	14
Staff—prefers men teachers in some subjects; more pleasant male staff attitude; mixed staff	21	4
Broader outlook on life; not so narrow; more balanced; healthier; more progressive	55	2
Preparation for life	43	−1
Better social atmosphere and social life, out-of-school activities, more co-operation	60	1 / −3
Better for work; lessons more interesting, more lively; work more enjoyable; competition between the sexes	54 / −4	43
Variety of interests, etc.; richer topics of conversation, discussion; more colourful; more lively; more opportunities for dramatics	59	
Smaller school		6
Discipline good; efficient		4
Greater freedom and less importance attached to detail; freer atmosphere; less pettiness; fewer unnecessary rules	34	7
Better facilities and opportunities	7	2
Girls less catty; less bitchiness, spitefulness and pettiness	13	
Healthier attitude to sex, less preoccupied with other sex	6	−1
Boys too rough, manners, discipline	−2	6
Others	9	21

* A minus sign indicates that the student's comment qualified his preference.

TABLE 11.11 *School preference: free responses (men)*

'*Both schools*' survey · Preference

	Mixed much and a little	Single-sex much and a little
Atmosphere—pleasant, happy, friendly, more relaxed, family, freer	50	3
Relationship between sexes natural; presence of girls, educative	42	
Prefers own sex; restricted by what girls might think		2
Pupil–pupil relations friendly, trust	7	
Prefer boys only		6
Staff—friendly, helpful, better pupil–teacher relations	17	4
Staff—prefer have some women	1	
Staff—prefer no women		2
Preparation for life—helps social behaviour; more adult	12	1
Broader outlook on life, more balanced; healthier	9	
Social—better social life, more varied activities; out-of-school activities	12	
Sports		5
Interests—variety of, more colourful, wider, enjoyable, discussion. More fun.	6	1
Work, better for—higher standard. No distractions	17 −2*	15
Discipline: better	6	6
Better facilities	4	
Better status of school		2
Sex—attitude to, better	3	
Others	7	6

* A minus sign indicates that the student's comment qualified his preference, i.e. modified it.

The free responses of the men portray a story similar to that of the women, except that the dominance of the co-educational side, though strong, is not quite as marked. Because of the similarity comment is curtailed. Again the largest section in favour of the single-sex school is that on 'work' where it equals that for the co-educational. Within this section on the co-educational side is the emphasis on a natural and friendly competition between the sexes, the more enjoyable lessons, mixed staff, etc., and on the other side the lack of distractions and good standard of teaching. The comments under 'better facilities', 'better status' and 'small school' (women) remind us of the presence of other variables contaminating the main comparison.

The proportion of comments favourable to the co-educational school as against those favourable to single-sex schools is so large that to select quotations in this proportion would either produce far too many co-educational ones for the chapter or far too few for the single-sex school arguments to be properly illustrated; the quotations on the single-sex side are therefore increased.

Women: favourable to co-education

SOCIAL 'A natural relationship grew up between boys and girls. The first thing that struck me on going to a single-sex school was the competition there was to try and "get" a boy-friend.'

'The presence of the opposite sex was so very helpful in obtaining a more balanced attitude to many things which I felt somewhat lacking in the girls especially as I had no brother at home.'

'Girls are far too spiteful when together for too long. Boys add competition as well as enjoyable company.'

'Very happy at co-ed. and first single-sex school but cattiness and sex obsession at the second single-sex school left me uncertain as to its merits. (Boarded at first girls' school)

'The relief from the boredom of seeing only females day in and day out.' (Girls' boarding at first)

'More friendly—I lost timidity—I always dread to think what would have happened if the school hadn't amalgamated.' (Am.)

'This allowed boys and girls to develop naturally side by side. The school was far happier when co-ed. It was an artificial situation in the single-sex school.' ('Split' school)

'Because the pleasant atmosphere. The boys were almost always smiling and helped us to "laugh things off" if ever we felt down.'

'Life in a mixed society is decidedly more colourful and helps to bridge the conscious gap between the male and female adolescent.'

'At the single-sex school the girls' only topic of conversation up to the age of 16 was boys.'

'The presence of the opposite sex meant the education in general was easily related to life, which it should be, and a natural attitude to the opposite sex grew out of it.'

PUPIL–TEACHER RELATIONSHIPS 'I felt that there was much more freedom and individuality. Children become independent.' (Co-ed. boarding)

'The narrowness and staid atmosphere of the single-sex school seemed to be crushing my personality.'

'We spent much more time in a state of depression, dejection, feeling unjustly treated, etc. at the single-sex school.'

'In the mixed school everybody was treated as a normal human being instead of being "hushed away" as it were in the single-sex school.'

'I think that the education and atmosphere in a co-educational school is more balanced and a better preparation for life. I only wish I had attended one right from the first form.'

'I felt at ease—the atmosphere was not so strained as in a single-sex school.' (Comp.)

'The attitude of the teachers. In the mixed school they took their work as a pleasure and in the single-sex one as a duty. This altered the atmosphere of the school.'

'Far more pleasant atmosphere between staff and pupils. Men and women together get things in proportion and there is less fuss over minute unimportant details.'

ACADEMIC WORK 'Mainly in the educational field—it is very valuable to know the opinions of the opposite sex in any subjects; this causes the widening of one's own knowledge.'

'There was much more vitality about lessons and debates. Standard of education was higher, people worked harder. Much more fun and team spirit in school activities.'

'In classes the boys were far livelier and amusing at times. The whole atmosphere of the school was more active and alive.' (Co-ed. boarding)

'There was definitely more room for discussion and I am sure that this helped in the maturation of individuals.'

'Wider choice of subjects and girl/boy rivalry aided work. Education led more to the life you lead after school (self-discipline taught from the start) rather than just academic abilities.' (Comp.)

'The atmosphere both from a work angle and socially is far better. I found that it made people work much harder on the whole.'

'Everything—socially and educationally—was easier and more friendly and people were willing to join in and help towards the group activities and learned to share and became less concerned about "me" and "what I do for me", but "what can I do to help this group?" '

'Social activity and liveliness in the classroom were more apparent in the mixed school. More scope for drama, discussion, work and practical work such as metal work and technical drawing.'

Women—favourable to girls' schools

SOCIAL 'There was more of a feeling of being an individual rather than being one of a huge institution.'

'The general atmosphere was considerably better to other problems of life, though sex was rather prominent.'

'Life was less tense in the upper forms without the other sex—one could concentrate better on work.' (Comp.) (Attended co-ed. boarding school for one year)

'The boys were resented and rather destructive to the building.'

'I preferred the attitude of the single-sex school but if it could have been run on the same lines but as a co-ed. school I feel that it could have been even better.'

'Jealousy plays a big part in the life of a co-ed. school and work does not always come first.'

WORK 'I concentrated far more on my work. On the other hand I think girls who do not meet boys at home *definitely* need a co-ed. school.'

'The attitude of girl to girl was better and of girl to boy was better. The work atmosphere was much much easier.'

'With the happier atmosphere, lacking in the pre-occupation of the other sex [sic] my work reached a much higher standard. It deteriorated on entrance to the mixed school.'

'One was much more able to concentrate on one's work and the work was of a much higher standard in consequence.'

'It was a "better" school, the pupils were "nicer" and the quality of the teaching was on the whole better.' (Girls' boarding)

The men's free responses are particularly frank; as with the women the responses about the single-sex schools are not limited to the proportion allowed to co-educational schools.

Men—favourable to co-education

SOCIAL 'The mannerisms and behaviour of us all towards a mixed society as opposed to a single-sex society was greatly improved. Life was also very enjoyable and interesting discussions arose.' (Am.)

'A healthy atmosphere between boys and girls, good pupil–teacher relationships, excellent school social life, all of which helped develop a healthy pride in school.'

'The whole attitude of both staff and pupils is different—far more pleasant and natural.'

'It meant an opening-out whereby a whole new social horizon was established.' (Am.)

'The presence of girls seemed to make the boys more civilized than they were in my single-sex school.'

'The learning to live together and realizing that the opposite sex is natural ¦and not unnatural and something that you must be shielded from.'

'The mixture seemed thoroughly normal and natural, which the single-sex school never was.'

'It prepared the pupil for the outside world. They could not go on just meeting members of their own sex; eventually they would have to mix; school is the best place for this.' (Am.)

'A much more congenial and relaxed atmosphere designed to produce human beings not computers.'

'The presence of the opposite sex shattered a lot of illusions and helped one make many adjustments to the realities of life—unpleasant as they may be!'

'Gives a chance for the rather timid person to acquaint himself with the opposite sex—*misconceptions in single-sex schools are a fact.*'

'Women and girls' influence calms down excess of lots of things.'

'The single-sex school I went to was frustrating in every way.'

DISCIPLINE 'It was a school in the most helpful and understanding sense. The single-sex school resembled a concentration camp with frightened guards.'

'The whole atmosphere of school was different—the staff–pupil relationship was much more tenable.'

'More open and friendly relationships, trust, sensible discipline.'

'Much more friendly attitude which is more conducive to work.'

'Less restriction—more of a family unit than the Regimental Barracks.'

SEX 'We were brought up in a community akin to that in which we were to live. Sexual relations are "normal"—boy goes out with girl—and not homosexual as in the single-sex.' ($3\frac{1}{2}$ years in boys' school, then $3\frac{1}{2}$ in co-educational)

'I did not like being at a co-ed. school when I was 13. However I think that the absence of girls in my last single-sex school had a bad effect on the pupils and on the teachers with regard to boy–girl relationships and problems of sex which arose in the school.' (Boarding)

'Generally a happier atmosphere. Boys less sex conscious. More natural than segregating sexes. Girls' presence tends to make boys be smarter, less foolish.'

WORK 'The co-ed. school had its atmosphere of healthy regard for other people and for learning. The single-sex did not.'

'Better atmosphere in which to work and play.'

'In the mixed school one felt more relaxed and at times had the feeling that you had to impress the opposite sex, and things and tasks you undertook would be tackled much more efficiently.' (Co-ed. boarding)

'You wanted to work harder often just to impress the girls, but it was a nice atmosphere especially in the Sixth.'

Men—favourable to boys' schools

SOCIAL 'The co-ed. school tended to be rather more impersonal than the single-sex school, also the single-sex school was smaller.'

'Less emotional atmosphere than from women teachers and from girls. Restricted by the thoughts of what the girls might think.' (Am.)

'A delay or rest period before being exposed to the human female.'

'The good atmosphere of boys enjoying life together. Girl-friends were always out of school and much more forgotten during working hours. There is a tendency for shyness to arise, however.'

'No distractions, better feeling between pupils and between pupils and staff. Better sports. More out of school meetings between pupils.'

PUPIL–TEACHER RELATIONSHIPS 'Less interference of staff within societies, etc. Absence of female staff.' (Am.)

'More sport and outdoor activities with teachers taking a greater interest in extra-curricular activities.'

'The fun we had was much better and the attitude of the teachers towards the pupils was a good deal better. The understanding nature of the teachers also made you respect them.' (Small school)

'Better staff–pupil relations. Friendlier atmosphere in class. More progressive work and harder work.'

WORK 'Classroom atmosphere much better—boys have much more fun when no girls are around. Girls are apt to tell teachers if anything is wrong.' (First two years co-ed.)

'In the single-sex atmosphere my academic work was of a far higher standard than at a co-ed. However, the fact that it was a boarding school may have influenced this.'

'There was far more work done, both academically and physically.'

'It enables a better standard of work all the year round rather than just at exams time and there is plenty of time for female company in out-of-school hours.'

PRESTIGE AND TRADITION 'Enjoyed the tradition and pride in belonging to the school.'

'I approve strongly of co-ed. schools. Academically O.K. They don't put this bullying business into everything. I am convinced that girls have something to offer, e.g. in discussion; their points of view often surprisingly different from boys'.' But he strongly preferred the single-sex school he went to and when asked to which type of school he would send his children he replied, 'To my school I hope. Keep up the tradition and all that. (Dad went there).' (Boys' boarding)

PUPILS' PREFERENCE

So far this chapter has described research on the school preference of ex-pupils who were student teachers, and the objection might be raised that these are not a fully representative cross-section of grammar school pupils. Replies to this argument are considered in Chapter 1, but the best answer is evidence from a wider representation of grammar school pupils. Work in this was begun, and although never completed owing to the calls of other research and lack of clerical assistance, it is not without interest.

The first part of this enquiry derives from a questionnaire which was completed by the pupils of a number of sixth forms in grammar schools. In order to make the returns as reliable and as impartial as possible the author visited most of the schools personally and administered the questionnaire himself. Replies were anonymous and pupils were assured that no one at school would be shown the papers. Among a number of other questions pupils were asked, 'Which do you think you would like better, a school of (a) Boys and girls together, (b) Boys or girls only?' The results follow the pattern set by the other enquiries (Table 11.12). This is stressed because the number of schools in the sample is too small for the enquiry to stand as an independent investigation; on the other hand the co-educational schools were almost unanimous. The schools in the table were the only ones approached.

The sixth forms in the co-educational, the boys' and the girls' schools, all proved to be in favour of co-education. In the single-sex schools the majority was sometimes comfortable, sometimes substantial; in the co-educational schools opinion was almost unanimous. Incidentally these were individual opinions, written without consultation with friends or those pupils at the next desks. They were accompanied by free responses, but as these add little to the evidence only a few are quoted.

The comments from the boys' schools were decidedly direct and often forceful; for example, one young man of eighteen who earlier had had experience of co-education wrote, 'A school should be a microcosm. Ours pretends to be but is a false one. We have only one half of the community represented. In the world outside we meet men and women. This should also be the case in schools.' Again, 'A pupil should leave a good educational school with the idea of life as a co-operative adventure, demanding the best efforts of both sexes.' A boy of eighteen writes, somewhat naively, 'So far I have been constantly in the dark as far as girls' general opinions are concerned. I believe emotional association with girls would remove much of the speculation about our opposite sex. As the system exists, end of term parties (with the correspond-

TABLE 11.12 *Pupils' school preference (Sixth forms)*

Type of school sampled	Type of school preferred				Percentage for co-education combined sexes
	Co-educational		Single-sex		
	Boys	Girls	Boys	Girls	
					%
Mixed schools:					
1	13	21	0	0	100
2	5	4	1	0	90
3 (Type B)	7	10	0	0	100
4	10	10	0	0	100
5	12	12	0	0	100*
Girls' schools:					
6		12		1	92
7		24		12	67
8		15		9	63
Boys' schools:					
9	22		4		85
10	14		2		88

* One undecided girl is not included.

ing girls' school) have a stilted atmosphere for those who rarely encounter girls except in cinemas, etc.'

The presence of the opposite sex in the same class may not be merely the distracting influence that some have supposed, as a number of boys thought co-education increased competition in class and raised the standard of work.

Two rather humorous replies against co-education cannot be left out. Brief, but to the point is, 'Because I prefer boys to girls.' The other is more interesting: 'I prefer to keep social life and education separate by dividing the day into two parts, viz. (a) up to 4 p.m. when I do *all* my work and spend all my time in the company of boys; (b) 4 p.m. to 11 p.m. which I spend in the company of my other friends. This variation relieves boredom and makes life very interesting.'

The replies from the girls' schools lacked the unintentional humour of those of the boys. Like the boys' replies, however, they emphasized the value of co-education as a preparation for life. 'If boys and girls were taught together, it usually teaches both to be less self-conscious and does away with any "silliness" they might otherwise show when each would be unexpectedly thrown together. It also teaches the sexes to be more appreciative of the view-points and ideas of the other.' Two comments found frequently were that co-education prepares students for university life and for life in general, and that there is a higher standard of work due to a sense of competition. On the other hand some of the minority thought the presence of the other sex might be a distracting influence. One girl wrote, 'Boys and girls get to know one another without having to roam the streets after dark or sit in the park.'

In the comments from co-educational schools there was almost unanimity on the advantage of co-education, the principal argument being the preparation for social life after school. A boy wrote, 'Association with girls in school often prevents a boy from being narrow-minded later and helps him to achieve self-possession and assurance. His outlook is also broadened.' The girls wrote in a similar strain, e.g., 'By attending mixed schools we come into contact with boys every day and it prepares us for mixing with men in later life. It gives us a chance of understanding men and their outlook on life.'

Among the few comments against co-education from co-educational schools, there was no discernible theme, but a variety of remarks such as, 'Teachers would be all men and I would prefer that,' and, 'There would be easier arrangement of time-tables such as P. T. and Woodwork.'

The second piece of work among pupils in grammar schools was a survey of opinion among the whole age range. This was undertaken because one of the objections to co-education, raised sometimes by men teachers from boys' schools, is that boys want to be with boys and to be taught by men. A variation on this theme is that boys of 12 to 14—and perhaps girls—like to play in groups of their own sex and shun the company of the opposite sex.[1] The writer's intention was to carry out this survey in a number of schools, administering a questionnaire personally, but lack of time has limited the work to one co-educational school. The outcome, however, is not without interest (Figure 11.2).

It is surprising that in spite of the smallness of the sub-group when the 239 pupils are divided according to sex and age, there is a consistency in the results and a trend which fits into the expectations of theory and of previous research. In the first place a decided majority of these boys and girls at all ages between 11 and 18 prefer a school for both sexes, thus refuting the argument that because the sexes prefer to play apart between the ages of 12 and 14, they would prefer separate schools. When they are placed together in a school, and therefore know what they are talking about, they appear to prefer the opposite sex to be there even if the

[1] See also chapter 12, p. 196.

two sexes play apart. As this work was done in only one school, however, confirmation from work in other co-educational schools is needed.

In the second place the graphs show that in spite of the strong preference for co-education there is a dip round about the age of 13. This might be due to boys having a stereotyped impression of

FIGURE 11.2 *Preference for co–education: pupils in co–educational grammar school*

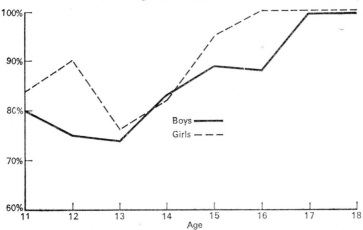

playing with girls as being effeminate, or to boys hesitating to admit at that age that they wanted girls about at all. But what of the girls? Is it similarly 'not done' amongst girls of that age to admit that they like having boys around? Whatever the reason, even at the lowest points of the graph—age 13—three-quarters of the boys and of the girls prefer a school of both sexes, and this preference increases steadily with age. Out of 124 boys in the age range 11 to 18, 103 preferred a mixed school and similarly 101 out of 115 girls. In view of individual differences in temperament, disgruntled individuals, and the instability of young teenagers, this is a very big majority.

Discussion

Though comparisons may sometimes be odious they cannot always be avoided, and there is a danger that established institutions that fare less well in the comparison may become emotionally involved and actively resentful. This would be a pity because reason takes to flight when emotion takes control, and the resentment would be founded on a misconception. For no one should think that this book is in any way a criticism of the dedicated work of the heads and staffs of single-sex schools; it represents rather an assessment of the possibility that the reorganization of these schools as co-educational schools might enable them to serve the children and the community still better. Incidentally it seems that most of the teachers would be happier in such schools (Dale, 1969).

Someone asked why pupils should decide whether secondary schools should be co-educational or single-sex. There is naturally no intention of allowing them to do so, but as consumers—people at the receiving end of education—they have a right to be heard, a right which is made much stronger by their relative maturity and their responsibility. They are mostly ex-pupils and sixth-formers, mostly future entrants to the teaching profession, strongly motivated to want the schools to be as good as possible. These are not 'good time' pupils or disillusioned premature or early leavers, but pupils who are sound academically and should have a better attitude to school than most other pupils. Moreover, the judgment of teachers themselves has also been taken, and there is a most marked similarity between the views of students and of teachers. In both cases the greatest reliance has been placed on the judgment of those who have had practical experience of at least one co-educational and one single-sex school.

In all the inquiries described in this chapter, each with a different sample of respondents, there is a decided preference expressed for co-educational schools. The reasons given seem logically sound— a better preparation for life in a bi-sexual world, a more natural atmosphere between boy and girl, a better attitude to sex, a school life which is more colourful, a staff–pupil relationship which is closer, more friendly, and a staff drawn from both sexes, which is true to life. The three types of school community— co-educational, boys', and girls'— are found to be much more different in 'community spirit' than most educationists considered possible, though we must also remember the wide variations of standard and of atmosphere within the schools of any one of these types.

This range within each could be a principal reason why a small minority of pupils who attended both types of school prefer their single-sex to their co-educational school. Another important reason, given by pupils and ex-pupils themselves, is that the order of schools attended is in itself a force tending to cause a preference for the last school attended, especially for the boys, so that if a student attended a co-educational grammar school for only one year and a single-sex school until he left the sixth, he might well indicate a preference for this last school. As a majority of pupils attended a co-educational school last in the 'Both schools' survey, this factor has been controlled by comparing pupils who attended a co-educational school first with those who attended a single-sex school first, then similarly for last schools.

Other pupils have expressed a preference for the single-sex school because it was small, some because it was an old school with tradition, a number of girls because the pupils were 'more my class' or 'more my type', and a few pupils because of better facilities. Those who are late arrivals at either type of school—especially girls arriving in the fourth form upwards—have difficulty in breaking into established circles and become unhappy; there is therefore a tendency for them to prefer their previous school, though this factor can be outweighed by others.

There remain a number who preferred their single-sex school for reasons which concern the co-educational-versus-single-sex controversy. These include some boys and a tiny minority of girls who said they preferred a school without the opposite sex. There are a number of factors which could cause this attitude. Apart from the handful of individuals who may already have homosexual or lesbian inclinations (and there is evidence that there are a few), there may be others who would prefer the company of their own sex only. They are a very small fraction of the total sample, and it might also be queried whether it is psychologically helpful to them to permit them to withdraw from a bi-sexual world. A related question is whether there might be a connection between high or low scoring on the introversion-extroversion scale and preference for co-educational or single-sex schools. In Chapter 9 on 'unhappy pupils' it seemed likely that unhappy pupils in girls' schools tended to be extroverted more often than unhappy pupils in mixed schools; immediately the opposite case comes to mind—is there a small minority of highly introverted pupils who would prefer to be in a single-sex school? Unfortunately there is no direct evidence available on this point.

The largest group in this minority who preferred their single-sex school is that which based their argument on academic work. Though there is an equal group on the co-educational side, there is a definite overlap here between co-educational and single-sex schools in the standard of teaching and the achievement reached. It would be unfair to the co-educational schools, however, if it were not pointed out that there is a distinct danger of confusion, in so far as a high standard of attainment in a single-sex school may be due either to a good standard of teaching or to a very selective entry, and the latter is a factor which is not an inevitable accompaniment of single-sex education. In large cities direct grant schools, which are almost always for historical reasons single-sex take the cream of the pupils, whereas there are few co-educational schools in this favourable position.

The objection could be made that the preference for the co-educational school might be due to its 'less strict' discipline and even to less stringent demands for academic work. There are three main arguments in reply: first, that research has shown that there is in fact no inferiority in academic standard that can be said to be due to co-education (cf. Dale, 1962a); second, that the students in the samples were academically inclined and would have had no hesitation in protesting if their co-educational schools had not efficiently fulfilled their teaching function; third, that, as shown earlier those teachers who have taught in both types prefer the co-educational and do not criticize the academic standards there.

It has been demonstrated that another factor in the problem—the pleasantness or unpleasantness of the school situation—could not have produced the very large preference for co-educational schools, because the pupils report that the co-educational schools were on average only a little better situated; moreover the large differences in preferences continue when the pleasantness of situation factor is held constant.

The preference for co-educational schools which has been revealed by these enquiries relates to the society in which the pupils and schools are placed. It depends partly upon society's attitude to the relations between the sexes, and to its attitude towards sexual problems, both natural and unnatural. It depends upon the force of tradition and the question of the equality of the sexes. Underneath this, however, is something which is even more fundamental because it is concerned with human nature—the query whether boys and girls naturally benefit more from being educated together or apart. These researches have tried to throw some light on this question, but within the setting of a certain type of civilization.

12

Attitude to the opposite sex

Almost a hundred years ago the Honourable Dudley Campbell, M.A., published a small and ephemeral but prophetic pamphlet entitled *Mixed Education of Boys and Girls in America*.[1] It had little practical result and the pamphlet has been forgotten, but many of its passages show that it was written by a percipient educationist who was, however, before his time. A few passages are here resurrected as a quaint but appropriate introduction to this chapter. Writing of educational influences he argues:

But there remains to be applied an influence entirely
ignored by the principal educators of this country, yet taking
rank amongst the most potent agencies for moulding the
human mind and character. The moral power of sex upon
sex would seem to be regarded as either useless or dangerous.
For all the care of the better known institutions, professing
to train and completely equip their pupils for the duties of the
future, a man might pass his life, from the cradle to the
time of taking his degree as a Master of Arts, without ever
seeing the face of a woman or hearing the sound of her
voice. Yet everyone would admit that such chance
opportunities as youths enjoy of associating with ladies are
of the utmost value; and that but for the time spent at home
before going to school, and, later, for the holidays, they
would grow up with very imperfect notions of civilization.
Moreover, it is often observed that boys without sisters are
less cultivated and refined than their fellows who in this
respect have been more fortunate.

Such reflections naturally suggest the inquiry whether
an influence so admirable and efficient, in spite of the
limited sphere allowed to it, might not be yet more serviceable
if permitted to work on a larger scale. Is the society of
woman like those Indian spices which, in order to be
beneficial, must be sparingly used? or is it like pure air,
which men are glad to have in abundance at all seasons of the

[1] London, 1874.

year? Why should an atmosphere so healthy at home be
thought perilous at school? Why should an agency admitted
to be good and even necessary in August and September
be counted as worthless, if not mischievous, in October
and November? If boys and girls, young men and young
women, may dance and sing and generally play and amuse
themselves together with advantage, is any special danger to
be apprehended if they should also study together? Might
not the refining influence of the one sex upon the other
be expected to continue, so that the boys aiming at a higher
standard of conduct would be less prone to selfishness,
bullying, and 'rowdyism' of whatever kind, while the girls
were less given to frivolity, sentimentalism, and gossip?
Might not the fact that each sex demands from the other a
loftier standard of action than it is contented with for
itself, have an effect in increasing the importance attached
by school opinion to study, so that the boys would shrink
from showing incompetence or sloth before the girls, or
the girls before the boys?

He then mentions the success of mixed schools in Scotland,
and even of some in England, a passage which the writer cannot
refrain from quoting:

An excellent instance is afforded by the admirable Home
and Colonial School in Gray's Inn Road, near King's Cross,
where 1000 pupils of both sexes are trained under the most
advanced and enlightened methods of instruction. An example
no less striking is afforded by the Birkbeck Literary
Institution. The classes there, held every evening, are
attended by both men and women. The number belonging
to the institution, whether for the sake of the classes or the
library, is about two thousand; and it would be difficult to
name a body of students, either more respectable in character,
or, considering the tax put upon their energies by daily
business, more zealous for self-improvement.

Previous chapters have inevitably referred to various aspects
of the attitude of the sexes towards each other, but here there is a
more direct approach. The results of three surveys are presented.

The equality of the sexes

MEN

In the Second College survey some 900 students in Colleges of
Education answered, as part of a questionnaire, the question, 'In

your attitude to the opposite sex do you think of them, in general,
as being Very superior/Superior/Equal/Inferior/Very inferior?'
They were invited to comment if they wished to do so. In Table
12.1 we see that the co-educated men had a slightly stronger
belief in the equality of the sexes than did the men who had been
in schools apart from the opposite sex, the main interest being in
the slightly greater spread of the estimates made by the men who
attended boys' schools, rather more of them estimating women as
superior and rather more estimating them as inferior to men.[1]
That part of the sample for which the information was available
was analysed by social class and no significant differences emerged
within either type of school. The students in the sample are,
however, already moving away from their original social class to a
new common one. Another relevant fact is that 38 per cent of these
men had spent one or two years in a mixed College of Education.

TABLE 12.1 *Attitude to the opposite sex*

Second College survey

The opposite sex is:	Replies from male students				Replies from female students			
	Co-educational schools		Boys' schools		Co-educational schools		Girls' schools	
	N	%	N	%	N	%	N	%
Very superior	0	0	0	0	1	0·3	2	0·3
Superior	8	2·3	22	4·0	120	30·0	174	28·2
Equal	286	83·4	435	78·5	275	68·7	435	70·7
Inferior	49	14·3	94	17·0	4	1·0	5	0·8
Very inferior	0	0	3	0·5	0	0	0	0
Totals	343	100	554	100	400	100	616	100

NOTE: The differences in the distributions between co-educational and
single-sex schools are not statistically significant, but on the men's side
they are not without interest.

The free responses showed little difference between the co-
educated and single-sex educated men, most of them saying that
the sexes are equal but different, are complementary, or that it
depends on the individual, but 22 per cent in each group of those
who commented regarded women as inferior—a higher proportion

[1] The tendency for the men from boys' schools to be more extreme in
attitude is not statistically significant but approaches it.

than in the estimates. A few quotations are given to lighten and in some cases illuminate the text, but here there seemed to be little point in treating them on a proportional basis. From the co-educated men we have:

'Always seemed so hard working, neat and conscientious: gave me a feeling of inferiority! Associated therefore with years just below rather than same.'

(Inferior) 'This is only a general answer. My own girl-friend, e.g. I consider equal, but most females bring their inferiority upon themselves and like it.'

(Inferior) 'Need more care in handling psychologically and emotionally.'

(Equal) 'I feel that male and female are complimentary [sic] to each other. Men have much to offer women and vice versa.'

(Equal) 'At school obvious the girls could hold their own with us. Since then I have found that in our own particular society women can hold their own with us.'

A few comments from the men educated in boys' schools were more extreme:

(Superior) 'Possibly due to the fact that not having had much contact with opposite sex and during adolescence I often feel uncomfortable in their presence.'

(Equal) 'Women are of poor character when in authority—petty.'

(Equal) 'I cannot think that we [men] are on one level and that they [women] are on another level. I only think of humanity on a common level.'

(Inferior) 'God created woman to be in subjection to man as the head of the family unit.'

(Equal) 'After two years in a mixed training college I have grown out of regarding girls as inferiors.'

WOMEN

About a thousand women students answered the same question as the men. Their results are also in Table 12.1 The table shows an almost identical distribution of attitudes for the two groups. It would appear that long exposure to the conduct of boys in a mixed school had done nothing to undermine the feminine assessment of the status of the male, nor had this continual social contact done anything to increase his status. Nor, on the other hand, does the seclusion of the girls in their girls' school seem to have had any effect at all on their estimate of the general status of males. In both groups, however, between a quarter and a third of the women admit to thinking of men as, in general, superior, and only 1 in 100 said they thought them inferior.

The data were then analysed according to social class. No association was found between father's occupation and respondent's view of men as superior, equal or inferior.

Free comments were made by a quarter of each school group, and they were similar in tone. In both groups the commonest statements emphasized the basic equality of the sexes, or implied that they are complementary, or that relationships depend on the individual, or that men are superior to women in some things and inferior in others. Such statements made up 43 per cent of each group's total comments. Thirteen per cent of the comments from the girls' schools group and 14 per cent from the mixed schools expressed a *preference* for men to be superior! About the same proportion actually said man was superior, some 9 per cent on grounds other than physical. A few representative comments are:

'Women will never be men's equals.'

'I tend to get an inferiority complex with most men, but it depends on the man as to whether it affects me.'

'I believe them to be superior in thought, at least the more intelligent ones, because they glean much more from the world around them in politics, government, literature, etc., and have a wider background than most girls but not all.'

'I have much more respect for them than for members of my own sex.'

'I like to be equal in the company of a member of the opposite sex but feel a husband should be superior.'(!)

'More original. Women on the whole mediocre and less interesting.'

'Members of the opposite sex are complimentary.' [sic]

Comment

By the time the ex-pupils have reached the age of eighteen to twenty there is little difference between the view of the co-educated and those educated in single-sex schools on the equality of the sexes. Some students from single-sex schools, however, said that their experience in a mixed College of Education had changed their ideas about the innate superiority of the male.

Attitude pleasant or unpleasant

In the 'Both schools' survey the ex-pupils were asked, 'In your single-sex [or co-educational] school was the general attitude of most of the pupils towards the opposite sex Pleasant/Fairly pleasant/Neutral/A little unpleasant/Unpleasant?' They were also invited to comment.

MEN

The estimates of the men are in Table 12.2. Figures are given separately for schools attended as juniors and those attended as seniors, because of the extent of the difference between them.

TABLE 12.2 *Pleasantness of attitude to the opposite sex (boys)*

'*Both schools*' *survey*

| | Replies about first school attended | | | | Replies about last school attended | | | |
| | Co-educational | | Boys' | | Co-educational | | Boys' | |
	N	%	N	%	N	%	N	%
Pleasant	38	45·8	24	20·7	66	63·5	24	35·8
Fairly pleasant	29	34·9	31	26·7	29	27·8	25	37·3
Neutral	12	14·5	35	30·2	9	8·7	4	6·0
A little unpleasant	4	4·8	21	18·1	0	0	13	19·4
Unpleasant	0	0	5	4·3	0	0	1	1·5
Totals	83	100	116	100	104	100	67	100

NOTE: The difference between the distributions for co-educational and boys' schools is statistically very highly significant both for 'first' and for 'last' schools. The difference between 'first' and 'last' schools themselves may well be due mainly to the change in pupils' ages.

Before interpreting the figures a brief comment on the wording of the question is needed. The words 'pleasant attitude' had for a few pupils a slight element of ambiguity; though it is evident from the free responses that most of the boys interpreted the words as meaning 'normally friendly', without any overtones, there were some who interpreted them as 'pleasant because they wanted to date girls'. Fortunately there is no doubt about the incidence of this minority response; the free responses show that it is much more characteristic of the boys' schools than of the co-educational, so that the 'pleasant' estimates are inflated more for the former than for the latter. Additional proof of this is to be seen in the much greater percentage of the ex-pupils who estimated the attitude in their boys' schools towards girls to be 'a little unpleasant' or 'unpleasant' compared with their co-educational schools. The differences in tone between these comments will be seen later in the quotations.

In both the co-educational and boys' schools the ex-pupils who attended as seniors estimated the attitude to girls to be more pleasant among the seniors than among the juniors. The attitude was least pleasant among junior boys in boys' schools, more pleasant among senior boys in the same schools, still more pleasant among junior boys in co-educational schools and most pleasant of all among senior boys in these schools, where some 91 per cent of the students estimated the attitude to be pleasant or fairly pleasant —mostly the former.

Co-educational schools

The seventy-seven free responses from co-educational schools were too few for satisfactory classification, but approaching half of them spoke of a good friendly relationship or that girls were treated as equals or that there was normal interest—often using these phrases. Small groups said that the attitude varied with age and that it depended on the personality of the girl; five said there was a 'romantic relationship'. Because of the central importance of this theme to the co-education debate one in five of these free responses are quoted, except that the relatively uninteresting 'neutral' category is omitted entirely to avoid overloading the text with quotations. The quotations are now proportionate to the total comments in each category for each type of school.

PLEASANT 'In the upper forms the two sexes could talk frankly about each other's problems of growing up which I consider has helped me greatly.'

'The general attitude was that the girls were an asset to the school.'

'As regards members of the opposite sex relations could not have been better.'

'In the Sixth—romances bound to arise. Everyone was broad-minded. Healthy atmosphere.'

'The girls joined in nearly all the "out-of-school" activities which the societies formed and both sexes got on well together.'

'The opposite sex was there and as we grew up in the school that was all there was to it, they were just accepted as being there.'

'There was an acceptance of the fact that it was natural for the two to be together.'

'Never met any woman haters—a few were shy or indifferent at worst—none actually aggressive.'

FAIRLY PLEASANT 'A matter for the individual, depending upon his or her age and social development—on the whole harmonious.'

'There were times when the girls could be a nuisance.'

'A few of the boys were quite open about the fact that they only wanted a girl for the sexual pleasure, rather than the social pleasure that went with it.'

'Some of the girls may have been unpleasant but the majority were enjoyable to work with.'

A LITTLE UNPLEASANT Only three comments came in this category and none of these was in fact 'a little unpleasant', the worst one being:

'The only reason for answering was that it was not neutral but rather disdainful: not really unpleasant at all but neutral would not be right.'

UNPLEASANT As there were no estimates in the unpleasant category, there are no comments either.

Boys' schools

The free responses about the boys' schools, attended by the same pupils who attended the co-educational schools, were of a different nature, the largest single category being accompanied by the estimate 'a little unpleasant'. (The number in the two pleasant categories, however, equalled those in the two unpleasant ones.) There was a wide variety of themes, varying from shyness and ignorance and 'annoying distraction', especially among juniors, through normal interest, friendly relationships and 'romantic', to 'sex mad' and attitude unpleasant sexually. This last type of comment was much more frequent than in the returns about the co-educational school. We must once again remember that this is what the ex-pupils report, and that boasting about sexual adventures which have no basis in reality does sometimes occur among boys in their late 'teens. Yet these are the same ex-pupils reporting on the predominant attitude in the two types of school they attended. Likewise more of the comments in the 'pleasant' category about the boys' schools had 'dating girls' or something similar as a theme whereas the dominant theme about the co-educational schools was 'normal friendly relationship'. Typical free responses are as follows:

PLEASANT   'Most of us met and went everywhere with our girlfriends.'

'It was pleasant in that the opposite sex were completely cut off from us.'

'Dating girls from the High School was common.'

FAIRLY PLEASANT   'The boys tended to look upon girls as a thing to be enjoyed sexually.'

'Sex mad in most boys.'

'We did have a sister school to which we were invited for the Christmas Dance. The atmosphere and attitude of these dances was quite good.'

NEUTRAL   'In my second school I had a much more mature attitude towards girls.' (Attended three schools, the second being co-educational)

A LITTLE UNPLEASANT   'Some were antifeminist, some sexually unhealthy in their attitudes, many immature.'

'Normal attitudes to the opposite sex were sometimes degraded by one or two depraved youngsters.'

'Unbalanced; myself a tendency to fantasies.'

'One or two tried to create the impression of having intimate relations with girls. Probably caused by lack of females in school, therefore ignorance of them.'

'They showed no consideration for girls as people, but rather treated them as animals.'

UNPLEASANT   'With reference to the word "unpleasant" reply is—"Better would be the word 'unhealthy' ".'

'Girls were all right for sex, otherwise they were "sissy".'

Two themes not represented in the above quotations were that the very junior boys were too young to be interested in girls and that some schools or boys were so cut off from girls that they were very ignorant about them. The extent to which an individual may encounter these latter difficulties is illustrated by the following response: 'I don't think I spoke to a single girl for five years.' A direct comparison of some interest is, 'It was completely different from co-ed. and I was frankly shocked by what I considered an unnatural attitude.' Because of the importance of the replies to this question a full tabulation is given in Appendix 2 (Table A.21).

Though surveys in this field should be replicated, it appears highly probable that the Victorians and Edwardians were wrong in their policy of segregating boys and girls in their secondary schools through their fears of encouraging sexual misbehaviour if the two sexes were placed in the same school. In this sample it is in the schools where the boys were deprived of the company of the opposite sex that their attitude is less desirable. It is deprivation of such company that makes them desire it all the more and at the same time tends to create—in their own words—unhealthy attitudes and an outlook towards girls which falls considerably below the 'normal friendship' which is the predominant phrase in the replies about co-educational schools.

The same results were obtained when supplementary questions were asked, such as, 'In your co-educational (or boys') school was the general attitude of most of the pupils (of your own sex) towards the opposite sex, "Rather preoccupied with the opposite sex?" ' and, with a similar preamble, ' "Boy–girl crazy?" ' The ex-pupils thought the senior boys in the boys' schools to be more preoccupied with the opposite sex and more boy–girl crazy than those in the co-educational schools, the differences being statistically very highly significant (cf. Table A.22).[1] When the phrase 'normal interest' was substituted they considered the interest in the opposite sex to be more 'normal' in the co-educational schools than in the boys' schools, the difference being statistically significant for juniors as well as for seniors. Only 8 men out of 177 thought that the attitude in the co-educational schools was not normal or were doubtful (cf. Table A.22).

In the same series of questions were included two which, though related, begin to explore different facets of boy–girl relations. The first was, 'Was the general attitude of most of the pupils (of your own sex) towards the opposite sex "antagonistic"?' Pupils again could choose their answer from True/Partly true/False/Doubtful. The second question substituted the word 'timid' for 'antagonistic'.

[1] Data for 'rather preoccupied', etc., are not given in the table.

The full results may be seen in Table A.23. Here it is sufficient to report that the distributions were closely similar for the two types of school, and though rather more ex-pupils said there was no antagonism in co-educational schools compared with boys' schools, the differences were not statistically significant either for first or last schools. Only 2 per cent of ex-pupils said it was true that there was antagonism, though 20 per cent said it was partly true.

With regard to timidity, segregation in a boys' school produced a greater degree of it according to the ex-pupils' reports, the differences being highly significant statistically for both juniors and seniors (see Table A.23). Some 10 per cent of the students thought this was true of the boys in their boys' school, compared with 1 per cent about the co-educated boys.

WOMEN

When we consider the women's results the question uppermost in our minds is naturally, 'Is the attitude of girls in girls' schools towards the opposite sex subject to the same kind of "deprivation effect" as in the case of the boys?' The answer given by their estimates in Table 12.3 is that at least in this sample it appears to have such an effect.

TABLE 12.3 *Pleasantness of attitude to the opposite sex (girls)*

'*Both schools*' *survey*

	Replies about first school attended				Replies about last school attended			
	Co-educational		Girls'		Co-educational		Girls'	
	N	%	N	%	N	%	N	%
Pleasant	136	45·6	117	30·2	206	57·4	107	42·0
Fairly pleasant	112	37·6	125	32·1	117	32·6	84	33·1
Neutral	39	13·1	85	21·9	31	8·6	18	7·1
A little unpleasant	10	3·4	53	13·7	3	0·8	39	15·4
Unpleasant	1	0·3	8	2·1	2	0·6	6	2·4
Totals	298	100	388	100	359	100	254	100

NOTE: The difference between the distribution for co-educational and girls' schools is statistically very highly significant for both first and last schools.

The ex-pupils reported that the attitude of girls in girls' schools towards boys was 'less pleasant' than the attitude of girls in co-educational schools, with regard to both junior and senior pupils. As with the boys an obvious query is, 'What did the ex-pupils mean by "less pleasant" and "unpleasant"?' As one young lady put it when writing of the girls' school she had attended: 'Great interest in boys but depends on your morals as to whether attitude pleasant or not.' Another woman, again commenting on her girls' school, and estimating the attitude to boys to be 'a little unpleasant', wrote, 'Not quite the right word. Bad effect in that many girls were boy-mad.' Fortunately the meaning of the estimates is elucidated by the free responses, a detailed examination of which showed conclusively that whereas in regard to the girls' schools a small minority estimated 'pleasant' and accompanied this with the comment 'boy-crazy' or something similar, this was absent, in regard to their co-educational school, the free responses being dominated by the 'normal friendly relations' category. The difference is epitomized in three 'direct comparisons' which are taken in advance of the main group in order to illustrate this point:

'Pleasant—seemed to be more boy-crazy.' (Girls' school)

'Pleasant—the attitude was "who were you with last night?"—a lot of discussion about boys whereas in a co-ed. they are accepted.'

'Unpleasant—boy-mad. When I returned from co-ed. was shocked at preoccupation for something I took for granted.'

As in the case of the boys this nature of the differences between the girls' and co-educational schools in the 'pleasant' category receives support from the fact that the girls' schools also have the greater percentage of estimates in the two 'unpleasant' categories.

Considering only the estimates in Table 12.3 at present, there is a decided difference between the pleasantness of attitude reported in the co-educational schools and that in the girls' schools, and as we have already seen this extends down into the 'unpleasant' section of the scale. The attitude is both 'pleasanter' at one end of the scale, and less unpleasant at the other, in the co-educational schools. The free responses confirm this in dramatic fashion, those about the co-educational schools being completely dominated by categories of responses such as 'natural friendly relationship', 'took each other for granted' and 'treated them as equals', while the replies about girls' schools were characterized much more by remarks indicating the effects of deprivation, e.g. 'boy-crazy', 'obsessed with sex' and 'unhealthy'. (See Table A.24.) Readers should not infer from this that the attitude affected all girls who went to girls' schools or that the staffs are in some way responsible; the point is merely that because of the form of organization—because of the deprivation of the natural companionship of the opposite sex—there appears to be a sharpening of the desire for them, with boys placed on an artificial pedestal. At the same time there is also evidence that some girls—especially those without brothers—have little opportunity for meeting the opposite sex and are even, in their own words, 'afraid' or 'terrified' of them.

In view of the importance of this question the free responses are quoted extensively, strictly in proportion for each category of estimate and each type of school, but again omitting the 'neutral' category. Those about co-educational schools are taken first.

Co-educational schools

PLEASANT 'In the lower school girls hero-worshipped the boys, but in the Sixth most girls very friendly with the boys although their boy-friends were usually from outside school. Often found schoolboys rather immature. Although we were able to have lively and poignant [sic] discussions about any subject.'

'The boys didn't particularly worry us or affect the way we conducted ourselves—we looked upon them as friends.'

'The boys, for the most part, became an accepted part of a school life, and therefore a pleasant atmosphere surrounded us.'

'Regarded them as companions with whom to work seriously and also share a joke. Sex relationships were the serious problem as most people had ties outside of school life.'

'We were all good friends, but we thought of them as if we were all one sex, and not as an object of the next date as we probably thought of other boys.'

'We all seemed to be on brother and sister terms, very friendly and pleasant towards each other.'

'Many girls got on better with boys than they did with girls.'

'On the whole the girls were less catty when the boys were around. In the 4th year they tended to show off a little, but mainly to impress boys higher up the school. In the Fifth and Sixth forms they treated them more as equals.'

'A lot of the boys in my form I had known from infant schooldays —then we were separated into single-sex schools and then we were mixed again. I find this most satisfying to really get to know a boy for about 13 years. You can in fact watch them developing. Some of these boys I had really disliked during my infant/junior education—yet now I like them all and feel we will always be friends. Perhaps this is not the same for others in my form—but generally I should say relationships were very good.'

'It wasn't often that someone would try to attract a boy or vice versa. We had very platonic friendships.'

'After the initial excitement at first contact, general attitude of acceptance as individuals instead of "boys" and as platonic friends.' (Am.)

'The boys were never looked upon as "from another planet" but only as friends and fellow scholars.'

'Enjoyed their company. Felt the boys really added to the lessons by comments and discussions.'

'One grew to accept the opposite sex, and got to understand their reactions to various situations. Therefore one knew how to behave towards them out of school as well as inside school.'

'It was more pleasant in the senior part of the school. The juniors treated members of the opposite sex in rather a childish manner.'

'One or two boys that some of the girls disliked, but on the whole we thought they were alright. Forgot that they were boys and treated them nearly in the same way that one would treat one's girl-friends.'

FAIRLY PLEASANT 'At an early age the opposite sex were just accepted, then we found an unpleasant argumentative period, but later on during the majority of my time there the attitude was pleasant, friendly.'

'At 14 and 15 tended to be giggly and pester the older boys, but towards their own age group boys and girls always behaved normally.'

'Some went mad the minute we amalgamated, however those mixed lower down the school regard the school as a mixed sexes school—we resented the boys for the most part.' (Am.)

'At first it was a novelty to be co-ed. but after this feeling had worn off the attitude was still pleasant.' (Am.)

'It varied at various ages. In the lower forms it was merely toleration and friendly rivalry but later in the school life closer relationships developed.'

'Pupils learned to accept the opposite sex as friends and not as prospective husbands and wives.'

'The natural interests of teenagers were allowed to exist within a "healthy" background.'

'Regarded them as equals, treated them as such.'

'Generally accepted them. A few of the girls (especially in D stream) were really tarty and either teased or embarrassed the boys.'

A LITTLE UNPLEASANT AND UNPLEASANT   'If you were not friendly with the opposite sex in a boy–girl relationship you were tended to be looked down upon and thought peculiar.'

These comments speak for themselves: the emphasis is decidedly on normality, with boys and girls growing up together in a family-like atmosphere. This is in spite of the existence of the 'amalgamated' schools within the sample of co-educational schools, where adolescent boys and girls were suddenly placed in school together for the first time and the relationship between the sexes might be expected to be troublesome. The tone of the comments about girls' schools is, however, quite different from the 'normality' of those about the co-educational schools:

Girls' schools

PLEASANT   'Absolutely "nuts" about the opposite sex.'

'Pleasant, if you would class obsession as pleasant!! '

'More than pleasant—most adored the opposite sex.'

'Most girls regarded boys as a "must" due to not seeing or being with them all day.'

'The boys seemed more glamorous when we had no contact with them.'

'Social events, etc., with boys' school; not other-sex starved anyway.'

'The boys' school who were invited to our socials and made mixed teams were always welcomed.'

'Man-mad more like it.'

'Most girls had steady boy-friends, whereas in the previous school it was almost unheard of.'

FAIRLY PLEASANT   'General tendency to great excitement the moment almost anyone in trousers appeared!'

193

'There was a little too much "romantic" glory attached to opposite sex which tainted their attitude to sex.'

'Sixths had grown to regard boys as normal human beings, Fourths still giggled over them.'

'There were extremes; some were boy-crazy, some scared to even speak to a boy, some normally interested.'

'Because we never saw any members of the opposite sex at all, many girls showed interest in builders etc. that they passed.' (Boarding)

'The girls peered through wire netting at the boys peering through from the other side.'

'Everyone boasted about "conquests" but most were painfully shy. All liked boys or would like to know them.'

A LITTLE UNPLEASANT 'Varied from bragging of sexual experience and pseudo-sophistication to indifference because of shyness.'

'Too grasping—too much like a hunt. Boy-friends were status symbols. As I didn't know a single boy that was another black mark for me.'

'If boy walked through the school some girls would immediately turn around, laugh and giggle and generally make a spectacle of themselves.'

'Most of the girls had obsessively morbid interest in boys—as I had grown up with them, could not understand this.'

'Kept away from boys—no attitude could grow healthily.'

'Any male underwent strong scrutiny—they appeared to be starved of male company, didn't know how to behave when with boys.'

UNPLEASANT 'Ridiculous—some were boy-crazy and ignorant; some were priggish, prudish and ignorant. The birth rate was higher than *every* other school in town, secondary modern included.'

In another part of the questionnaire the question dealt with in this section was supplemented by several others. In answer to the question, 'In your co-educational (or girls') school was the general attitude of most of the pupils (of your own sex) towards the opposite sex, Rather preoccupied with the opposite sex?' Respondents chose their answer from True/Partly true/False/Doubtful. Whereas only 9 per cent replied 'true' about their co-educational school, this rose to 38 per cent from the girls' schools. While the proportion estimating 'partly true' was roughly the same for the two types of school, one-third said the statement was false about their co-educational school (compared with one-eighth) and 17 per cent were doubtful (compared with 7 per cent in the case of girls' schools).

Another question, using the same preamble, substituted the words 'girl/boy crazy', with the same choice of replies. Only 5 per cent of the pupils said this was true of the girls in their co-educational school and 29 per cent in their girls' school. The replies for 'partly true' were 26 and 42 per cent respectively, while 52 per cent said the girls in their co-educational school were not boy-crazy compared with 19 per cent about their girls' schools. As might be expected, more of this attitude was reported in the senior schools of both types than in the junior schools. Rather interestingly the social class breakdown showed a slight tendency for this attitude to increase with lower social class girls in the girls' schools but to *decrease* in the co-educational schools.

When the question was phrased in a different way, using the words 'normal interest', 79 per cent said 'true' about their co-educational schools, compared with 42 per cent, and 18 per cent 'partly true' compared with 39 per cent (Table A.25). There was little difference between the reported attitudes of seniors and those of juniors, nor could any social class differences be discerned in either school.

In the same series of items two attacks were made on somewhat different aspects of boy/girl relationship. The first substituted the word 'antagonistic' for the phrase 'normal interest'. There was, however, a remarkable similarity in the distributions of the estimates for the girls in the two types of schools, some 1 per cent of the ex-pupils endorsing 'true' (i.e. 'antagonistic'), and some 17 per cent 'partly true'.

The second new aspect was 'timidity', where the reported difference in attitude was considerable and statistically very highly significant both for juniors and seniors, there being much more timidity amongst girls in girls' schools (59 per cent estimating 'true' or 'partly true') than amongst those in co-educational schools (27 per cent). For both 'antagonism' and 'timidity' the comparison between co-educational and single-sex schools gives a similar result with the girls as with the boys. Fuller results are in Table A.26. To conclude this section of the chapter brief consideration is given to two other questions which relate only to the co-educational schools; though there may appear to be some duplication here, the questions are not identical to those which have gone before, and these linked questions increase the dependability of the results.

Attitude to presence of the opposite sex

It is sometimes said that boys aged about 12 to 14 do not want the company of girls, implying also that they do not want their presence. Though a detailed examination of this could not be attempted[1] a start was made by including for co-educational schools the item, 'The presence of the opposite sex of pupils in my school was Liked very much/Liked/Tolerated/Disliked/ Disliked intensely.' The results for both boys and girls are in Table 12.4.

TABLE 12.4 *Liking for presence of opposite sex*

'Both schools' survey

Estimates about co-educational schools	Replies from male ex-pupils				Replies from female ex-pupils			
	First schools (juniors)		Last schools (seniors)		First schools (juniors)		Last schools (seniors)	
	N	%	N	%	N	%	N	%
Liked very much	21	25·3	44	42·7	103	34·4	139	38·8
Liked	47	56·6	50	48·6	163	54·6	196	54·7
Tolerated	14	16·9	7	6·8	30	10·0	20	5·6
Disliked	0	0	2	1·9	2	0·7	2	0·6
Disliked intensely	1	1·2	0	0	1	0·3	1	0·3
Totals	83	100	103	100	299	100	358	100

NOTE: The difference between the distributions for first and last schools does not quite reach the conventional level of statistical significance for males and is insignificant for females.

MEN

In Table 12.4 the male ex-pupils of co-educational schools show a most marked liking for the presence of girls in the school, only one in 186 saying that it was disliked intensely and two saying it was disliked. Some 82 per cent said their presence was liked or liked very much among the juniors, and 91 per cent among the

[1] Some evidence has been put forward in Figure 11.2.

seniors, so that although it is true that their popularity increased with age, they could scarcely be said to be unpopular at the junior stage. The smallness of the numbers precluded a social class analysis.

WOMEN

The women's result is closely akin to that of the men—a similar negligible percentage of dislike (with two out of the three seniors who expressed dislike coming from amalgamated schools) and the same huge preponderance of liking, in both junior and senior schools. As with the men's estimates, however, one can detect among the senior girls a slight increase in the liking for the presence of boys, when compared with the junior girls. Division of the respondents into three social classes according to parental occupation revealed a decided consistency between classes in the 'popularity poll'.

Aspects of attitude to the opposite sex (Schools project)

In order to probe a little more deeply into the effect of separation from the opposite sex compared with companionship, large numbers of present female pupils in some forty grammar schools were given items such as, 'Boys are much too noisy', 'Boys cannot be trusted', 'Boys are unpleasant', 'Boys are nicer than girls', 'Boys are cleverer than girls in school work', 'Boys are better leaders than girls', 'Boys are not as catty as girls', 'Boys are braver than girls', 'Boys are cruel', 'Boys are interested in the wrong things', and 'I would prefer to be a boy'. Other items, some of which were the same, with the word 'girl' substituted for 'boy', were given to the boys. The possible answers were, Agree strongly/Agree/Doubtful/Disagree/Disagree strongly. Unfortunately the test administration time at the researchers' disposal was inadequate for the request of free responses, so that the items lack the elucidation which has so frequently come from this source. The items should therefore be regarded as probes designed to find differences between the groups which might profitably be explored further.

The results were disappointing, in that there were few statistically significant differences between the co-educated and single-sex schools, either for boys or for girls. Possible reasons for this were discussed in the previous volume and are concerned mainly with the intake into the samples of the two types of school. From the four age groups 11 plus, 13 plus, 15 plus and 17 plus were derived forty-four comparisons between girls in co-educational and girls in girls' schools and only five were statistically significant. In spite of this there are two trends which deserve comment. One of these is the tendency for the girls from girls' schools to have a somewhat more romantic view of boys, and those from co-educational schools to have a more down-to-earth outlook, seeing boys' faults as well as their virtues. The second tendency is for the girls in girls' schools to have slightly more extreme opinions. The items which yielded significant differences included that about boys being much too noisy, which produced two out of the five mentioned—in the 13 plus and 15 plus age groups—where the co-educated girls endorsed this more frequently than did those from girls' schools. The third of the five occurred when the co-educated girls aged 15 plus supported more strongly the idea that boys cannot be trusted—though this did not apply among girls from social class 3 or among the other age groups. The fourth was that girls (aged 13 plus) in girls' schools were more inclined to think boys braver than girls, though the other age groups did not agree. Lastly, in the same age group more of the girls in mixed schools agreed that boys are 'interested in the wrong things', though there was very little difference between the co-educated and single-sex educated in the three other age groups.

Four of the boys' items were the same as for the girls except that the word 'girl' replaced 'boy', namely girls are 'nicer', 'cannot be trusted', are 'cleverer', and the boy 'would prefer to be a girl'. Different but in the same vein are, 'Girls are catty and spiteful', are 'kinder', are 'boring', are 'interested in unimportant things', 'giggle and talk too much', and are 'more sensible'. The results strike the same note as those of the girls.

There are only seven statistically significant differences out of forty in the four age groups. One of these comes from the 15 plus boys, where those in boys' schools said that girls are nicer than boys, and the 13 plus and 17 plus boys had the same trend though it was not by convention statistically significant. A second occurred in the boys aged 13 plus where more of those from boys' schools disagreed strongly that girls are boring, supported by a similar non-significant trend in the 15 plus and 17 plus boys. It should be said, however, that a big majority in both types of school did *not* believe that girls are boring.

Two more of the seven differences occurred among boys aged 13 plus and 15 plus in response to the item saying that girls are cleverer than boys in school work, this being endorsed by more boys in the co-educational than in the boys' schools, but this was far from a majority in both types of school. In the same age group the co-educated boys also agreed to a greater extent than their opposites that girls were more sensible than boys; this was, however, still only a relatively small minority opinion. The idea that boys might prefer to be girls had very little support in any age group at either type of school—much less than the 11 to 15 per cent of girls who would have preferred to have been boys.

As with the girls, there was a slight tendency for the boys in boys' schools to be more extreme in their replies, and to present a more romanticized picture of the opposite sex.

Summary

To conclude the chapter let us draw a few threads together. In the Second College survey the ex-pupils from single-sex and those from co-educational schools have closely similar opinions about the basic equality of the sexes, though some men from boys' schools said that their belief in the inherent superiority of the male had been changed by their residence in a mixed college. This question differed from most others in that it asked the ex-pupils about their *present* opinions rather than asking them to make a judgment about their experience in a certain school. The tendency of the ex-pupils of boys' schools to express rather more extreme opinions appears again, even though this difference in spread between the opposite groups did not quite reach statistical significance.

In the question about the pleasantness of the attitude of most of the pupils towards the opposite sex we return to ex-pupils' judgments about the schools which were attended. The male ex-pupils from the 'Both schools' survey considered the attitude towards girls to be more pleasant in their co-educational schools because of a good family relationship there, while the number of judgments describing the atmosphere as a little unpleasant or worse were more numerous about the boys' schools. The same type of 'deprivation effect' is to be seen among the women, there being more 'unpleasant' or 'rather unpleasant' estimates made about the girls' schools than about the co-educational.

The series of supplementary questions about the attitude of pupils towards the opposite sex, which included the one about 'boy/girl crazy', consistently produced the same results—that the attitude was more normal and healthier in the co-educational schools. At the same time this less normal attitude in the single-sex schools appears to be accompanied by a greater timidity about the opposite sex which in a small minority of girls (and a few boys) even becomes fear.

A related problem—whether the younger boys and girls want the presence of the opposite sex in a co-educational school—has been tentatively examined, and although this presence is rather less popular in the junior than in the senior school, a large majority of the junior boys and almost all junior girls welcome it.

For reasons discussed in the previous volume (Dale, 1969), which are mainly concerned with sampling, the Schools project discovered few differences between the attitudes of samples of present pupils of co-educational and single-sex schools towards the opposite sex, though it should also be emphasized that the inquiry was limited to a few aspects. However, a trend was observed for pupils in single-sex schools to use the extremes of the scale slightly more often than those in co-educational schools. Further comment is reserved for the concluding chapter.

13

Social relationships between boys and girls

As might be expected the area of social relationships between boys and girls is considered by both teachers and pupils to produce decided advantages for co-education. A single-sex school clearly cannot give a normal education in these relationships without moving towards co-education. Unless there are serious moral dangers in educating adolescents of both sexes together—and there is not at the moment any research finding to show that this is so—it is necessary for the protagonists of single-sex education to find other powerful arguments to compensate for this considerable deficiency.

This chapter endeavours to supply a little research evidence about the effect of these social relationships, mainly by examining them within the co-educational school itself, using evidence from ex-pupils. A start is made with the influence of the girls on the boys within the co-educational school.

Influence of girls on boys

In the 'Both schools' survey grammar school ex-pupils who were then in Colleges of Education were asked the following question about their schooling: 'Do you consider that the influence of the girls on the boys in this school was, in general, Very good/Good/Fairly good/No effect/Bad/Very bad?' This question might have been better if 'fairly bad' had been included. However, Table 13.1 shows that these mature ex-pupils, looking back on their schooldays, judged that the girls had a good influence on the boys. This was the view of both men and women, and was fundamentally the same for junior ('first') and senior ('last') pupils. The men praised the influence of the girls rather more than the women did. Only three women and no men out of 648 replies from women and 181 replies from men estimated that the influence was 'very bad', and the percentage of either sex who considered it 'bad' does not rise above 6.4 per cent. It was shown in the previous volume that this is also the opinion of grammar school teachers and especially of those who had taught in co-educational schools (Dale, 1969, Ch. 4).

TABLE 13.1 *Influence of girls on boys*

'*Both schools*' survey

Estimates of ex-pupils	Replies from men about co-educational schools				Replies from women about co-educational schools			
	First schools		Last schools		First schools		Last schools	
	N	%	N	%	N	%	N	%
Very good	11	14·1	20	19·4	20	6·8	34	9·6
Good	30	38·5	34	33·0	89	30·4	122	34·4
Fairly good	26	33·3	38	36·9	107	36·5	119	33·5
No effect	6	7·7	8	7·8	59	20·1	70	19·7
Bad	5	6·4	3	2·9	16	5·5	9	2·5
Very bad	0	0	0	0	2	0·7	1	0·3
Totals	78	100	103	100	293	100	355	100

OPINION OF THE MEN ABOUT THE GIRLS' INFLUENCE ON THE BOYS (FREE RESPONSES)

A classification of the free responses made by the ex-pupils as a comment on their estimates is given in Table 13.2. We see that an overwhelming proportion of the men thought the girls had a good influence on the boys. By far the largest group—82 in all—were of the opinion that the behaviour, manners, language or appearance of the boys were improved. In the 'social' section, while 10 made some criticism about 'boys showing off' or girls likewise, no fewer than 8 of these gave favourable estimates about the overall influence of the girls, and there is a strong emphasis on the advantages of learning to mix naturally with the opposite sex, the reduction in shyness and the healthier attitude. On the academic side the dominant opinion is that the conscientiousness of the girls and the friendly rivalry between the sexes improved the standard of work of the boys, while only 5 of the 199 comments mentioned 'distraction from study'. Here we have forces acting in opposite directions, but in the opinion of the men the good influence on academic progress far outweighs the bad, an opinion which is supported by the results of research on the comparative attainment in co-educational and single-sex schools.

TABLE 13.2 *Influence of girls on boys: Men's free responses*
'*Both schools*' survey

Type of comment	No. of comments
Behaviour	
Improved boys' behaviour, manners, language	65
Appearance	
improved boys' appearance	17
Social	
social life improved	5
social development, easier mixing with opposite sex, less shy, co-operation, mutual understanding	35
healthy attitude to opposite sex, less preoccupation with sex	6
few immoral girls, a few troublesome	2
boys show off before girls	8
girls tried to impress boys	2
Academic	
made boys work harder, girls more conscientious	12
friendly competition	13
distraction from study, lower standard of work	5
girls less ambitious pupils	2
interchange of ideas	2
Depends on age, etc.	7
Others	18
Total	199

A few quotations, again chosen in proportion to the totals in their sections, illustrate the text.

BEHAVIOUR AND APPEARANCE 'Much of the roughness of an all-boys school was removed on the change to a new co-ed. school; different staff came and some of the tradition disappeared.' (Am.)

'Tended to calm the boys down, and also gave incentive to work.'

'A calming influence—*on the whole* improved behaviour.'

'If anything, a modifying effect, on manners, language, bullying, etc.'

'Seemed to keep the boys more in discipline than the school rules.'

'There was a minimum of bad language and an excess of good manners.'

'Increased good manners and decreased bad language.'

'After a certain age (13–15) the boys began to take notice of the girls and respond by (a) trying hard in class, (b) improving their appearance.'

'We all combed our hair after games and wore what we thought the girls would like.'

SOCIAL 'Brought home to me a larger meaning of social behaviour and appearance.'

'Although there was favouritism towards the girls, at last we recognized them as human and not stupid. We saw the upper school mixing much more. We were made to mix in dancing lessons.'

'Gave a good atmosphere.'

'We were in contact with girls all day, therefore we did not find it embarrassing or awkward speaking to members of the opposite sex.'

'To a greater extent there was no effect, but sometimes there was the odd incident where a boy would do something wrong to attract the attention of certain girls.'

'We had an insight into their life. Therefore our outlook became broader. Social events were more natural. Culture varied—more like "life".'

ACADEMIC 'The girls had an extra competitive effect on the boys in both the classroom and in other school activities. I had never felt this before, but I am sure it did nothing but good.'

'Gave a competition in work, which was stimulating to great effort and produced a much freer social life in the school.'

'I think it was bad in so far as it brought the level of the work over the year down which meant that we had to study much more intensely at examination times.'

The tone of the comments is serious and these men obviously think that the girls in their schools had a distinctly good influence. Though there are a few dissenters they form a minute fraction of the whole.

OPINION OF THE WOMEN ABOUT THE GIRLS' INFLUENCE ON THE BOYS

The women ex-pupils answered the same question; their judgments about the influence of the girls on the boys are to be seen in

Table 13.1. Like the men the women thought the girls had a good influence, though some of them are not as certain as the men—the 'no effect' group has risen to 20 per cent of the whole as against the 8 per cent amongst the men. However, those who thought the influence was bad were only 6 per cent for juniors and 3 per cent for seniors—almost identical with the men's figures.

As the free responses from the women are sufficiently large they have been classified in more detail than those of the men in order to give readers a better picture of the reasons underlying the estimates.

The women's judgments in Table 13.3 show that most of them are thinking of the effect of the presence of girls in improving the behaviour, manners, language and appearance of the boys. Secondary in size, but still numerous, are those who write of the healthy academic rivalry of girls with boys and also those who thought the presence of the girls (with the boys) encouraged a natural friendly atmosphere, co-operation between the two sexes and a better understanding of girls by boys. Of lesser importance, but not negligible, are the comments of those women who thought that mixing with girls made the boys less shy and raised their academic standard, but on the negative side there was some showing off and a little distraction. Both these latter groups were again small fractions of the whole.

The large groups of comments are represented by approximately one quotation for every twenty (after consolidation) and the smaller ones by one in ten, in order to give the latter adequate representation.

BEHAVIOUR AND APPEARANCE 'The girls' presence tended to "calm" the boys and teach them to be gentlemen.'

'It made the boys courteous and considerate. Headmaster very firm about this.'

'Girls did help the boys to be more considerate towards them so in fact they acquired a sense of respect.'

'The girls were often able to calm the boys down if riots broke out!'

'Girls make gentlemen out of the boys and also have a "good grooming" influence, e.g. long hair, dyed, etc., would be ridiculed by the girls.'

'They took more care of their appearance and learnt to take care of their manners.'

TABLE 13.3 *Influence of girls on boys: Women's free responses*

'*Both schools*' *survey*

Type of comment	No. of comments
Behaviour	
girls steadying influence	30
improved behaviour, manners, language	137
no bullying	2
bad effect	4
Appearance	
improved appearance, dress	55
Social	
not shy	24
natural atmosphere, friendly, respectful, co-operation	56
understood girls better	12
pleasant friendship	2
not preoccupied with opposite sex, not girl-crazy	4
helped boys grow up	12
good co-operation in societies, etc.	6
boys not interested (especially junior)	13
boys interested in girls' sports	3
some showing off	37
no respect for girls	2
thought girls stupid	1
girl-crazy	3
boys dominant	2
Academic	
raised standard, by example	14
healthy rivalry	83
broadened their interests, more balance	9
co-operation	4
no distraction	2
some distraction	10
poor work by boys	1
interests different	1
Moral	
low morals of young girls	1
Depends on age, individuals	5
Don't know	10
No effect	23
Others	56
Total	624

'When school changed to a boys' school I stayed on and noticed that their manners, behaviour and dress became lax.'

'When I look at some of the products of all-boys schools here at College I realize what a good lot ours were on the whole. They were made to be polite and considerate in the beginning and eventually it came naturally. Talking to whose who have left I feel that they appreciate this too, for they are more sure of themselves at all times, especially at social functions.'

'Boys took a little more pride in their dress. Cultivated better manners towards girls, e.g. opening doors, giving up seats, etc. Some did not bother though.'

'Boys tended to be rowdy by themselves. Also disliked being lazy, unintelligent in front of girls.'

'Girls have a sobering influence.'

SOCIAL 'The boys were always aware of the girls' presence and treated them with respect.'

'Because boys and girls mixed together there was no preoccupation with the other sex as sometimes happens in a single-sex school.'

'Boys were aware of the need to respect girls, even though they did not always carry this out in the early years.'

'Boys accepted girls, girls accepted boys. There was no shyness or restraint. We learnt together in an easy atmosphere.'

'It created a more natural atmosphere. They didn't tend to be too shy when talking to girls outside school.'

'I feel it made them understand girls. They worked alongside the girls quite happily. They developed as they grew older a well mannered and naturally friendly attitude to the girls. The boys also learnt not to be embarrassed by girls or company of them. I feel it helped to give them a healthier attitude.'

'I think on the whole influence of the girls was good. Tended to make boys accept the girls naturally. They also learnt some courtesy towards the opposite sex; less rough perhaps than boys from single-sex school.'

ACADEMIC 'Boys appeared to fear being beaten in exams. etc. and were encouraged to work.'

'There was healthy competition between the sexes regarding work—rivalry but also co-operation.'

207

'Most boys seemed to work harder in order to try and gain superiority.'

'Academically they stretched the boys in discussion, etc. Socially they tended to make them more mature.'

'Attention in class was continually being detracted [sic] from the lesson. General attitudes and behaviour were appalling.'

'They seemed to grow up far more quickly. Childish pranks were in general over by the 4th Form.'

'Boys in my peer group tended to ignore us. If they did pay attention to girls they were usually teasing or "showing off". I suppose politeness (under supervision!) to girls was a temporary "good effect".'

'The girls often encouraged the boys to bad behaviour and showing off.'

The boys showed off and wanted to appear "big" to impress the girls.'

Influence of boys on girls

The corresponding question about the boys was: 'Do you consider that the influence of the boys on the girls in this school was,

TABLE 13.4 *Influence of boys on girls*
'*Both schools' survey*

Estimates of students in Colleges of Education	Replies from men about co-educational schools				Replies from women about co-educational schools			
	First schools co-educational		Last schools		First schools co-educational		Last schools	
	N	%	N	%	N	%	N	%
Very good	8	10·7	14	13·9	16	5·5	33	9·4
Good	18	24·0	24	23·8	103	35·1	130	37·2
Fairly good	33	44·0	37	36·6	104	35·4	112	32·0
No effect	10	13·3	17	16·8	40	13·7	41	11·7
Bad	6	8·0	9	8·9	26	8·9	34	9·7
Very bad	0	0	0	0	4	1·4	0	0
Totals	75	100	101	100	293	100	350	100

Very good/Good/Fairly good/No effect/Bad/Very bad?' The male ex-pupils thought that in their co-educational schools the influence of the boys on the girls was good, only some 8 to 9 per cent thinking it bad, while some 13 per cent (junior) and 17 per cent (senior) thought the boys had no effect. The distribution of estimates of those who were at the schools as juniors and those who were seniors is almost identical (Table 13.4)

TABLE 13.5 *Influence of boys on girls (men's opinions)*

'Both schools' survey

Type of comment	No. of comments
Behaviour	
improved, stabilizing	18
Appearance	
improved	9
Social	
good social development	6
good atmosphere, co-operation	5
girls less preoccupied with opposite sex, understanding, natural mixing	21
less petty-minded, more balanced education	4
less shyness	8
girls rejected 'tearaways'	1
some 'showing off'	4
girls' 'crushes' on older boys	4
jealousy over boy-friends	1
boy/sex crazy	2
Academic	
standard improved, widened interest	5
friendly rivalry	11
bad example of boys	2
moderated girls' preoccupation with work	2
some distraction	2
Sex	
healthy attitude	2
promiscuous impression of some girls	1
some boys corrupted girls	1
good except some boys' sexual offences	1
No effect	12
Others	12
Total	134

The chief reasons for this opinion (Table 13.5) were given as improved behaviour and appearance of the girls, the natural mixing of the sexes with a consequent reduction in shyness, and the friendly rivalry in academic work. The total number of men, however, was only 172, which produced only 134 free responses, so that the numbers in each category were small.

Quotations in the proportion of one in five (approximately) are given from sub-categories containing four or more comments.

BEHAVIOUR AND APPEARANCE 'It made them less petty minded and also made them more mature.'

'Made this *fairly good* rather than good, because girls, even in a single-sex school, *seem* to have a more balanced attitude to opposite sex (so influence of comprehensive is less) but this may only be an appearance, as I also believe the confidence of the comprehensive girl is not just *superficial* but an *inner* confidence arising from working with boys.'

'In general the girls adopted a more sensible attitude to the opposite sex. There was no childish giggling and blushing.'

' "Woke up" some of the quieter ones—thus producing much more balanced community.'

'Girls became more aware of dress sense and far more prepared for out-of-school social life.'

'Kept girls neat and tidy.'

SOCIAL 'Boys are part of everyday life outside of school, to ostracize them in school is to deprive girls socially. Social development is very important especially in later teens.'

'Toughened up the girls' contact with boys, made girls less "romantic".'

'We treated the girls as people and not strange beings.'

'I do think girls build up false impressions about the opposite sex. The presence of the genuine article does I think help in part to break this down.'

'There was a good atmosphere, problems on both sides were discussed freely, seriously and intelligently. The atmosphere was very natural.'

'In quite a few cases the influence was good for it brought some girls out of their shells.'

'In early adolescence the girls tended to become preoccupied with boys—but at least they were always in contact with them—little shyness.'

ACADEMIC   'Raised the standards of the girls.'

'The girls wanted to beat the boys so they worked harder.'

'The boys had an extra competitive effect on the girls in both the classroom and in other school activities.'

Though comments in the adverse categories are too few to be included by the fixed percentage criterion, readers are reminded that there are some, as indicated in Table 13.5.

OPINION OF THE WOMEN EX-PUPILS ABOUT THE INFLUENCE OF THE BOYS ON THE GIRLS

The estimates given by the women ex-pupils about the effect of the boys on the girls (Table 13.4) resemble those given by the men— the same low percentage of ex-pupils thought the influence bad, and a slightly smaller percentage of women than men thought there was no effect. Another slight difference was that rather fewer women considered the influence to be 'very good' as opposed to 'good'; this difference was not considered important enough for testing statistically.

The women's free responses give a definitely favourable opinion about the influence of the boys on the girls in the co-educational schools they attended, though they also indicate some lesser negative aspects. (Table 13.6). Amusingly we find that the improved appearance of girls is an outstanding effect, but combining 'improved behaviour' with 'prevented silliness towards the opposite sex', and 'girls less catty, less giggly and less spiteful' produced an even larger group of comments. The dividing line between 'behaviour' and 'social' is admittedly arbitrary and there is a marked overlap. Classified under 'social' the largest group of comments is concerned with the girls' relationship with boys being normal, girls regarding them as fellow-workers and normal friends, and not being 'boy-crazy', while another sizeable group regards as important the broadening of girls' outlook and ideas. As was indicated at the beginning of the paragraph, these judgments are not unanimous, a few women saying that some girls were boy-crazy, and that some showed off, while other women thought boys set a bad example and encouraged girls to misbehave. In view of the criticism that has in the past—unfairly—been directed against the academic standards of co-educational grammar schools, it is interesting to

TABLE 13.6 *Influence of boys on the girls: (women's opinions)*
'Both schools' survey

Type of comment	No. of comments
Behaviour	
improved behaviour	21
improved appearance	92
too concerned about appearance	3
some tried to attract boys	10
some noisy, rough	5
girls less catty, spiteful, less giggly, silly	46
Social	
prevented silliness towards opposite sex, more natural	65
socially good	4
girls interested in boys' sports	2
boys as normal friends, fellow workers, co-operation	16
understood boys' point of view	13
broadened girls' outlook, ideas; maturity	41
not boy-crazy	15
helped timid girls	5
took notice of boys' opinion	2
bad influence lower forms	3
better in higher forms	3
worse in higher forms	2
some showing off, silliness, rivalry	6
boy-crazy	9
girls encouraged to misbehave	10
boys bad example	5
girls got inferiority complex	3
girls mixed with older boys	1
girls ignored boys and vice-versa (junior)	5
Academic	
good rivalry in classwork	97
helped girls' science	1
encouraged discussion	10
work more interesting	3
boys' humour in lessons, lively	5
lowered standards	1
girls shy about some work	2
distracted girls from work	23
no distraction	2
Others	
(comments inapplicable etc.)	51
difficult to say, generalize	10
too young (juniors)	2
no effect	9
Total	603

see the large body of opinion which praises the friendly academic rivalry of the two sexes, equally in junior and senior school, though the minority view that girls were distracted from their work is not negligible. Little positive pointers that have constantly occurred in this context in answer to related questions, and in other of the writer's researches, are the girls' appreciation of the way class discussions are improved by the presence of boys, and the welcome the girls give to the boys' sense of humour.

The proportion of free responses quoted is one in twenty, but sub-categories with ten or fewer replies have had to be omitted.

BEHAVIOUR 'The girls were inclined to behave in order to make a good impression on boys, especially if rather keen on one particular boy.'

'Nearly 99 per cent of the girls took more care over hair, clothes, etc.'

'Girls' dress improved, although perhaps more for the purpose of attracting the boys, rather than for the good of their souls.'

'The girls tended to act a little more dignified. They didn't shout or run.'

'Girls were less catty and more careful about appearance.'

'Most of the boys were quite rough and as might be expected some of the girls often showed this streak in them.'

'Girls seemed less catty and much less boy-crazy and more mature. Boys' good manners helped femininity.'

'Boys made life less petty and catty. Made girls conscious of having good table manners, etc., because theirs were very poor. Sense of humour from boys infected school.'

SOCIAL 'Boys were accepted as friends, just as we made girl-friends. They helped us to widen our knowledge regarding the opposite sex.'

'I can't think why; boys and girls seemed to provide more natural atmosphere for each other. Sex was not distorted as can happen in single-sex schools. There was more sense of unison, boys and girls working together, both important.'

'Made the timid girls less self-conscious and encouraged them to have more social life.'

'It taught us to get along with the opposite sex, which is important for future life.'

MSS—H

213

'The girls became interested in the boys' hobbies etc., so had a wider knowledge of life than girls from the nearby girls' school.'

'In general the boys, particularly those with some knowledge of the sciences on a deeper level, had wide knowledge of the Arts too. This broader view showed the girls the limitations of their own knowledge and encouraged them to extend it.'

'They did not seem as "boy-mad" as some girls from girls' schools.'

'The girls were too "boy-crazy" and far more concerned with what they looked like for "Johnny" than what sort of work they presented.'

ACADEMIC 'The girls made a little more effort to look neat and tidy, and worked a bit harder to make sure they kept up with the boys.'

'Having boys in the form made you work harder at the subjects which boys are taken to be better at, e.g. Science, Maths.'

'Girls tried to obtain better results than boys. Element of competition inspired by opposite sexes.'

'In science subjects they were encouraged to "be as good as the boys" who tended towards those subjects.'

'The boys were very good in contributing to class and out-of-school activities, and the girls learned to understand and appreciate their opinions, as the boys did the girls'.'

'In many cases the influence of the boys interfered with the work of the girls and concentration in lessons.'

It has been the practice in previous chapters to publish all those free responses which make a direct comparison between the co-educational and single-sex school. Those relating to this chapter are so numerous and often so repetitive of what has gone before that their presentation as a special section would have overburdened the chapter; some, however, have already been included with the other responses.

Schools project

An attempt was made to compare pupils still at co-educational schools with those still at single-sex schools about their ease of relationship with the opposite sex. They were asked to reply to four items; for the boys these were: 'When I meet girls at a party

I don't know what to say,' 'I feel very awkward when I am with girls', 'I feel perfectly at ease when I am with girls,' and 'I prefer talking to girls rather than to boys.' The possible answers were: 'Very true/Often true/Sometimes true/Seldom true/Not true.'

It was hypothesized that the co-educated pupils would socially be much more at ease with the opposite sex, but the results were quite inconclusive. No differences between the co-educated girls and those from girls' schools were statistically significant, and only two between the boys' groups—more 15-year-old boys from boys' schools preferred talking to girls, and fewer 17-year-old co-educated boys felt awkward when with girls. The reasons for the lack of clear and consistent differences are complex. They appear to include the existence of two opposing forces, first that the separation of the sexes may by perpetuating ignorance, tend to make each sex not at ease with the other, and second that deprivation of the company of the opposite sex may make boys and girls keener to get this company, thereby generating a powerful motivation to overcome shyness. There is in addition a flaw in the multiple choice range of possible answers, because the alternative 'seldom true', for example, could be ambiguous in so far as (a) it was 'seldom true' the pupil felt awkward, because he hardly ever spoke to a girl, and (b) it was 'seldom true' that he felt awkward as a proportion of the many times he spoke to a girl.

Another possible explanation for the lack of reliable differences at the school stage may be that in the co-educational schools the pupils are brought face to face with the problems of social relations with the opposite sex and have a more realistic appraisal of their own position, whereas the girls in girls' schools meet the opposite sex on 'special occasions' rather than on a day-long basis.

Comment

The evidence that the presence of girls improves the appearance, conduct and discipline of the boys is very strong, coming as it does from both male and female ex-pupils and from teachers. Though the evidence that the presence of boys effects a corresponding improvement in the girls is less strong, its existence cannot be denied; the tidiness of the girls and their dress are noticeably better and, according to those women who have attended both a girls' and a co-educational school, they become less catty and vindictive and less inclined to group in cliques. The world, however, is not a simple place, and jealousies over boy-friends are naturally more frequent in co-educational schools. As with so many aspects of the central theme there is an obvious need here for more research.

The lack of supporting evidence from the Schools project on the more specific questions related to the general theme of the chapter may be due to a combination of causes among which the two already mentioned in the previous section—the flaw in the wording of the answer scale and the contrast between the day-long facing of the problems in the co-educational school and the occasional evening venture for girls from girls' schools—may be the most important.

14

Comparative attitude to sex

Whatever reasons may be given openly for opposition to co-education at the secondary stage, there appears to be a deep-seated fear among some people that such schools might lead to an increase in sexual misbehaviour and to an undue interest in sex at too early an age. The introduction to the previous volume included a passage on ways of gathering objective evidence about which kind of school atmosphere encourages or diminishes these tendencies. At an early stage in the inquiry the writer decided that an investigation of that kind would need a research team drawn partly from specialists in social work, and as there were no funds available for the purpose he turned towards a method which was less objective but by no means without value as a preliminary survey of the field. Surprisingly this research has yielded results which are so conclusive in their verdict that they are much more valuable than might otherwise have been the case.

Incorporated in the 'Both schools' questionnaire was the item, 'In which school do you consider the pupils had the healthier attitude towards sex?' The respondents were all intending teachers who had been pupils in both co-educational and single-sex secondary schools (excluding secondary modern), and they were asked to choose one of four alternative replies: Doubtful/Don't know/Single-sex school/Co-educational school. Their replies were obviously sincere and considered, and although there might be quibbles about the exact meaning of 'healthier' there can be little doubt that an unhealthy atmosphere towards sex is undesirable in any school. The estimates themselves, however, do not necessarily indicate that any one of the atmospheres is actually unhealthy—merely that one is healthier than the other. Not until the free responses are examined shall we be in a position to interpret the estimates more precisely.

The attitude of girls

As will be seen from Figure 14.1, a large majority of the women (76 per cent) judged the attitude towards sex to be healthier in their co-educational school than in their girls' school, a mere 7 per cent recording the opposite belief. The only intervening

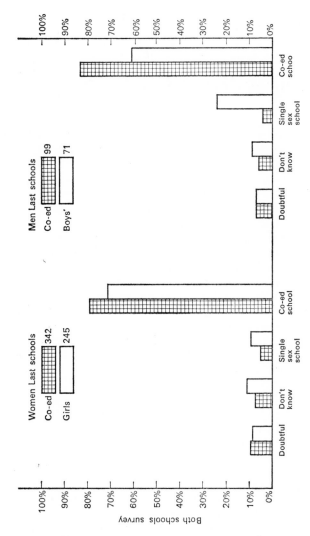

FIGURE 14.1
Healthier attitude to sex:
'Both schools' survey

218

variable which the writer can think of which might be advantageous to the co-educational schools is that a larger percentage of
them have a rural or semi-rural catchment area, but this would in
itself be unlikely to produce so great a difference. In these social
surveys there are usually so many forces exerting an influence on a
problem, and pulling in different directions, that rarely does one
find group differences of such magnitude. In spite of the extent of
the differences we must remember that for some individuals and
maybe for some schools the influence of co-education might be
overcome by other forces, among which the individual personality
of the pupil and his or her individual experience are obviously
important.

There was a greater tendency for women who had been senior
pupils in co-educational schools to judge the attitude to sex to be
healthier in such schools (than in girls' schools) than for women
who had attended girls' schools as seniors, though even among the
latter only some 9 per cent thought the attitude was healthier in
girls' schools.

TABLE 14.1 *Attitude towards sex (women's opinions)*
'Both schools' survey

Estimate	Type of comment	No. of comments
Co-educational school healthier	co-educational school healthier	20
	natural behaviour, no preoccupation with sex	29
	sex discussed and not kept secret	26
	boys—friends, not obsessed sex, girls equals	25
	outlook broadened; narrow attitude in single-sex	16
	greater knowledge of opposite sex, more realistic	12
	mixed classes in sex education	3
	boys more accessible, not a challenge	2
	not healthy, but more so than single-sex	1
	not healthy, except when junior	1
	girls in girls' school boy-mad, frustrated, segregation unnatural, sex dominated conversation, silly ideas	6
	single-sex—crushes on females, some unhealthy consequences	1
	worse at boarding school	1
	many girls left because pregnant in girls' school	1
	attitude crude, less at co-ed.	2

219

TABLE 14.1 *Attitude towards sex (women's opinions)*
'Both schools' survey

Estimate	Type of comment	No. of comments
	afraid of men at single-sex school	1
	depends on individual	1
	Other	5
Total		**153**
Girls' school healthier	sensible, though danger of ignorance	2
	all-female staff, easier to discuss	1
	pleasant and much more tolerable	1
	nicer class of girls	1
	more emphasis on dirtier side in co-ed.	2
	too preoccupied with sex in co-ed., choosing boys	2
	in co-ed. sex considered undesirable	1
	at age when discussed sex sensibly	3
Total		**13**
Don't know	don't know	6
	more open discussion in co-ed.	4
	co-ed. less embarrassment	1
	depends on upbringing; slightly healthier co-ed.	1
	physical interest single-sex, ethical interest co-ed.	1
	separation in single-sex, therefore went crazy in co-ed.	1
	single-sex perhaps healthier—only wishful thinking	1
	more self-conscious at co-ed. and preoccupied with sex	1
	single-sex some preoccupation with boys, but work better	1
	possible single-sex—dirty stories spread more in co-ed.	1
	boys discussed in single-sex because absent	1
	no difference, mixed outside school	1
	depends on home background	2
	not healthy at either	1
	cannot remember co-ed.	2
	varying ages	3
	presence of opposite sex has no effect	1
Total		**29**

TABLE 14.1 *Attitude towards sex (women's opinions)*
'*Both schools*' survey

Estimate	Type of comment	No. of comments
Doubtful	doubtful	1
	perhaps co-ed. healthier	1
	indifference at co-ed.	1
	possibly juniors co-ed. healthier	1
	co-ed. little interest sex, reasonable attitude single-sex	1
	lower forms single-sex bad attitude but improved with age	1
	a bit unhealthy in co-ed., single-sex too young	1
	in neither was sex discussed in class	1
	no interest in sex at 13	1
	depends on association out of school	1
Total		10
No estimate	*Other*	
	both the same	2
	difficult question	1
	depends on individual	1
Total		4

The free responses again enable us to interpret more accurately the significance of the estimates. From Table 14.1 we see that the larger groups among those women who judged the attitude to be healthier in their co-educational schools were those who emphasized normal behaviour, the lack of preoccupation with boys, the open discussion, broadened outlook and greater understanding of boys as people. The small minority who found the girls' attitude healthier in their girls' school are too few for their comments to be considered representative of such schools—there were only thirteen.

The classification in Table 14.1 is more detailed than usual, so that there is less need for the quotation of comments, especially quotations in strict proportion to category totals, and only a few of the more discerning or more interesting are given. The first three go to the root cause of the difference between the attitudes prevalent in the two types of school: 'When you see boys every day the novelty wears off,' 'Boys were part of everyday life in the co-ed school, and at times were completely forgotten about,' and 'Mixing with the opposite sex one comes into closer contact than in the single-sex school—it changes one's ideas completely— found I had more respect towards them and a healthier attitude towards sex.' A fourth quotation enlarges this: 'Greater maturity together, therefore far less mystery and intrigue. Accepted each other as personalities and not so much men and women.'

One woman makes the point that the personality of the girl herself can be a strong influence for good or bad: 'Whatever school a girl goes to she makes her own moral values. A girl can be just as "wild" in a girls' school as a co-ed—depends only on the individual,' but she seems to take the argument much too far at the end—as if the environment had no influence.

Two extreme comments are about girls' schools, but they do not rest on any representative basis: 'There was definitely a high proportion of girls leaving school because of pregnancy in the single-sex school, or being married as soon as leaving school, than ever in the co-ed.,' and, 'My single-sex school had unmarried mothers, promiscuous women, a few lesbians, several nuns, one or two mentally unstable young women, and not a few women incapable of friendship with men. I have seen all these come from the form I was in at this school.' One would be sceptical of taking this last comment at its face value if it were not for the transparent honesty of the rest of the woman's replies. A few comments show that sometimes an undesirable atmosphere can also exist in a co-educational school, for example: 'In co-ed. sex was treated as a joke, i.e. "dirty" jokes, etc. were numerous. Obscene remarks from the boys to the girls also evident.' This school, however, was an 'amalgamated' school. In general, remarks of this kind are not characteristic of either type of school, a fairer and more reliable picture being represented by the estimates.

ANALYSIS BY PARENTAL OCCUPATION

When the data are broken down by parental occupation as in Table 14.2 no consistent trend associated with social class appears. The slight drop in the support of the class 2 ex-pupils, i.e. broadly the clerical class, for the healthiness of the attitude in the co-educational schools is intriguing as it occurs among those who were at a co-educational school last as well as among those who attended a girls' school last; but no further examination was made. Any association of the judgments with social class influences would probably be reduced by the tendency for the student teachers themselves to be moving towards the same class. However, the judgment that the attitude towards sex is healthier in the co-educational schools is very decided in each parental occupation grouping.

TABLE 14.2 *Healthier attitude to sex (women's responses): Analysis by parental occupation*

'Both schools' survey

| | Replies from women (from 'co-educational last' schools) in Occupational Class | | | | | | Replies from women (from 'single-sex last' schools) in Occupational Class | | | | | |
| | 1 | | 2 | | 3, 4, 5 | | 1 | | 2 | | 3, 4, 5 | |
	N	%	N	%	N	%	N	%	N	%	N	%
Doubtful	15	8·0	7	10·0	7	8·5	8	6·6	9	18·0	4	5·7
Don't know	13	6·9	6	8·6	7	8·5	13	10·7	6	12·0	8	11·5
Single-sex school	7	3·7	6	8·6	2	2·4	11	9·0	5	10·0	7	10·0
Co-educational school	153	81·4	51	72·8	66	80·6	90	73·7	30	60·0	51	72·8
Totals	188	100	70	100	82	100	122	100	50	100	70	100

The attitude of boys

The estimates of the male ex-pupils were almost as overwhelmingly favourable for the co-educational schools as were those of the females (see Figure 14.1), though the percentage of the men who judged the attitude towards sex in their boys' schools to be

TABLE 14.3 *Attitude towards sex (men's opinions)*

'Both schools' survey

Estimate	Type of comment	No. of comments
Co-educational school healthier	co-educational school most definitely a healthier attitude	11
	perhaps, or slightly more balanced attitude	4
	no secrecy, good healthy relationships	11
	less depravity or homosexual tendencies	8
	mixing made attitudes broader	10
	unhealthy attitude of some of staff of single-sex school	1
Single-sex school healthier	as opposed to co-ed. experience	9
	slightly better attitude	1
Don't know	don't know	3
	varied with individuals	2
Doubtful	doubtful	3
	but slightly in favour of single-sex school	1
Total		64

healthier than in their co-educational schools rose to 24 among those who attended their boys' school as seniors. The number in the sample was too small to permit any meaningful breakdown of the data according to parental occupation.

The free responses were naturally few, but were again informative (see Table 14.3). Most of the replies said that there was a healthier attitude towards sex in the co-educational rather than in the boys' schools, with a more balanced or broader outlook, less secrecy and good friendly relationships. As a sub-section of this majority, eight replies, being one-ninth of the total, said there was less depravity or homosexual tendencies in the co-educational schools. A minority of ten men thought that the attitude was healthier in their boys' school; of these, eight attended the boys' schools as seniors.

Free responses typical of those which said the attitude was healthier in the co-educational schools are quoted below. The proportion of those favourable to boys' schools, given afterwards, has been increased above their due allotment to improve the coverage of the argument. The free responses in favour of co-educational schools are as follows:

'There is less depraved sex-talk amongst the boys—fewer jokes etc. The attitude is far healthier altogether.'

'Close relationships with members of the opposite sex leads to a better understanding of each other's roles in society. A balanced adjustment ensues.'

'They grew up with it, having a respect rather than a desire for one another.'

'Is it healthy to have girls leave school to have babies? I understand there was a homosexual teacher at single-sex school, and I know there were many homosexuals in that school.'

'Some members of staff in the single-sex school had an unbalanced outlook towards sex.'

'The attitude in the single-sex was at least 75 per cent homosexual inside school, and girl-mad outside school.'

'Homosexual tendencies in single-sex schools were obvious and often quite open.'

'Some of the boys in single-sex school seemed more interested in themselves than in girls.'

Four of the ten comments favouring the attitude in the boys' schools were:

'Everyone at the co-ed. school seemed sensitive to the subject. At the boys' school the attitude was one of respect tempered with coarseness.'

'This may be because our attitude grew healthier as we grew older.'

'Promiscuity much more rife in co-ed. school.'

'Even though they were less well acquainted with the opposite sex their attitude to them was far more polite and they were treated with greater respect.'

As with the girls, although a large majority of the men estimate the attitude to be healthier in their co-educational schools there is a small minority whose experience leads them to the opposite view.

A researcher who limited himself to this topic would wish to give additional solidity to the evidence by examining data such as the incidence of unwanted pregnancies, the incidence of juvenile delinquency connected with sex, and even—perhaps as a long shot—investigate whether the incidence of prostitution and of homosexuality was startlingly higher among ex-pupils from one type of school rather than the other, with relevant variables held constant. However, as this evidence is not available we can only say that the data examined in this chapter are strongly in favour of the co-educational school. It should be added that the attitude to sex in co-educational schools does indeed need to be healthy for these schools to be viable institutions.

15

Some sociological questions

The questionnaire used in the 'Both schools' survey contained several items which had an element of sociological significance. One of these—the least sociological—was, 'The school tried to dominate my whole life,' to which respondents could answer one of the following: Agree strongly/Agree/Doubtful/Disagree/ Disagree strongly. The results obtained from this are in the first section of the chapter and three sections following will each be devoted to another item.

'The school tried to dominate my whole life'

The demarcation line between the part of a pupil's life which is controlled by the day school and those parts which are controlled by other institutions, such as the family, the Church, the youth club etc. is, as we saw in a previous chapter, exceedingly ill-defined. Have the school authorities any legal right to demand that a pupil should wear a school cap or hat, to and from school, i.e. before he enters the school precincts and comes clearly under the authority of the head of the school? If the family says 'No cap, or hat' and the head insists on the said article, whose legal position is the better? Is a school head within his or her rights in insisting that schoolboys or schoolgirls do not walk through the town eating ice-cream (a) in the dinner-hour, or (b) after school hours? Has a school head any legal right to ban entry to certain rather low-class or noisy cafés during either of these times? If a headmaster sees a boy misbehaving in the streets after school hours, not in such a way that would merit police intervention, has he any *legal* right to stop his car and intervene? More important, if a pupil commits any of these offences, has a head any legal right to punish the offender? Have heads, in a well-intentioned effort to bring up their pupils in the way they should go, arrogated to themselves powers which strictly belong to the family? These questions are not usually asked, probably because the heads of families, the community at large and even most of the pupils recognize that heads are acting for the good of the pupils and for the good of the community. It

Some sociological questions

could happen, however, that an over-zealous head could go too far, and lose this tacit support of families and community. What then?

Another aspect of this item is whether the time demanded by the school *after school hours* is so great that the pupils' good leisure-time activities are seriously curtailed or even prevented. Is this a desirable result of schooling? Some schools frown on pupils attending youth clubs in the evenings because of the effect on homework. Innumerable pupils give up piano lessons when they reach the fourth or fifth because they cannot both practise an instrument and do their homework. Some compromise is probably inevitable but have we sufficiently considered the impact of home-work on other legitimate and desirable activities of the pupils? By encroaching on this leisure-time do schools seriously limit those legitimate hobbies and pursuits through which pupils' individu-alities might normally develop? Do they overstrain their pupils?

There are other ways in which a school could 'dominate the life' of a pupil—by consciously or unconsciously dominating his or her outlook and thoughts. In this respect the writer believes we are much better off than most other countries.

We are concerned, however, with a comparison between co-educational and single-sex schools made by ex-pupils who had attended both. Unfortunately the results are once again limited to

TABLE 15.1 *'The school tried to dominate my whole life'*

'Both schools' survey (women)

| Estimates | Replies about 'first' schools attended | | | | Replies about 'last' schools attended | | | |
| | Co-educational schools | | Girls' schools | | Co-educational schools | | Girls' schools | |
	N	%	N	%	N	%	N	%
Agree strongly	3	1·0	28	6·9	6	1·7	16	6·2
Agree	19	6·4	75	18·5	17	4·7	51	19·6
Doubtful	23	7·7	77	19·0	45	12·5	45	17·3
Disagree	157	52·5	181	44·7	189	52·7	120	46·1
Disagree strongly	97	32·4	44	10·9	102	28·4	28	10·8
Totals	299	100	405	100	359	100	260	100

NOTE: The difference between the estimates about co-educational and girls' schools is statistically significant beyond the ·001 level, both for first and for last schools.

the estimates as there was insufficient time for the ex-pupils to add their free responses to this or the three other items of this chapter. We therefore do not know what type of domination the ex-pupil is referring to if he or she agrees with the statement; yet this overall exploration indicates interesting possibilities for further research. The results for the women are given in Table 15.1.

Table 15.1 shows that the female ex-pupils were strongly of the opinion that their girls' schools 'tried to dominate their whole life' more than their co-educational schools did, whether they were at the schools as junior pupils or as seniors. The possible significance of this has been outlined in the introduction to the chapter and the evidence is inadequate for more precise statements. The finding corresponds with trends found in other parts of the research, e.g. that single-sex school authorities exert more disciplinary power in running their schools.

The results from the male students are given in Table 15.2.

TABLE 15.2 *'The school tried to dominate my whole life'*

'Both schools' survey (men)

Estimates	Replies about 'first' schools attended				Replies about 'last' schools attended			
	Co-educa-tional schools		Boys' schools		Co-educa-tional schools		Boys' schools	
	N	%	N	%	N	%	N	%
Agree strongly	1	1·2	11	9·2	1	1·0	4	5·6
Agree	6	7·2	20	16·8	11	10·6	12	16·9
Doubtful	12	14·5	24	20·2	18	17·3	10	14·1
Disagree	42	50·6	50	42·0	47	45·1	32	45·1
Disagree strongly	22	26·5	14	11·8	27	26·0	13	18·3
Totals	83	100	119	100	104	100	71	100

NOTE: The difference between co-educational and boys' schools is statistically highly significant (beyond ·01) for first schools, but not significant for 'last' schools, though in the same direction.

Here the men give their co-educational schools as less dominating, a result statistically highly significant for 'first' schools but not significant for 'last' schools, though the difference is in the same direction. (This latter difference, however, in the setting of the general findings of the survey and in the light of the differences between the 'first' schools, i.e. junior pupils, is unlikely to have occurred purely by chance.)

The next item was, 'I felt that the school created a gap between myself and my home.' The five possible answers were the same as in the previous section.

Gap between pupils and home

It is sometimes said that the children of manual workers tend to make poorer progress in the grammar school than the children of upper-class parents because they find themselves out of place in the middle-class atmosphere prevalent there. Provided this is not accepted as the only reason or even the most important one, it may be correct. We hear less, however, of the effect of the school on the relationship between the manual worker's child and that child's home. Is it true that the school all unwittingly creates a gap between the child and his home? If it is true, must it be accepted as part of the price to be paid for progress?

Here the analysis is limited to the ex-pupils' opinion about this gap and whether it is felt to be greater in co-educational or single-sex schools (Table 15.3).

TABLE 15.3 *Gap between pupil and home*

'*Both schools*' (*women*)

Estimates	Replies about women's 'first' schools attended				Replies about women's 'last' schools attended			
	Co-educational schools		Girls' schools		Co-educational schools		Girls' schools	
	N	%	N	%	N	%	N	%
Agree strongly	7	2·3	21	5·3	4	1·1	9	3·5
Agree	23	7·7	37	9·2	24	6·7	21	8·1
Doubtful	26	8·7	92	23·0	31	8·6	46	17·8
Disagree	142	47·7	188	47·0	173	48·2	132	50·9
Disagree strongly	100	33·6	62	15·5	127	35·4	51	19·7
Totals	298	100	400	100	359	100	259	100

NOTE: The difference between the distributions for co-educational and girls' schools is statistically highly significant both for 'first' and for 'last' schools.

Table 15.3 shows that although a large majority of female ex-pupils from both types of school disagreed that their schools created a gap, they were appreciably more sure that their co-educational school did not have this effect than about their girls'

schools. A breakdown of these estimates according to the occupational class of the ex-pupils' fathers revealed only a slightly
greater tendency for the girls belonging to social class 3, 4 and 5 in
the girls' schools and also those from this class who were seniors
in the co-educational schools to agree that a gap was created by
the schools.

The men's results resemble those of the women in that although
only a small proportion of them agree with the statement as
applied to either type of school, they disagree more strongly when
it is applied to their co-educational schools. The difference, however, is statistically significant only for 'last' schools (Table 15.4).
Breakdown of the data by occupational class of the ex-pupils'
fathers could not profitably be undertaken because of the smallness
of the sample.

TABLE 15.4 *Gap between pupil and home*

'*Both schools*' *survey* (*men*)

	Replies about men's 'first' schools attended				Replies about men's 'last' schools attended			
	Co-educational schools		Boys' schools		Co-educational schools		Boys' schools	
	N	%	N	%	N	%	N	%
Agree strongly	2	2·4	3	2·5	2	1·9	1	1·4
Agree	7	8·5	17	14·3	6	5·8	6	8·6
Doubtful	10	12·2	25	21·0	5	4·8	11	15·7
Disagree	36	44·0	50	42·0	44	42·3	35	50·0
Disagree strongly	27	32·9	24	20·2	47	45·2	17	24·3
Totals	82	100	119	100	104	100	70	100

NOTE: The difference between co-educational and boys' schools is not
statistically significant for 'first' schools but is highly significant for 'last'
schools.

Comment

The discovery that these ex-pupils, both men and women, consider that their co-educational schools are less likely to create a gap
between pupil and home than are their single-sex schools is not
necessarily produced by the type of organization found in those
schools—the two are shown to be merely associated. It might be
that the rather lower social class composition of the co-educational

schools in itself has this effect. Here is yet another field awaiting further research, though the next two items throw a little further light on the problem.

'I felt I didn't belong socially'

In this tug-of-war between school and home there is a danger that the pupil might find himself alienated from both. What proportion of the ex-pupils felt that they 'didn't belong socially' when at school? Was this proportion different in co-educational and single-sex schools? The data gathered in Tables 15.5 and 15.6 indicate that fewer of the ex-pupils, whether they were men or women, felt that they 'didn't belong socially' at their co-educational schools than at their single-sex schools. Again, we cannot say precisely why this is so. As expected there is a tendency for those men who attended as seniors at both co-educational and boys' schools to feel that they belonged socially more than the juniors felt they belonged, while the women's groups showed little difference between junior and senior pupils.

It is a matter of some interest to discover which social class of children felt that they 'didn't belong socially', though again only the sample of women is large enough for this purpose. Accordingly Table 15.7 was prepared.

To simplify the table 'first' and 'last' school estimates are merged, a procedure possible because in this instance the distributions of the estimates for first and last schools were sufficiently similar even when these were broken down according to occupational class. The figures give no support to the hypothesis that there might be a systematic trend associated with occupational class, for example that girls in the lower occupational classes might feel out of place at both mixed and girls' grammar schools. Amusingly enough, in girls' schools rather more pupils of class I felt they didn't belong socially (one-quarter of this class) than did pupils of the other social classes, though the difference is not statistically significant. There is, however, a salient difference between the estimates for the co-educational and those for the girls' schools, namely that the ex-pupils are much more emphatic ('disagree strongly') that their co-educational schools did not make them feel they didn't belong socially, than they were about their girls' schools, and this is remarkably consistent for all three occupational class groups.

Social image of the school

A fourth item of a similar nature was: 'I disliked the social image the school tried to capture,' which used the same scale of answers

TABLE 15.5 '*I didn't belong socially*'

'*Both schools*' *survey* (*women*)

Estimates	Replies about women's 'first' schools attended				Replies about women's 'last' schools attended			
	Co-educational schools		Girls' schools		Co-educational schools		Girls' schools	
	N	%	N	%	N	%	N	%
Agree strongly	12	4·0	22	5·4	8	2·2	16	6·2
Agree	28	9·4	71	17·6	27	7·5	27	10·4
Doubtful	30	10·0	57	14·1	28	7·8	47	18·1
Disagree	129	43·2	182	45·1	151	42·3	117	45·2
Disagree strongly	100	33·4	72	17·8	144	40·2	52	20·1
Totals	299	100	404	100	358	100	259	100

NOTE: The differences between the co-educational and girls' schools are statistically highly significant for both 'first' and 'last' schools.

TABLE 15.6 '*I didn't belong socially*'

'*Both schools*' *survey* (*men*)

Estimates	Replies about men's 'first' schools attended				Replies about men's 'last' schools attended			
	Co-educational schools		Boys' schools		Co-educational schools		Boys' schools	
	N	%	N	%	N	%	N	%
Agree strongly	1	1·2	11	9·2	2	1·9	3	4·2
Agree	8	9·8	24	20·2	4	3·8	9	12·7
Doubtful	7	8·6	23	19·3	7	6·7	7	9·9
Disagree	33	40·2	49	41·2	43	41·3	29	40·8
Disagree strongly	33	40·2	12	10·1	48	46·3	23	32·4
Totals	82	100	119	100	104	100	71	100

NOTE: The difference between the distributions for co-educational compared with boys' schools is statistically significant beyond the ·001 level for 'first' schools and is in the same direction for 'last' schools, but here falls just below the conventional significance level.

TABLE 15.7 *'I didn't belong socially'* (women): Tabulated by occupational class

'*Both schools*' survey

Categories of agreement	Replies from women about co-educational schools (percentages)			Replies from women about girls' schools (percentages)		
	Occupational classes			Occupational classes		
	1	2	3, 4 and 5	1	2	3, 4 and 5
Agree strongly	3·2	1·5	4·1	6·6	5·8	4·1
Agree	8·6	7·4	8·9	18·1	10·9	11·0
Doubtful	6·9	13·2	8·3	12·1	22·5	18·0
Disagree	43·5	40·4	43·2	45·4	41·2	47·1
Disagree strongly	37·8	37·5	35·5	17·8	19·6	19·8
	100%	100%	100%	100%	100%	100%
Number	347	136	169	348	138	172

TABLE 15.8 *Social image of the school*

'*Both schools*' survey

Estimates concerning dislike of the image	Replies from women about the schools attended				Replies from men about the schools attended			
	Co-educational schools		Girls' schools		Co-educational schools		Boys' schools	
	N	%	N	%	N	%	N	%
Agree strongly	27	4·1	112	16·9	9	4·9	25	13·2
Agree	60	9·2	129	19·6	20	10·8	32	16·8
Doubtful	103	15·9	125	18·9	30	16·2	47	24·7
Disagree	329	50·6	242	36·6	92	49·7	64	33·7
Disagree strongly	131	20·2	53	8·0	34	18·4	22	11·6
Totals	650	100	661	100	185	100	190	100

NOTE: The difference between the distributions for co-educational and girls' schools is statistically highly significant (this is also true when 'schools attended first' or 'last' are taken separately); that between the boys is highly significant for 'first' schools and for combined groups but just fails to reach the conventional ·05 level for 'last' schools.

233

as the previous items. Table 15.8 indicated that both men and women ex-pupils showed more dislike of the social image projected by their single-sex schools than of that in their co-educational schools, though as many as 45 per cent of both men and women disagreed with the statement as applied to their single-sex school. On the other hand, whereas only 13 per cent of women and 16 per cent of men agreed that they disliked this image in their co-educational schools, these percentages rose to 36 and 30 respectively about their single-sex school. (If we were thinking in terms of 'absolute' standards, we would need to consider the probably favourable nature of the student teacher sample.) In this item those men who attended the co-educational or boys' schools as seniors were more ready to support this 'social image' than were those who attended as juniors, but with the women from both types of school there was a slight tendency in the opposite direction—the 'image' becoming slightly less liked by senior pupils.

An analysis of the women's sample according to the occupational class of the parents of the students was again made. Contrary to expectation, in neither type of school was the social image disliked more by the students from the manual working occupational classes. *Within the present sample* we could find no discernible association with parental occupational class.

Comment

In brief, about a quarter of the women thought their girls' schools 'tried to dominate their whole life' but only some 7 per cent thought this of their co-educational schools; the men produced similar results for 'first' schools, but for 'last' schools a difference in the same direction as that for women was not statistically significant. Likewise more of the women said their girls' schools created a gap between school and home than said the same of their co-educational schools, though they were not so certain of this as about the girls' schools 'trying to dominate their whole life'. With both sexes there was a more emphatic rejection of the idea (i.e. disagree strongly) where the co-educational schools were concerned. The same trend was to be seen in the replies to the item, 'I felt I didn't belong socially,' both for men and women, and this was again repeated for the item, 'I disliked the social image the school tried to capture.' Though a 'halo effect' might conceivably be increasing these differences in favour of the co-educational schools, it is not likely to be creating the gaps themselves, and one has also to ask first the origin of such a halo favourable to co-educational schools and second to consider whether, if such a halo affects the results, it might well be considered part and parcel of the differences between co-educational and single-sex schools. If an ex-pupil considered he or she 'didn't belong socially' in the single-sex school attended, but 'did belong socially' in the co-educational school, this is what really matters to the pupil, whether or not this feeling has been increased by, for example, a generalized liking for the co-educational school. The results reported are what the pupils say about their experience, and as such represent a legitimate comparison of the two types of school.

16

Preparation for the adult world

Research on co-education in this country commenced in the twenties with Tyson's study (1928) of comparative attainment, and continued in a desultory fashion on this theme, only widening its horizons with Moreton's inquiry into the attitudes of teachers to co-education in 1939. No large-scale research on the comparative effects of the two types of schooling on the attitudes and social and emotional development of the pupils appears to have been done anywhere until the work of Moreton (1939), Lotz (1953) in U.S.A., Dale (1948, 1949, 1966 and 1966a) and Atherton (1971). This chapter presents the results of several investigations in one part of this area, all of them examining the extent to which the ex-pupils and pupils considered their school education prepared them for life in the adult world.

The Second College survey

The section of the Second College survey with which we are now concerned related to the attitude of men and women towards the opposite sex, as portrayed by their answers to three questions, viz.:

Did your school life help or hinder you in your relations with the opposite sex? Reply was on a five-point scale from 'very helpful', through 'no effect' to 'great hindrance'.
Do you find it easy to work with the opposite sex? Do you think you would find it easy, in general, to work under the direction of a member of the opposite sex? A seven-point scale was used for these two questions, ranging from 'very easy' to 'very difficult'.

Space for voluntary comment was provided under the last of these questions, partly in order to discover the reasons behind the expressed attitudes, and partly to discover ambiguities or other faults in the questions. The replies of the women are examined first.

THE WOMEN

The results were treated in two ways, first by calculating for each question the percentage of women recording each preference on the scale; second, by weighting (e.g. five for 'very helpful', decreasing to one for 'great hindrance'), and then calculating mean scores for different groups. Though the allocation of the weights is somewhat arbitrary it has compensating advantages for the comparison of large groups, especially combined with the first method.

Results

Table 16.1 shows how women from the two types of school answered the question, *Did your school life help or hinder you in your relations with the opposite sex?*

TABLE 16.1 *Type of schooling and women's relationships with men*

Second College survey

	N*	Percentages				
		Very help- ful	Help- ful	No effect	Slight hin- drance	Great hin- drance
Effect of school life on relationships with men						
women from co-ed. schools	403	31·3	44·7	22·6	1·2	0·2
women from girls' schools	623	1·6	8·7	50·9	32·4	6·4

		Very easy	Easy	Fairly easy	Doubt- ful	A little diffi- cult	Difficult	Very difficult
Ease of working *with* men								
women from co-ed. schools	407	40·0	41·0	17·0	1·0	1·0	0	0
women from girls' schools	610	31·3	32·7	25·4	4·8	4·6	1·0	0·2

Ease of working *under* a man's direction								
women from co-ed. schools	405	44·7	41·6	10·6	2·2	0·7	0·2	0
women from girls' schools	626	40·9	42·1	12·1	3·2	1·1	0·3	0·3

* The totals are not the same for all tables because of differences in the numbers who replied to particular questions.

It requires no great wisdom to forecast which type of school would give the superior estimates, but the extent of the difference is unexpected. Whereas only some 10 per cent of the ex-pupils of girls' schools said their school life was helpful in this respect, the proportion from mixed schools was three-quarters. At the opposite end of the scale almost four in every ten women from girls' schools said their school life was a hindrance, while the proportion from mixed schools was little more than one in every hundred. The difference between the distributions from the two types of school is statistically significant well beyond the ·001 level.

It was known that the social class distribution of the two groups differed, and there might have been a systematic bias. We therefore grouped the women according to the occupational class of their

TABLE 16.2 *Effect of type of schooling on women's relationships with men: Analysis by occupational class**

Second College survey

		Occupational class of father				
		1	2	3	4 & 5	Total
Co-ed. schools N		61	32	91	19	203
Girls' schools N		160	44	148	18	370
	Maximum	Weighted mean scores†				
Effect of school life on relationships with men	5					
Women from co-ed. schools		4·16	4·31	4·27	4·37	4·26
Women from girls' schools		2·65	2·80	2·65	2·50	2·66
Ease of working *with* men	7					
Women from co-ed. schools		6·18	6·44	6·34	6·25	6·29
Women from girls' schools		5·94	5·71	5·85	5·76	5·87
Ease of working *under* a woman's direction	7					
Women from co-ed. schools		6·39	6·47	6·44	6·55	6·44
Women from girls' schools		6·31	6·33	6·24	6·11	6·28

* Data were available for only part of the sample. The categories were: Class 1 professional, administrative, managerial and teachers; class 2 clerical workers; class 3 skilled manual workers; class 4 semi-skilled; and class 5 unskilled.
† Weighted mean scores 7 to 1 on seven-point scale and 5 to 1 on five-point scale, the high scores being the more favourable.

fathers, and calculated the weighted mean scores. These are shown in Table 16.2.

The most striking feature of Table 16.2 is the steadiness of the score from one class to another, within each of the two school groups; further, as one would expect, within each class there is a wide gap between the women from girls' schools and those from mixed schools. It has been mentioned before, however, that the parental occupational class influences are reduced in importance because the respondents all belong to the same (or closely related) future occupational class; also pupils from the lower occupational classes will be a much more restricted sample than those from the higher occupational classes. The figures are therefore reported as true for the present sample and not as representative of the attitudes of the various social classes.

Do you find it easy to work with the opposite sex? The answers to this question are shown in Table 16.1

The hypothesis that women educated in mixed schools would find it easier to work with the opposite sex than women educated in girls' schools finds partial support in these data; the difference between the two distributions is statistically significant beyond the ·001 level.

The possibility of systematic bias from social class factors was again examined. The results, given in Table 16.2, show that, within this sample, occupational class had very little effect on the women's estimate of their ability to work with men. Within each class, however, the women from the mixed schools consistently gave a slightly higher estimate than did women from girls' schools.

It is still traditional and 'normal' in Britain for women to work *under the direction* of a man. There also appears to be a tendency for some—perhaps many—women to dislike working under another woman, but to like working for a man. The questionnaire asked, 'Do you think you would find it easy, in general, to work under the direction of a member of the opposite sex?'

Table 16.1 shows that rather more women from the mixed schools in this sample than from girls' schools thought it would be easy to work under the supervision of a man; but here emphasis should be placed on the similarity between the groups rather than on the small and statistically insignificant difference.

A social class breakdown of the data is given in Table 16.2. There is again a notable consistency in the pattern of the scores.

Respondents were invited to amplify their answers to this question, and about one-quarter of each of the two school groups did so. The comments from these two groups resemble each other closely, apart from one small section of answers. This consisted of some 6 per cent from the girls' schools who expressed difficulties (and even fear in one case) at working under a man; three of these women said it was easier after having attended a mixed college. But the basic similarity is to be seen in the predominant theme of the replies—that men are better in authority, fairer, more patient, gain more respect and are easier to work with. No less than 53 per cent of the replies from the women from co-educational schools come into this category, and almost 49 per cent of those from the girls' schools. A minority of respondents from each group attacked the women instead of praising the men, complaining of cattiness, bossiness, 'bitchiness' and being temperamental and difficult. A few quotations are given:

'I prefer to be dominated by a member of the opposite sex rather than try to dominate him.'

'Men dealt more justly and fairly than women. Women in high positions are usually domineering.'

'Men tend to be more fair in their judgments and certainly not "bitchy".'

'Very difficult to work under a woman.'

'Better than under one of my own sex.'

Other comments of interest were:

'Since being at a mixed college I have found it easier to get on with the other sex. I'm not so shy and self-conscious.'

'I don't get on so easily with the opposite sex as I have a slight fear of them which is not good in a working relationship.'

'Had this been filled in on just leaving school I would have said "very difficult" but four years in mixed Colleges have now overcome the setbacks, but I have taken three years to do so.'

In this last comment there is a hint that the very slight (non-significant) difference between the two groups might have been greater if it had been measured at the time the pupils left school.

The women in this study who attended girls' schools regarded themselves, on the average, as decidedly handicapped in their social life with the opposite sex, and, to a lesser extent, in working with the opposite sex. This is what we might have expected, but it has now for the first time been demonstrated. A factor to be noticed is that almost all the women in the sample, whether from mixed or single-sex schools, were day pupils from grammar schools; the difference in attitudes between the two groups might be greater in the case of boarders. It is still open to the protagonists of girls' schools to argue that the finding might not apply to all types of pupil, though judging by the figures this would seem extremely unlikely. We must also remember that girls' schools may have the advantage in other aspects which have not yet been investigated.

The scores of the women appeared not to vary according to the occupational class of the fathers. We cannot, as we have seen, generalize this finding to the grammar school population as a whole because of the restriction of the sample in respect of occupational class.

Critics might object that the higher estimates of the mixed school group about the ease of their relationships with men could be produced, not by any difference in educational provision, but by girls who felt at ease with the other sex choosing to go to mixed schools rather than to girls' schools. Fortunately we know that in most areas the girls had no choice. In the remaining areas it is likely that, at the age of eleven, the choice would be made for scholastic work and 'atmosphere' or 'tone' rather than because of the girls' attitude to the presence of boys in the school. Where the girls' school is 'Direct Grant', it will tend to take automatically the top thirty or more in the area's 11-plus examination, and few pupils would decline this offer. Further evidence on some of these matters is, however, desirable. We now turn to the men's results for the same questions.

THE MEN

The hypothesis examined was the same as in the case of the women, that educating the two sexes together at the secondary level (as opposed to educating them apart) would affect their social relations and their attitude to each other, and that these effects might to an appreciable extent persist in adult life. Procedure was again by questionnaire, administered in large groups to prevent collusion, with a pledge of anonymity. The sample was drawn from male student teachers in five Departments of Education and sixteen training Colleges, consisting of 569 ex-pupils of boys' schools and 351 from mixed schools. They were asked the same questions as the women and the results were treated in the same way.

Table 16.3 summarizes the answers of the two groups of men.

Almost 40 per cent of the men educated at boys' schools thought their school life hindered them in their relationships with women, while nearly three-quarters of those from mixed schools believed that their social life had helped them in this respect. Difference between the two groups is statistically significant $(P < \cdot 001)$.

Working *with* women was considered difficult by 9 per cent of the men from boys' schools but only 3 per cent of those from

TABLE 16.3 *Type of schooling and men's relationships with women*

Second College survey

N* Percentages

	N*	Very help-ful	Help-ful	No effect	Slight hin-drance	Great hin-drance
Effect of school life on relationships with women						
men from mixed schools	347	27·4	46·9	20·2	4·6	0·9
men from boys' schools	569	2·5	10·7	47·4	31·1	8·3

	N*	Very easy	Easy	Fairly easy	Doubt-ful	A little diffi-cult	Difficult	Very difficult
Ease of working *with* women								
men from mixed schools	351	30·5	37·6	25·6	3·1	2·6	0·3	0·3
men from boys' schools	542	21·0	34·3	28·2	7·4	7·6	0·9	0·6
Ease of working *under* a woman's direction								
men from mixed schools	345	11·0	26·7	24·7	22·6	7·5	3·2	4·3
men from boys' schools	561	6·6	20·3	26·4	19·4	12·7	8·2	6·4

* The totals are not the same for all tables because of differences in the numbers who replied to particular questions.

mixed schools. The difference between the two groups is statistically significant (P < ·001) if those who expressed doubt or difficulty are taken together in contrast with all the others. Working under women also differentiated the two groups; 27 per cent from boys' schools thought this difficult, but only 15 per cent from mixed schools; the difference is significant (P ·001)

Table 16.4 compares these results with the equivalent figures from the parallel study of women's attitudes. Men considered single-sex schooling a greater handicap than did women in their subsequent working relationships *with* the opposite sex.

The data were examined to see whether the expressed attitudes were associated in any systematic way with the occupational class of the men's parents. Table 16.5 shows the number of men in each of the two groups who came from each of four occupational classes; and it also gives the weighted mean score for each of the three questions.

TABLE 16.4 *Type of school and relationships between men and women: Comparison of men and women*

Second College survey

	Men		Women	
	Mixed schools Per cent	Boys' schools	Mixed schools Per cent	Girls' schools
School life a hindrance in relationships with opposite sex	5·5	39·4	1·4	38·8
Difficult to work *with* opposite sex	3·2	9·1	1·0	5·8
Difficult to work *under* opposite sex	15·0	27·3	0·9	1·7

TABLE 16.5 *Effect of type of schooling on men's relationships with women: Analysis by occupational class*

Second College survey

		Occupational class of father				
		1	2	3	4 & 5	Total
Mixed schools	N	32	22	69	17	140
Boys' schools	N	59	20	114	20	213
	Max.	Weighted mean scores				
Effect of school life on relationships with women	5					
Men from mixed schools		4·06	4·05	4·12	4·18	4·10
Men from boys' schools		2·53	2·50	2·49	2·55	2·51
Ease of working *with* women	7					
Men from mixed schools		5·97	5·95	5·89	6·06	5·94
Men from boys' schools		5·84	5·43	5·39	5·40	5·50
Ease of working *under* a woman's direction	7					
Men from mixed schools		4·63	5·09	5·15	5·18	5·02
Men from boys' schools		4·32	4·26	4·41	4·90	4·42

Occupational class appeared not to be associated with any change in these men's estimates of how their school life had affected their relationships with women, but for each class the men from mixed schools gave consistently higher, i.e. more favourable replies than

243

did those from boys' schools. In respect of work *with* women, there was no observed association between class origins and the replies of the men from mixed schools, but among the men from boys' schools those whose fathers were in occupational class 1 had a mean score significantly higher than that of all the others combined ($P < \cdot 05$). Those from mixed schools again scored consistently rather higher than the others. Ease of working *under* a woman's direction also was greater in every occupational group among men from mixed schools; of men from both groups, those in the lower occupational classes tended to score higher, the difference being slightly short of statistical significance.[1]

From the 561 ex-pupils of boys' schools who made estimates there were also 199 free comments on the question of ease of work *under* women. Almost half of these said that sex made no difference or that it depended on the individual's competence or age, but about a quarter replied expressing difficulties, namely that women were inferior, had no natural authority, were petty, domineering and emotional, and not impartial. Of the 345 male ex-pupils of mixed schools, 101 made comments, half of them of the type described above as 'sex made no difference', etc., and like the boys' schools about a quarter mentioned difficulties. A few of the more interesting comments are quoted. From the boys' schools group:

'Women possess an inherent quality of orderliness and method, and love of detail which is unbearable over long periods and eventually terminates in the realm of "hair splitting".' ('Difficult')

'Women were created to be in subjection, not to rule.' ('Very difficult')

'The artificial atmosphere of the single-sex grammar school at first made my present situation intolerable.' ('Very difficult')

'Woman's place is in the home.' ('A little difficult')

'Women cannot govern.' ('Doubtful')

From the mixed schools group:

'Speaking as a senior army officer. My service experience, particularly overseas, has made me very wary of women in positions of authority; there has been less give and take with them and they were unfortunately inclined to be biased in their judgments.' ('Doubtful')

---

[1] $t = 1 \cdot 81$ opposing classes 4 and 5 with class 1. An examination of the occupational class trend for all men by analysis of variance gave a statistically non-significant result.

Many more of the comments from both groups were of the type, 'Easy, provided she was older and more experienced in the work being done.'

The great majority of the men who completed the questionnaire would be between 18 and 20 years of age. Few would be under 18 and few over 23. Their judgment would be mature, and their memories fresh enough for them to give valid and reliable estimates relating to their life in school. Only one of the questions, however, was based explicitly on school life; the others asked present attitudes. The comments made throughout the questionnaire and the consistent patterns produced by the results indicate that the students were thoroughly interested in their work and showed a high sense of responsibility.

On the other hand the sample, like that of the women, was limited to one type of ex-pupil, and though it can be claimed that this method ensured reasonable equality of sample between mixed and boys' schools it can with equal cogency be argued that one cannot be certain that the findings would be similar for a complete cross-section sample of pupils, even though it appears likely that the findings could be generalized. As with the women, this occupational narrowness of the sample may also have had some influence on the 'reluctance' of the men's estimates to vary with the occupational class of the fathers.

The men from boys' schools in this sample believed that their school life was less helpful to them in their relations with women than did the men who attended mixed schools. Similarly the former considered that it was less easy to work with, and to work under, women than did the latter. In other words, this effect tended to persist after leaving school, though we don't know for how long. In the comments a few individuals said that being students in a mixed college, after having attended a boys' school, had helped them to establish easier social relations with women.

We need to remind ourselves again that attitudes such as those with which this chapter is concerned are powerfully affected, not only by the schools, but by the society around them. The men would have been much less likely in Victorian times, for example, to have been willing to work under the direction of women.

The Schools project

In the Schools project over one thousand pupils aged 13 plus and 17 plus were asked: 'Apart from employment do you think your school prepares you sufficiently for the adult world? Agree strongly/ Agree/Doubtful/Disagree/Disagree strongly.' Pupils were also encouraged to add a free response.

For both boys and girls aged 13 plus more of those in the single-sex schools than in the co-educational thought their education did not prepare them for life in the adult world, but neither difference was statistically significant (see Table A.27). For students aged 17 plus the trend was the same, but the difference between the male groups is almost statistically significant and that between the female groups is statistically highly significant (see Figure 16.1). The change between the ages 13 plus and 17 plus might reasonably be thought due to the immaturity of the former group for making a judgment of this kind.

Readers will see that in Figure 16.1 only a negligible percentage of the senior girls in both types of school 'agreed strongly' that their school prepared them sufficiently for life in the adult world, and that whereas 22 per cent of those in girls' schools endorsed 'agreed' this percentage was doubled by the girls in co-educational schools. Correspondingly few of the senior male students in either type of school endorsed 'agree strongly', but whereas only a little more than one third of those in boys' schools estimated 'agree', this figure rose to over one-half for boys in co-educational schools. At the age of 17 plus the sample consists mostly of those who stayed at school until they reached the sixth.

FREE RESPONSES

What were the students' reasons for their estimates? Fortunately their free responses, unmistakably responsible in manner, provide us with a good picture. For both sexes there is a wide variety of reasons for disagreement, ranging from narrowness of curriculum and outlook to lack of the teaching of good manners and sex instruction. The analysis is confined to the older (17 plus) group, as the younger group were rather immature for this question; the girls will be considered first.

Of those girls who agreed that their school prepared them sufficiently for life in the adult world, 16 of those in girls' schools wrote supporting statements, and 31 in co-educational schools. There is little of real interest and information in these individual replies, but the free responses of those who estimated they were doubtful, disagreed or disagreed strongly, are informative, and are given in detail in Table 16.6.

Here the pupils educated in co-educational and those from girls' schools have much in common. In the social area both groups complain that there is no preparation for life's responsibilities and problems, that there is little outside the curriculum, with some lack of guidance on marriage problems, sex, careers and colleges. Girls from girls' schools, however, emphasize more strongly that there is

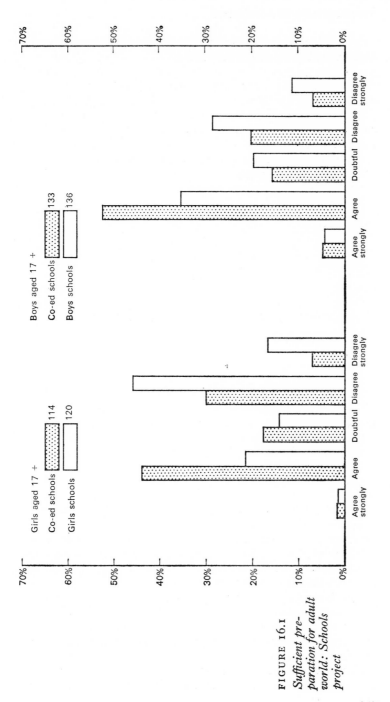

FIGURE 16.1
*Sufficient pre-
paration for adult
world: Schools
project*

TABLE 16.6 *Sufficient preparation for world? Girls aged 17 plus: Free responses denoting disagreement*

Schools project, 1966

	Co-ed. schools	Girls' schools
Social		
no experience of life outside school, or preparation for outside responsibilities	10	8
too coddled, sheltered, no freedom, too formal, too organized		7
little outside the curriculum, not enough social activities	9	20
little or nothing on marriage, sex, social behaviour, careers, income tax, college	10	4
no contact with opposite sex		6
Curriculum		
Over-emphasis on curriculum (see under Social) more variety of topics needed—too narrow, no relation to life, discussions on life	4	7
need more current affairs, civics	1	2
Discipline		
treated like children—bad preparation for life in adult world	4	3
treated like puppets		1
Others	2	5
do their best but ideas wrong		1
no freedom of thought		1
conduct yes, growing up no		1
have to learn for yourself		2
Totals	40	68

little outside the curriculum, and are alone in protesting about being coddled, sheltered or organized, and in saying they cannot be trained for life in the adult world if they are deprived of social contact with the opposite sex. Both groups believe the curriculum should be less narrow, be more related to life, and should include more current affairs. Again, in the complaints about discipline a few individuals in each group complain that being treated like children is no proper training for life in the world. A few responses are quoted to illustrate the dissatisfaction. (The principle is maintained that the number of quotations should be in proportion to the number of comments made.)

Preparation for the adult world

Co-educational schools

'In our school we are treated in a childish manner by the head-master.'

'Exams are not going to prepare us for the outside world. A lesson on the rights and wrongs of sex life should be held.'

'We are not taught anything about social behaviour.'

'If you fail your exams you are almost totally unprepared.'

Girls' schools

'Little taught on the hardships of life.'

'We are taught nothing of sex.'

'Being in a girls' school—absolutely hopeless!'

'An all-girls school is always a setback.'

'I am taught nothing of etiquette, cooking and current affairs.

'Too much stress laid on academic work.'

'We are confined more or less to our subjects.'

The free responses of the boys (Table 16.7) are strikingly similar to those of the girls. Agreement with the statement was recorded by 38 boys in co-educational schools and by 28 in boys' schools. If those who estimated 'doubtful' are included with the two categories of disagreement there were 35 from co-educational and 66 from boys' schools. The latter made more protests about the lack of preparation for life's responsibilities and problems, but the smallness of the numbers in the sub-categories makes further comment inadvisable.

The quotations are again limited to those expressing concern over deficiencies.

Co-educational schools

'Financial economics should be taught to all.'

'You should be shown different parts of life and other people's ways.'

'One period a week could be put away for sex education.'

'The onus is on intellect and we have no grounding in the techniques for getting on with older people outside school—that we have to do ourselves, which we cannot really do until we are allowed into pubs at 18.'

TABLE 16.7 *Sufficient preparation for world? Boys aged 17 plus: Free responses denoting disagreement*

Schools project, 1966

	Co-ed. schools	Boys' schools
Social		
no experience of life outside school, or preparation for life's responsibilities and problems	2	15
too sheltered, restricted, narrow	4	3
little outside curriculum, social, etc.	5	8
little on morals, sex education, careers, manners	9	3
no contact with opposite sex		5
Curriculum		
over-emphasis on curriculum (see under Social)		
too narrow, no relation to life, theoretical	4	6
need more current affairs, world problems, civics	3	2
insufficient discussion adult world		2
Discipline		
treated like children	2	7
too lax		1
independence not taught		4
Others	3	6
some but not enough	1	
little influence on character		1
depends on teacher		1
up to individual	2	2
Totals	35	66

Boys' schools

'I think we should have more lessons on house buying, banks, insurance, etc.'

'It should be comprehensive and mixed for this.'

'Probably not, because this is a single-sex school.'

'Prepares you for sadism perhaps. No attempt (except by fear) to instil citizenship.'

'Too much emphasis on exams, not enough on world affairs.'

'Some more positive form of sex education should be taught.'

'I think subjects such as cookery should be taught.'

'In the adult world the sexes are not kept apart.'

Comment

As with most of this work there is much to be learnt from
the estimates and comments which is quite outside the co-education
controversy. A substantial proportion of present pupils and of
mature ex-pupils are dissatisfied with their secondary education as
a preparation for life in the adult world. Both past and present co-
educated pupils, however, show appreciably less dissatisfaction
than do their contemporaries from single-sex schools.

17

Marriage

'At first sight of the word marriage at the head of this chapter the reader may understandably have wondered what connection there was between the chapter title and the subject of the book. On reflection, however, he will appreciate that the bringing up together of boys and girls, and indeed young men and young women in the same educational institution might have a permanent effect upon the knowledge that each sex has of the ways, the philosophy and motivations of the other, and that this knowledge might produce a lasting change in the attitude of the sexes towards each other, and consequently influence the keenness of the desire for marriage, and the happiness of marriage. It is of course recognized that the biological urge will be immeasurably more powerful than any effect of schooling.

This chapter, then, differs from most of the preceding ones in being concerned not so much with the immediate attitudes of pupils or of ex-pupils towards their schools but primarily with more lasting effects which may have resulted from their type of schooling. If any difference, say in the degree of marital happiness or in the desire for marriage, exists between the products of single-sex and co-educational schooling, this will be of some interest, though readers will not be unaware that there are many other factors affecting marriage, so that the sample examined would need to be very large in order to randomize out individual differences of temperament, the hazards of misfortune etc., while allowance must be made for factors such as age, social class and length of marriage.

Second College survey

The first attack on the problem was made in the Second College survey, when some 2,000 student teachers who were ex-pupils of secondary schools other than secondary modern were asked, 'Do you wish to marry, provided you can find a suitable partner?' Estimates were requested on a seven-point scale ranging from Very much/Much/A little/Undecided to Very much opposed. The distribution of the estimates of ex-pupils of single-sex grammar schools was compared with that from mixed grammar schools.

For some purposes a comparison of the means of weighted scores was also used. Replies were anonymous and free comments were requested where opposition to marriage was signified. Married students were excluded.

The method of procedure is admittedly not the best, but it was then the only one possible in view of the limitations of finance and time; the section was frankly regarded as exploratory. A more detailed investigation carried out by one of the writer's research students is outlined later in the chapter.

WOMEN'S ESTIMATES

The hypothesis was that social interaction between the sexes at school might slightly increase their desire for marriage, compared with pupils from single-sex schools. For the 972 women the difference was unexpectedly in the opposite direction, though not statistically significant (Chi-square was 5·832 for 6 degrees of freedom); 67·4 per cent of the girls from girls' schools wished 'very much' to marry, and 61·5 per cent from mixed schools, but most of this difference was reversed in the 'much' estimates. In both groups only about 2 per cent gave any of the three 'opposed' estimates. It may be that deprivation—or lack of contact with the opposite sex—slightly increases the desire for marriage and parenthood amongst women, but confirmatory evidence is needed. The effect is interesting but too small to be of practical significance.

As the social class distribution is different in single-sex compared with mixed grammar schools, part of the information was analysed according to this variable. No significant social class differences were found, nor did the variable have any appreciable effect on the main comparison except to reduce the difference slightly. These data were then divided into ex-pupils 'with siblings' and 'without siblings', for the parental skilled artisan class only. Ex-pupils of girls' and mixed schools were combined, as their means and distributions were so similar. The mean score on 'wish for marriage' of those 'with siblings' (163) was 6·42, and 'without siblings' (56) 6·50, i.e. more favourable to marriage, but the difference was far from statistically significant. Almost 6 per cent of those with siblings were undecided or opposed, while none of those without siblings were opposed and only 3·6 per cent were undecided. Unfortunately we do not know how many of the siblings of the women students were male, but there may be here once again a slight hint that lack of social contact with the opposite sex tends to drive people towards such contact more powerfully than the actual experience of it—which may, after all, be tragic or unhappy in some cases.

In all only seventeen comments were given which opposed marriage. The general theme of these is sometimes a frank avowal of selfishness, but more often a mere wish to stay independent or to indulge in an alternative, such as travel. Fear of having children and dislike of the idea of sexual intercourse are both mentioned. Noteworthy are: 'I'm not made for self-sacrifice—natural outcome of marriage for women.' 'Too limited—no scope for independent activity.' 'There are so many things I want to do that to be tied down to one person would not be good for me or him,' and 'I cannot see myself settling down with one person and being happy for the rest of my life.' The smallness of the number of comments severely limited their value.

MEN'S ESTIMATES

In contrast to the women the men's results were in the direction of the hypothesis that co-educational schooling would make them slightly more favourable to marriage. The difference between the two groups was, however, very small and not statistically significant. Of the 304 men from mixed schools, 63·3 per cent wished to marry 'very much', while of the 479 men from boys' schools only 59·5 per cent were in this category. A mere 0·6 per cent of the mixed schools group were opposed to marriage, and 2·3 per cent from the boys' schools. When the two distributions were divided into the favourable and the opposed, the difference between men from mixed and men from boys' schools gave a Chi-square of 3·07 which, for one degree of freedom, is somewhat short of statistical significance.

Analysis by father's occupational class produced a striking similarity between the average scores of the classes within each type of school, but a persistent small difference between the schools within each social class. (As mentioned before, any effect of social class would be reduced because all the students were intending teachers.) These differences between types of school, separately, were not statistically significant, but support each other by their consistent pattern.

Of the 783 men who participated, only thirteen opposed marriage. Two of these thirteen came from mixed schools, and wrote, 'I feel I want to carry on my studies so that I am taxed fully. To have to devote time to a wife and family would hinder me' (A little opposed); and, 'I enjoy my own company and freedom. I don't want the responsibility' (Much opposed). Of the eleven men from boys' schools who opposed marriage (out of 479 who answered), three failed to give their reasons, though requested to do so. The chief reasons advanced are loss of freedom, both personal and financial. There was one objection to 'monogamous marriage', and one man was 'appalled at the thought of such a relationship'. Another was 'very much opposed' because he was too moody and because his parents' marriage had been an unhappy one.

Comment

The slight tendency to greater variability of scores among the group from single-sex schools is interesting and in the case of the men approaches statistical significance. With the latter some opposition to marriage could be caused by a tendency to homosexuality among a small fraction of the pupils in boys' schools. Although there is a very slight indication of this in one comment and in comments about other items in the questionnaire, the evidence is insufficient for any definite conclusion. It was thought that the number of respondents from boys' schools who failed to reply might provide another pointer, when compared with the number of male non-respondents from mixed schools, on the hypothesis that homosexuals would refuse to answer a question on marriage. The difference was in the expected direction, 2·1 per cent from boys' schools, compared with 1·3 per cent of the boys from mixed schools, but it is not statistically reliable,[1] nor in any event could one be at all sure that the difference was due to the homosexual factor. Complaints regarding homosexuality tend to come, however, from boarding rather than day schools, and the former represent only 5 per cent of the present sample from boys' schools. (Of the ten respondents from boys' schools who failed to give any estimate only one was a boarder.) The questionnaire was not, of course, designed to elicit information on this specific point; and even if homosexuality were underlying the cause of opposition it is unlikely that this reason would be stated.

Findings closely similar to those on the marriage question resulted from asking the same sample, 'If you marry—or if you are married—do you wish to have children?' The girls' schools were slightly keener towards parenthood than women from co-educational schools through a slightly greater percentage replying 'very much' as opposed to 'much', there being no difference between the two types of school at the 'opposed' end of the scale, and the overall difference being small and statistically non-significant. For the men there was again a small difference in the opposite direction at the negative end of the scale, some 3.1 per cent of those educated in boys' schools giving one of the 'opposed' estimates, and 0·9 per cent of those from co-educational schools. If the distributions are split into the *realistic* dichotomy of 'against parenthood' versus

---

[1] Chi-square 0·67 for one degree of freedom.

Marriage

the rest, the difference falls only a little short of statistical significance. Though the chance element certainly cannot be ruled
out there seems here to be a case for more detailed research.

The Atherton survey[1]

The research into this topic was taken a stage further by
Atherton, one of the writer's research students at the University
College of Swansea. He made an inquiry into the happiness of
marriage, comparing co-educated men and women with those from
single-sex schools. His sample was over 1,100 men and 1,400
women, selected impartially by a large number of doctors scattered
throughout England and Wales, and the procedure was partly by
anonymous questionnaire and partly by attitude scale. Results of
this work are now available.

The first of two key questions was, 'Do you think that the
type of school (mixed or single sex) helped or hindered you in
everyday relations with the opposite sex?' Respondents could
choose their reply from, 'Helped/Hindered/Neither or Don't know.'
For both men and women about 70 per cent of the co-educated
group thought their type of school had helped them, 2 per cent
thought it had hindered and 25 per cent said 'neither' or 'don't know'.
Of the group educated in single-sex schools the percentage of both
men and women who said their schooling had helped them fell to
10, while the 'hindered' replies rose to 30 per cent, with the
'neutral' group at over 50 per cent.[2] Some people might say that this
result is merely what one would expect—that educating boys and
girls together would naturally help them to establish a good social
relationship with the opposite sex and that single-sex education
would hinder this. The writer would agree, but would add that it is
always useful to obtain confirmatory evidence for these beliefs,
and that it sometimes happens that such beliefs are shown to be
without foundation in fact. A vague belief is also much more open
to counter-argument. In the present instance there are certainly
supporters of single-sex schools who have argued that co-education
made little or no difference because boys and girls these days have
plenty of opportunities to meet the opposite sex outside school.
This new knowledge, however, makes it more difficult for anyone
to sustain this argument. Both the direction of the finding and the
decisive difference between the two groups are a replication, with a
more representative sample, of the writer's findings as seen especially in the answers to the question. 'Did your school life help or

[1] Cf. the summary in *Where?*, 28 October 1966.
[2] The difference is statistically significant beyond the ·001 level.

hinder you in your relations with the opposite sex?', given in Chapter 12.

With Atherton's second key question it is perhaps not so obvious that the type of schooling might make a difference between the co-educated and those educated in single-sex schools. He asked, 'Do you think the type of school (mixed or single-sex) helped or hindered you in making a happy marriage?' Respondents could reply, 'Helped/Hindered/Don't know'. Many people would think that other factors are so powerful that the influence of the type of school would be negligible. Atherton, however, found that for both men and women roughly 40 per cent of the co-educated judged that their schooling had helped them in making a happy marriage and only 1 per cent thought it had hindered, while among those educated in single-sex schools about 10 per cent thought their schooling had helped, over 5 per cent thought it had hindered and over 75 per cent said 'neither' or 'don't know'. For both men and for women the differences between the distributions of the co-educated and single-sex educated groups were statistically significant beyond the ·001 level. These questions, however, were only supplementary to the main procedure which was the administration of a self-rating questionnaire or 'attitude scale'. This scale for the self-rating of marital happiness also yielded results which gave strong support to these findings. The scale included one question directly on marital happiness and others on such topics as the sharing of interests by husband and wife, agreement on money matters, attitude to in-laws, religion, friends, any regret at having married and either actual separation or divorce or the thought of either. In this way a more objective element was introduced into the survey.

By far the most important difference he found was that between the 'happiness of marriage' scores of the co-educated and those educated in single-sex secondary schools, where schooling went on for five years or more, the co-educated had the better score. (A similar result obtained for those educated in grammar schools only, maybe because they were the principal group with prolonged schooling.) The difference between the two groups who had been at secondary schools for five years or more was statistically highly dependable.[1] The group of women lowest in happiness score were those who had attended convent schools, but even when these were removed (as being non-typical even for the groups educated in single-sex schools) the difference between the women educated at co-educational grammar schools and those educated in single-sex grammar schools remained statistically significant. In spite of the

[1] Beyond the ·01 level for men, ·02 for women and ·001 for men and women together.

consistency of these results an interpreter must tread warily in reaching his conclusions as there are so many other powerful forces acting for or against the happiness of a marriage, such as social class, age and religion, that it is necessary for a number of different researches to come to similar results before a finding can be regarded as established. Atherton's work, though praiseworthy, should be regarded as pioneering a way in a relatively new and difficult area of research.

The Schools project

In the questionnaire administered to groups of girl pupils in some twenty-four grammar schools in South Wales and the West Riding, three items were included which relate to the title of the chapter. They are, 'Marriage is necessary for happiness in later life', 'A woman cannot be married and also successfully carry on with a career', and, 'I feel that marriage and children are more important for a woman than a career'. Girls could choose their answer from a five-point scale ranging from 'agree strongly' to 'disagree strongly'. Their estimates yielded no conclusive results, none of the differences between co-educational and girls' schools being statistically significant for girls aged 17 plus and girls aged 15 plus. A similarly inconclusive result was produced when pupils were divided into social classes, and also when social class 3 (fathers skilled artisans) was split into those with siblings and those without.

Curiously enough, however, when the replies of the 15-year-old girls were analysed by social class, siblings and also geographical area, it was seen that whereas in South Wales there was a trend (remarkably consistent for each social class) for girls in girls' schools to be slightly more favourable to marriage than girls in the sample of co-educational schools from that region, in the West Riding this trend was reversed, again with consistency for social class groups. This reversal may have arisen through the small number of schools of each type in the sample, but whatever the reason it is abundantly clear that no conclusions can be based on such conflicting results (none of the differences was statistically significant).

Comment

An overall view of this evidence suggests that co-educational schooling at the secondary stage produces some improvement in the happiness of marriage, but more research is needed before this finding can be confirmed. More evidence is also needed on the extent of this difference—if indeed it is proved to exist, so that we can judge what weight to give it in the co-educational versus single-sex schools controversy.

The two following chapters may seem to break a certain thread of continuity in the book but they are included in it because like the rest of the material they are concerned with the social and emotional development of children in the two types of school, and are placed at the end because they are both based on a test technique which is not used in the rest of the book.

18

Anxiety about school

The anxious child is a hostage to fortune, liable to physical illness as well as to nervous complaints. No matter how able the child or how high the academic attainment, the future is not bright unless the anxieties can be removed or the anxiety habit modified. Though the home usually has the most important influence on the child, that of the school can be powerful either for good or ill. It is strange that educationists have for so long neglected to see that this good emotional and social development—central to sound education—might be profoundly affected by the alternatives of single-sex or co-educational schooling.

The area of emotional and social adjustment is vast in itself and no pretence is made that the subject is covered in this and the following chapter, nor any claim that the results from this one sample of forty-two schools are conclusive. We need other and larger samples of schools and also, as pointed out elsewhere, more 'objective' measures of emotional adjustment, such as analyses of truancy, juvenile delinquency and school attendance, though in view of other influences that bear on the problem, for example social class and urban versus rural environment, any straight comparison between co-educational and single-sex schools might be misleading.

In this study pupils at the age of 11 plus and 15 plus were given paper and pencil tests of temperament—including anxiety about school—and retested two years later. There are therefore results for the complete group at the first testing, for the remaining pupils two years later, and for a longitudinal sample similar in composition to that secured at the second testing. The tests were a modified Boxall for the juniors, and the Mooney Problem Check List and High School Personality Questionnaire (2nd edition) for both juniors and seniors.

The juniors

THE BOXALL TEST

The results of the Boxall test (for test see Appendix 1) and an analysis of previous research have been reported elsewhere (Dale, 1969), but a summary of the results is given here.

All the tests were administered by the writer and his research assistant, the pupils were told not to give their names, and the importance of the work was stressed. They worked under examination conditions, with no staff present, and their attitude was excellent. On the first occasion twenty pupils were tested in each single-sex school and twenty of each sex in the corresponding co-educational schools, making a full original sample of 1,120 pupils aged 11 plus. Anxiety towards school was measured by the number of situations in which the pupil admitted to feeling anxious, rather than by weighting each item for severity. Each affirmative reply scored one point, making a maximum of 23.

The results of the first testing (when the pupils had been in school for between a few days and two months) are shown in Table 18.1.

TABLE 18.1 *Mean anxiety score by school and occupational class (age 11 plus)*

Schools project

	Pupils*	Class 1		Class 2		Class 3		Classes 4 and 5		All classes
		N		N		N		N		
Girls in girls' schools	275	43	11·63	73	12·20	120	12·86	35	14·40	12·63
Girls in mixed schools	275	42	10·81	70	11·88	116	13·01	45	12·22	12·27
Boys in boys' schools	278	30	11·23	98	10·98	117	12·45	29	12·79	11·83
Boys in mixed schools	275	33	10·45	66	10·74	136	11·87	38	11·26	11·38
All schools	1,103	148	11·05	307	11·43	489	12·52	147	12·60	12·03

Header above table: Fathers' occupational class

* Includes a few unclassifiable pupils.

With each sex the mixed schools have the lower score, this being consistent through all parental occupational classes except for girls of class 3 (skilled manual). Taking the classes separately none of the differences between mixed and single-sex schools is statistically significant for the boys (though the *t* ratio is substantial), and for the girls the only significant difference is the greater anxiety of girls in classes 4/5 in girls' schools compared with those in mixed schools. The consistency of the trend in favour of the mixed schools is so strong, however (seven out of eight differences are in this direction), that it is certainly of interest.[1]

Arithmetic

Questions 2, 3, 8 and 19 were on anxiety about arithmetic. Here the scores of girls in girls' schools and those in mixed schools were unexpectedly almost identical, while for the boys there was a surprisingly highly significant difference in favour of those in mixed schools (see Table 18.2).

TABLE 18.2 *Responses to questions on anxiety about arithmetic (age 11 plus)*

Schools project

	Anxious	Not anxious
Girls in girls' schools	610	500
Girls in mixed schools	603	510
Boys in boys' schools	597	518
Boys in mixed schools	535	579

The pupils of every occupational class contributed to this difference between the boys' groups. In the mixed schools the boys showed a clear increase of anxiety about arithmetic as occupational class became lower, apart from the lowest class (but the difference between extreme classes was statistically significant), with a similar but slighter and more irregular trend in boys' schools.

School (sub-analysis)

Another four questions (4, 5, 20 and 21) had been pre-selected as the more important ones reflecting anxiety about school in general, as compared with those indicating difficulty with work, etc. Here the girls from mixed schools had a significantly lower anxiety score, but the difference between boys, though favouring mixed schools, was not statistically significant (see Table 18.3). These findings are not stressed as the pupils had been at the school only a short time and it cannot be definitely stated that this greater anxiety of the pupils from single-sex schools was not present on entry. In view of the slightly superior entry to the latter (in social class and intelli-

[1] Even though analysis of variance (discarding one-fifth of the group to secure even numbers) yields a non-significant result.

gence) and the whole tenor of this research, the writer's opinion is that the most likely explanation is to be found in a more congenial 'reception' atmosphere, on the average, in the mixed schools.

TABLE 18.3 *Responses to questions on anxiety about school in general (age 11 plus)*

Schools project

	Anxious	Not anxious
Girls in girls' schools	424	676
Girls in mixed schools	379	721
Boys in boys' schools	442	667
Boys in mixed schools	405	691

The longitudinal sample

We pass on to consider the *change* in anxiety about school, i.e. as measured by the whole test, experienced (or recorded) between the two testings. This sample is smaller because of pupils who had left, were absent or, for a variety of reasons, did not arrive at the testing room, and because changes in school organization caused the withdrawal of six schools. The results were at first puzzling. The co-educated boys were at the start rather less anxious about school than those in boys' schools and were also slightly less anxious two years later, but the gap had narrowed; neither the gap nor the slight change was statistically significant. The two girls' groups started with the same average score, but two years later those in girls' schools were slightly less anxious than those in mixed schools, though again the differences between the groups and the change in average scores were quite unreliable. Nor did the results present a regular pattern for each occupational class—both boys and girls of classes 4 and 5 in mixed schools being appreciably less anxious about school than those from single-sex schools, while the closing of the gap in the boys' case was due largely to pupils from the clerical occupational class. The most notable feature was the high consistency in the decline in recorded anxiety between the ages 11 plus and 13 plus for pupils from both groups (see Table A.28).

An exhaustive analysis of the data showed several likely reasons for this departure from the usual trend. One of these held good for most age groups of boys and girls in the research, namely that in spite of the matching of the schools for social background the pupils of the single-sex schools were of rather higher social class than those from the co-educational schools;[1] the girls from girls' schools were also slightly higher in intelligence (see Tables A.1 and A.2 in Appendix 2). Both these factors would be operating to increase the anxiety of the co-educated pupils, thereby handicapping the co-educational schools in a straight comparison with single-sex ones. The study itself shows a persistent tendency for anxiety to school scores to increase from occupational class 1 to occupational classes 4 and 5.[2] On the other hand, a breakdown of the data by occupational class showed that the decrease in recorded anxiety in the two years was slightly greater for boys' and girls' schools in three out of the four occupational class groups when these were separated out, though each of these sub-groups would still contain a slight advantage in intelligence level on the girls' school side.

The likelihood that anxiety would also be increased when I.Q. is lower is substantiated by a number of studies already referred to in Chapter 9 (McCandless, 1956a, b; Sarason, 1960; Cowen, 1965), but in this *longitudinal* sample only the comparison between the girls in co-educational and girls' schools is affected, as the boys' groups have almost the same average I.Q. Additional evidence illustrating this tendency in the case of the girls has already been given in the chapter on unhappy girls.

A third factor played a part when the groups were compared at the first and at the second testing, namely a curious imbalance in the drop-out problem. The drop-outs are those who were reported by the heads as left or absent and those who for any other reason failed to appear in the test room (see Table A.29). The twenty-five girl drop-outs from co-educational schools had an average anxiety score at the first testing which was markedly below that for the whole group, while the average for the twenty-one from girls' schools was well above that of their group. Remarkably, the same held good for the boys, and in neither instance was it due to a few extreme cases, but reflected a general tendency. Whatever the reason for this it disturbs the representativeness of the sample, placing the co-educational schools at a disadvantage.

An examination of the results of individual questions revealed that these were pulling in different ways. Taking the four questions pre-selected for special study in the first testing (full sample) we now find that with the boys in this longitudinal study there is a decided fall in the number in boys' schools who became frightened

[1] Equality for girls aged 15 plus in 1964 in the *longitudinal* sample.

[2] The difference between occupational class 1 and classes 4/5 combined is smaller for co-educational schools and not statistically significant for their girls or boys, but it is almost significant for boys in boys' schools and reaches significance for girls in girls' schools.

when the teacher was cross and this brings them equal with the boys from co-educational schools at the second testing.[1] Similarly with the item on 'often worrying about school' there was less increase for the pupils in boys' schools, bringing them below the opposite group (this of course would include those who worried about work). On the other hand the boys from boys' schools showed a greater increase in pupils who said they hated having to go back to school when they had been away (not quite statistically significant), and less reduction in those who thought that coming back to school after the holidays was frightening. The change for the co-educated boys on this last item was statistically highly significant. This question was the only one of the four in which there was also a decided change in the position of the girls' groups, the girls' schools registering no change in the number of 'frightened' pupils, while the co-educated girls, who started with a score equal to that of their opposite numbers, had a large reduction.[2] The results from this item, from both boys and girls, may have some connection with the finding that discipline is more strict in single-sex schools. Though the *rates of decrease* amongst the two girls' groups to the item 'I hate having to go back to school when I've been away' are similar, rather fewer of the 13-year-old co-educational girls than those from girls' schools endorsed the statement at the second testing.

To summarize, the results of the first testing of the whole sample at 11 plus tended to favour the co-educational schools both in the test as a whole, and in the sections on anxiety towards arithmetic and on anxiety towards teachers, but the longitudinal study's raw scores on the complete test have a slightly opposite tendency though this is statistically unreliable and not consistent for all social classes or all items. It should also be noted that when an analysis was made of each of the four pre-selected questions on anxiety towards teachers, the only statistically significant changes in anxiety were recorded by the co-educated boys who showed a decided reduction in the proportion who said they were frightened at going back to school (a change highly significant); by the boys from boys' schools in the reduced proportion who were frightened when the teacher was cross and by the co-educated girls in the reduction in the proportion of pupils frightened at the idea of going back to school. There was also a nearly significant change statistically among the boys from boys' schools in the increased proportion

[1] Those wishing to study the figures should refer to Table A.30. The drop in the score of the boys from boys' schools is significant at the ·025 level. (This Chi-square used as data the *change* in individuals' scores.)

[2] The reduction for the co-educated girls was statistically significant (by Chi-square allowing for correlation).

of those who hated having to go back to school. The scores at 13 plus for the whole test still showed the co-educated boys slightly less anxious than their opposite numbers, but there is a somewhat greater advantage for girls in girls' schools over those in co-educational schools, neither difference approaching reliability. Evidence has been put forward, however, to show that the girls in girls' schools decreased their scores over questions connected with work, while the scores of the co-educated girls decreased more with items concerning school in general.

We must remember that differences between the groups in average intelligence (girls only), parental occupational class and the type of 'drop-out' pupil all placed the co-educational pupils under a handicap. Further interpretation is given at the end of this juniors' section.

THE MOONEY PROBLEM CHECK LIST

In the Schools project all pupils completed a Mooney Problem Check List.[1] This is a schedule of 210 personal problems, from which the pupils selected any which were troubling them. These are classified into seven problem areas of thirty items each, from 'school' to 'home and family', 'boy–girl problems' and 'people in general'. Examples of the items in the 'school' area are, 'Trouble with mathematics', 'Afraid of failing', 'Too much homework', 'Don't like school', 'Afraid to speak up in class', 'Not getting along with a teacher'. It is with this 'school' section that we are principally concerned, but a brief analysis is made of the test results as a whole and these are also given in tabular form in Appendix 2 (Tables A.31 and A.32). We are here concerned with the longitudinal sample.

The data for the juniors were divided into parental occupational class groups, namely classes 1 and 2 (managerial etc. and white-collar), class 3 (skilled manual) and classes 4 and 5 (semi-skilled and unskilled). As there are seven problem areas this produced 21 mean scores for each type of school for each sex. Of the total of 42 means for boys, 37 rose from age 11 to 13, the number of problems recorded by boys from boys' schools rising rather less than those recorded by the co-educated boys,[2] *except about school*, where the trend was slightly reversed. If we suppose there were 100 boys in each school, 17 of those in boys' schools indicated an increase of one more problem about school compared with the boys

[1] An anglicized version prepared by the writer in conjunction with the N.F.E.R.

[2] The difference between the two boys' groups at age 13, for *all* problems, favoured the boys in boys' schools, but was far from statistically significant.

in co-educational schools, the average number of problems per boy being about four at the first testing and six at the second. Without exception the 21 means of the co-educated boys rose as the occupational class became lower. A result of such a consistent trend is rare and future researchers will need to watch this variable carefully in many kinds of research projects in schools.

For the junior girls in all problem areas for every occupational class, and in both types of school, there is a marked increase of recorded problems between the ages of 11 and 13. The greater intellectual capability (e.g. of speed, of reading and of underlining problem items) of the 13-year-olds might have accounted for some of this, but it is unlikely to be the whole explanation. In five of the seven problem areas the increase of mention between 11 and 13 years of age is slightly less for the sample from girls' schools; in one area (people in general) there is virtual equality of increase, the *school area again being exceptional,* the co-educated girls registering a smaller increase in problems than did the girls from girls' schools. The size of this difference is about the same as that found with the boys.[1] In both co-educational and girls' schools there was a tendency for the girls' means for the two higher occupational classes to be lower than those for classes 4 and 5.

For both boys and girls problems relating to the opposite sex increased slightly more in the co-educational schools than in the single-sex, but this was not consistently maintained within all three occupational class groupings. The problem area showing the largest differences between the two groups in the increase of problems reported was 'home and family', where both girls and boys in the co-educational group had a bigger increase than those educated in single-sex schools. This is in line with the larger proportion of lower-class pupils in the co-educational schools.

As one of the items in the Mooney was similar to one in the questionnaire, it was examined separately for the girls. It was 'School is too strict'; the results are in Table 18.4, the girls in girls' schools being more positive about this than those in mixed schools. This is, of course, the view of the consumers; those making the rules probably have different ideas. Those reporting the school as 'too strict' were, however, only a small proportion of the total (one-fifth in the girls' schools).

A similar examination of the item 'don't like school' for the junior boys groups (longitudinal) at the second testing gave fewer co-educated boys agreeing with the item than boys from boys' schools, but the difference was too small to be reliable.

In a separate section the Mooney 'test' asked pupils, 'What problems are troubling you *most?*' They were instructed to 'write about

[1] Not statistically significant.

TABLE 18.4 *'School is too strict'**

Girls aged 13 plus, longitudinal sample

	Girls in co-educational schools	Girls in girls' schools
Agree	26	42
Disagree	189	173
	215	215

* The difference is statistically significant.

two or three of these if you care to'. Under no circumstances were they pressed to do this, but many pupils gave one or two. (They had been told not to put their names on the tests, which would be read by no-one except the researchers.) We might have expected that the total number of these serious problems would rise sharply between the ages of 11 and 13, but this was true of only the boys. For the juniors, the co-educated boys had slightly fewer serious problems than the boys in boys' schools, including 'boy–girl relationships', but the differences were small except in problems about school, where a negligible initial difference (9 co-educated boys picking out some aspect of school as a special problem compared with 13 in boys' schools) became one of 68 to 84 at age 13.[1] This is the area of greatest change for both sets of boys.

Sub-classification of the problems about school (now allowing more than one problem per pupil in the few cases where these fell into different sub-categories) revealed that the problems were predominantly concerned with work and examinations (about 80 per cent) in both types of school. Poor relationships with teachers or dislike of the school in general were singled out as special problems by only 2.2 per cent of the pupils in the co-educational schools and only 5.5 per cent in boys' schools. In the former these form one-fifteenth of all the special problems recorded in this detailed examination of school problems and in the boys' schools one-eighth, but as numbers recording these personal problems were small the data is not mentioned as being statistically of importance in its own right.[2]

[1] The difference between the groups at the age of 13 is almost statistically significant.
[2] The difference between the two groups of boys in the proportions recording personal relationship problems is, however, not far from statistical significance.

268

As indicated above, a large majority of the problems, in both types of school, were about work, e.g.:

'Not spending enough time in study.'

'My most troubling problem is not getting high enough marks in exams. I am afraid that I will go to the wrong stream and then I will not be able to do what I like when I grow up.'

'Worried about school etc. and about subjects I don't like such as Maths.'

'Getting low marks when my parents expect me to do better.'

Those about pupil–teacher relations are illustrated by:

'Need more younger teachers. Old-fashioned teachers are no good because they do not understand us.'

'I am worried about being nervous when trying a test. The teachers do not help matters as some of them act as if they are in charge of a concentration camp, they do not look happy, have sad faces and they grumble to themselves.'

'I don't like school very much because it is too strict. Some masters keep whole forms in when only one boy has misbehaved.'

'School is too strict. You should be able to have more freedom.'

One amusing reply came from a co-educated boy: 'The school is too patriotic, i.e. we have to play Rugby when we would rather play football.'

The junior girls did not show the sharp rise in special problems between the two testings which was shown by the boys. The co-educated girls recorded the larger number of *special* problems[1] at both ages, though the opposite was the case when they were concerned with *all problems* (whether 'special' or not). The differences between the two girls' groups came largely from the 'home and family' section. The girls' schools recorded fewer 'boy–girl' special problems at 13 plus, and under 'school' they also had a minimal advantage, far from statistically significant. Both results were again the opposite to the results of the larger Mooney test and must therefore be viewed with some caution, especially as the co-educated girls have distinctly the better result when the number of special 'school' problems for each of the two groups is expressed as a percentage of its total number of special problems. As with the boys the problems are mainly about work and tests etc., those about personal relations at school being rare. We must remember, however, that young pupils, particularly girls, might be reluctant to

[1] See Table A.32a in Appendix 2.

put such problems down on paper as they might be afraid of staff or head seeing these. (For example one headmistress stayed for some time in the test room of the writer's research assistant, although it had been made clear that this might affect the results.)

THE HIGH SCHOOL PERSONALITY QUESTIONNAIRE

All pupils in the Schools project were also given the High School Personality Questionnaire (H.S.P.Q.), and a longitudinal sample consisted of all those who had completed it both in 1964 and 1966. The test yields scores on fourteen personality dimensions, but in this chapter we are dealing only with anxiety, the score for which is a composite of several of these fourteen 'source traits'. The whole test is essentially a self-rating questionnaire, containing items such as 'Do your hands sometimes tremble and your heart beat fast when you get excited about speaking up in class?' There is a choice of three replies: Yes/Perhaps/No. In this case we are not able to derive a score about 'anxiety to school' alone.

The longitudinal samples of junior boys had almost identical scores for the two types of school at the first testing; two years later, at age 13, the boys' schools showed a larger increase in anxiety[1] (see Table A.33). Occupational class 3, however, had a slightly opposite tendency. The junior girls also started off with similar mean scores and like the boys' schools, the girls' schools increased their anxiety score more than the co-educational, but the difference was small and not statistically significant; nor were the results for the separate occupational class groups at all consistent.

Summary (juniors)

The overall analysis is complicated. Clearly no dramatic differences in anxiety between junior pupils of co-educational and single-sex schools have been shown to exist. With regard to the boys the most interesting feature is that in the Mooney Problem Check List the problems recorded by boys in the co-educational schools increase more than those of the boys in boys' schools in every area *except that of the school*, where they increase less. Surprisingly the H.S.P.Q. test shows the boys from boys' schools increasing more in their score on *general* anxiety than those from co-educational schools, but all these differences are small. Readers should note, however, that the Mooney tends to emphasize the statement of problems by the pupil, while the H.S.P.Q. emphasizes

[1] The difference between the changes in scores for the two groups from age 11-plus to age 13-plus is almost statistically significant ($t = 1.77$), allowing for correlation within each group.

Anxiety about school

his anxiety towards them. The powerful influence of occupational class is to be seen throughout the tables, e.g. the differences in score between 11 plus and 13 plus for the co-educational boys in the Mooney test increase consistently with occupational class in all areas in 13 out of the 14 possible comparisons. This is a built-in handicap for the co-educational schools in comparison with the single-sex, though it is not a necessary concomitant of co-education.

The picture is much the same for the girls. In the two tests about general anxiety the differences between the co-educated and pupils from girls' schools are small and are built up from a number of forces which pull in opposite directions. As opposed to the slight advantage of the girls' school in the Boxall test of anxiety to school (longitudinal sample only) we have the fact that in the Mooney Problem Check List it was only in the area of school problems that the co-educated pupils had a smaller increase than the opposing group. It is noteworthy that in the case both of boys and girls it is in the 'home and family' section that the single-sex schools gain their biggest advantage, and one would expect this from their higher social class.

The score on anxiety to school (Boxall test) appears to be built up of several factors which research needs to separate out. It looks especially as if a distinction needs to be made between anxiety about academic progress in school (of several kinds), and anxiety about relationships with people—either staff or pupils. The sub-analysis of items concerned with fear of teachers, being frightened of school, etc., gives a distinct advantage to the co-educational schools, which means they are losing somewhere else, and this is likely to be in the area of academic work, where the lower social class of their pupils, and, with the girls, their lower average I.Q. would of themselves be likely to lead to greater anxiety about school. In the chapter on unhappy girls this factor is shown to be of importance in co-educational schools. In this comparison we should again keep in mind the peculiarly one-sided nature of the drop-out problem.

There are some suggestions—but not proof—in the data that co-education reduces worry about boy–girl problems for boys, but has little effect in this way for girls. This also needs further research, with special regard (once again) to the different occupational class composition of the two types of school.

The seniors

THE MOONEY PROBLEM CHECK LIST

Senior boys

The senior pupils were not given the modified Boxall test. The results from the Mooney Problem Check List had some interesting features (Table A.34). With the boys there was a consistent fall in the average number of problems recorded in each of the seven areas of problems, in each of the two[1] occupational class divisions, for the boys from both types of school—28 averages in all— between 15 and 17 years of age.[2] (Note that these pupils are in a sense specially selected since they chose to stay at school till at least 17.) The average number of problems recorded by the co-educated boys of 15, rather lower than that of the boys in boys' schools[3] (except for small differences in the opposite direction for 'boy–girl relationship' and 'school'), fell slightly more than the scores of the latter, the most favourable change for the co-educated boys being the comparative falls in the two problem areas mentioned.[4] For occupational classes 1 and 2 combined, five of the means (out of 7) fell more in the co-educational sample, with two the reverse, while for occupational classes 3, 4 and 5 combined the two samples differed little in the incidence of change. In every one of the seven problem areas the co-educated boys recorded fewer problems at age 17[5] than did those from the boys' schools, though the averages for *school* problems were not far from equality.

In reply to the question, 'What problems are worrying you *most*?' the same general tendency was continued, the co-educated boys indicating clearly fewer problems in overall total at both 15 and 17 years of age.[6] This was most marked in school problems and continued in 'boy–girl relationships',[7] but there was also an unexpected

---

[1] Here classes 1 and 2 are combined and 3 with 4 and 5.

[2] Statistically significant, by analysis of variance; (and also for girls).

[3] Substantial but not statistically significant ($t = 1.394$).

[4] The analysis of variance for the 'school' problems section showed also a significant sex difference with girls recording fewer problems, but the difference between co-educated boys and those from boys' schools was not statistically significant. The sex difference, however, could conceivably have been affected by a systematic difference in the administration of the tests for the two sexes—there being a different administrator for each. (The research was not assessing sex differences.)

[5] The overall difference approached significance ($t = 1.582$).

[6] Almost statistically significant at 15 plus but not at 17 plus.

[7] Not statistically significant for boy–girl relationships at 15 plus or 17 plus.

272

difference in the same direction for 'Home and Family'. The differences were maintained in each of the occupational class groups.

Senior girls

The same trends are to be seen when we examine the results of the senior girls in the main test (Table A.35). The co-educated girls had very slightly more problems in total at 15 years of age, mostly from the sections 'people in general', 'home and family', and 'work and future', but this was slightly reversed in 'school' problems, with an equality under 'boy–girl'.[1] By the age of 17 plus however, the co-educated girls were appreciably lower in overall total, and lower in all the problem areas except 'people in general' where there was equality. Easily the largest difference between the two types of school in the seven problem sections at the age of 17 *was that of 'school'*[2] and this was also an area in which the change over the two years was the second most favourable to the co-educated girls, the most favourable being 'people in general' (though, as indicated above, the *change* in this last category produced only equality).

A detailed examination of the answers to the four pre-selected items which emphasized 'the school in general' or personal relationships, rather than work, produced fewer co-educated girls who said they were 'not getting along with a teacher'[3] and fewer who thought the school too strict.[4]

Strangely, when these girls were asked to write down those problems which troubled them most, the co-educated girls indicated more in total than did the girls from girls' schools both at 15 and 17 years of age, though the difference had been halved in the two years.[5] It is possible that the co-educated girls were less inhibited about writing the problems down—perhaps less afraid of the consequences if the tests were seen by staff! However, in the 'school' problem section there was equality at age 17, and the co-educated girls had very slightly more problems in the 'boy–girl' area, though this was far from statistically reliable. The principal areas where the girls from girls' schools recorded fewer special problems at 17 years of age were 'people in general' and 'money, work and the future'. In the 'school' problems the co-educated girls recorded more at 15 years[6] and the same as the girls from girls'

[1] None of these differences approached statistical significance.
[2] This verges on statistical significance.
[3] Highly significant at 15 plus and significant at 17 plus.
[4] Not statistically significant at 15 plus but highly significant at 17 plus.
[5] Neither difference reaches statistical significance. See Table A.35a.
[6] Far from statistically significant.

schools at 17 years. In both years these school problems were a slightly lower percentage of the total number of problems for the co-educated group. A detailed analysis of these special school problems, for both co-educated girls and those from girls' schools, yielded a very high proportion of problems directly concerned with school work and examinations, and few about personal relations with teachers. There were no distinct differences between the two types of school in the nature of the special *school* problems.

THE HIGH SCHOOL PERSONALITY QUESTIONNAIRE

In the High School Personality Questionnaire[1] the co-educated senior boys had lower *general anxiety* scores both at 15[2] and at 17 years of age than those at boys' schools; this trend was consistent for both occupational classes, but the *rate of change* favoured the boys' schools, though it was too small to be reliable. Readers are again reminded that this measure of anxiety includes, for example, worry about work as well as about personal relationships, and one of the forces to be considered would be the influence of the lower social class of the co-educated boys in increasing their general anxiety as they approached their important external examinations.

The senior co-educated girls, like the co-educated boys, had lower general anxiety scores both at 15 and at 17[3] years of age, and this was clearly to be seen in each of the occupational class groupings. With the feminine sex, however, the rate of change quite strongly favoured the co-educated girls, the gap between the two types of school being greater at 17 plus than at 15 plus.[4] The co-educational schools had the more favourable rate of change in both occupational classes of this age group.

The finding that the difference in favour of the co-educated girls is greater than that in the case of the co-educated boys (as contrasted with the respective single-sex schools), is in conformity with the trend found at numerous points in these inquiries.

[1] A scientifically constructed American paper and pencil test designed to measure 14 personality factors.
[2] Substantial, but only that for the 15-year-olds reaches the accepted level of significance.
[3] The difference between the co-educated girls and those from girls' schools at age 17 is statistically highly significant.
[4] The difference between the changes in anxiety score for the two types of school (i.e. in the extent of change) is statistically highly significant. ($t = 3 \cdot 002$ allowing for correlation.)

Summary (Seniors)

Among the seniors the co-educated boys showed themselves less anxious both in the main part of the Mooney test and in the section where they were asked about their special problems, but the difference between them and the boys from boys' schools was found to be not statistically significant.[1] The co-educated boys also recorded a rather greater reduction in anxiety between the ages of 15 plus and 17—again not large enough to be statistically reliable, but counter to the trend one would expect from the comparative occupational class distributions of the two samples.

In the H.S.P.Q. test the co-educated boys also had lower scores on general anxiety at 15 and at 17 years of age, but in this case the rate of decrease slightly favoured the boys' schools, though the same qualifying remarks apply as with the Mooney test.

Viewing the results as a whole the co-educated girls were rather less anxious than those from girls' schools especially in the area with which we are most concerned—school, and a more detailed examination of that area showed that the difference was most marked in personal relationships at school. This finding was at first masked by other sources of anxiety such as, in the broad field, anxiety about home and in the narrow area of 'school' by factors such as anxiety about work, which would be accentuated in the co-educational sample by lower social class and lower average intelligence. The finding is in complete agreement with the relevant sections of the other surveys, such as 'happiness in school', 'school atmosphere', and 'friendliness of teachers' and the detailed investigation into 'unhappy pupils'. It should not, however, be exaggerated, as the difference between the two samples in anxiety in general, or even in anxiety towards school in general, is not large.

[1] By analysis of variance.

19

Neuroticism and introversion–extroversion

In addition to the data on anxiety the paper and pencil tests yielded scores on many other personality characteristics, notably on neuroticism and introversion–extroversion. The two latter scores were obtained from the High School Personality Questionnaire and the Maudsley Personality Inventory. The tests were administered by the writer and his research assistant to the sample of pupils in schools (Schools project). Throughout the chapter we shall be concerned with the longitudinal sample, i.e. those pupils who appeared for testing on both the first and the second occasion two years later.

It is undeniable that normally heredity and the home environment will exert the most powerful influence on the personality characteristics of an individual, but the part played by the school may be far from negligible though we know surprisingly little about it from research evidence. Since co-educational and single-sex grammar schools differ substantially as communities—in happiness, atmosphere, discipline, teacher–pupil relationship—it is possible that they may exert different effects on the personality characteristics of the individuals composing them. When comparing the scores of the two types of schools on such characteristics special attention needs to be paid to two other variables which may affect the comparison—the comparative intelligence levels of the groups and the occupational class of the fathers.

Neuroticism

BOYS

The boys' scores on neuroticism, as measured by the High School Personality Questionnaire, are given in Tables 19.1 and 19.2. At age 11 the boys in the co-educational schools had a marginally lower score than those in boys' schools, but by age 13 the difference had increased and become statistically significant ($\cdot$05 level). This does not signify that the boys from boys' schools were neurotic—

TABLE 19.1 *Neuroticism scores — junior boys*

H.S.P.Q.

Age	Schools	Class 1		Class 2		Class 3		Classes 4 and 5		All*	
		N	Mean	N	Mean	N	Mean	N	Mean	N	Mean
11+	Co-ed.	28	22·19	57	23·72	106	22·61	34	23·16	226	22·93
	Boys'	27	23·64	78	22·62	88	23·64	24	22·23	220	23·13
13+	Co-ed.	28	20·19	57	21·67	106	20·78	34	20·79	226	20·94
	Boys'	27	23·33	78	21·34	88	21·93	24	20·79	220	21·82

NOTE: At age 13 plus the co-educated boys have a statistically significant lower neuroticism score overall, but this is not consistent for all social classes.

TABLE 19.2 *Neuroticism scores — senior boys*

H.S.P.Q.

Age	Schools	Classes 1 and 2		Classes 3, 4 and 5		All*	
		N	Mean	N	Mean	N	Mean
15+	Co-ed.	56	20·71	77	20·85	134	20·83
	Boys'	70	22·47	67	22·11	137	22·29
17+	Co-ed.	56	19·81	77	20·28	134	20·11
	Boys'	70	21·35	67	21·03	137	21·20

* Includes some unclassifiable.

NOTE: At age 15 the co-educated boys had a statistically significant lower neuroticism score, but the gap had closed a little by 17 plus and was then not quite statistically significant.

merely that they had a rather higher score than the co-educated boys on this long scale which runs from 'unduly stable' to 'highly neurotic'.

At age 15 the co-educated boys of the middle school had lower scores for neuroticism than did the boys in boys' schools and the difference was again statistically significant; but the gap between the two samples had narrowed a little by the time they were 17 years of age and now was not quite statistically significant. The overall result of the testing at the four ages shows a clear trend towards rather lower neuroticism scores among the co-educated boys; this seems to differ from the finding of Furneaux (1961) but it should be noted that his was an incidental finding which did not examine other variables which might have had an influence, such as the average intelligence level of the students from the two types of school. In the present longitudinal sample, however, these scores are nearly equal for the boys, though not for the girls.

It should be noticed also that in this partly controlled situation there is no steady trend among the boys for neuroticism scores to increase as the occupational class of the father becomes lower. This is in contrast to the trend in anxiety scores which was commented on in the previous chapter.

As a second measure of neuroticism the Maudsley Personality Inventory was administered to the 15-year-old boys and two years later to the same group again (Table 19.3).

TABLE 19.3 *Boys' neuroticism—mean scores* (*Maudsley*)

Age	Schools	Classes 1 and 2		Classes 3, 4 and 5		All*	
		N	Mean	N	Mean	N	Mean
15+	Co-ed.	56	26·18	77	25·27	134	25·76
	Boys'	70	26·41	67	29·09	137	27·72
17+	Co-ed.	56	26·16	77	25·84	134	26·05
	Boys'	70	26·06	67	29·16	137	27·58

* Includes some unclassifiable.

As in the H.S.P.Q. test the boys from the boys' schools have the higher neuroticism score at age 15, but the difference between this and the score of the co-educated boys was on this occasion a little short of statistical significance ($t=1·754$). Taking classes 3, 4 and 5 alone, however, the co-educated boys had a statistically significant lower neuroticism score. At 17 years of age the co-educated boys still had the lower score, but the difference between the two groups was slightly reduced, being on the verge of statistical significance for students from occupational classes 3, 4 and 5, but negligible for classes 1 and 2.

We also find that in the boys' schools the neuroticism scores of the senior boys on this Maudsley test (at ages 15 and 17) increases as the father's occupational class becomes lower, but there is a smaller trend in the opposite direction in the co-educational schools. It is by no means the first time in these inquiries that there have been hints in the data that pupils of occupational classes 4 and 5 seem to react a little differently in co-educational as compared with single-sex schools. On the other hand the occupational class trend in the Maudsley is not confirmed by the results of the previous test (H.S.P.Q.) though the latter is admittedly a non-specialized test and therefore less reliable.

GIRLS

The girls' neuroticism scores on the High School Personality Questionnaire are given in Tables 19.4 and 19.5.

TABLE 19.4 *Neuroticism—mean scores (H.S.P.Q.)*

Junior girls

		Class 1		Class 2		Class 3		Classes 4 and 5		All*	
Age	Schools	N	Mean	N	Mean	N	Mean	N	Mean	N	Mean
11 +	Co-ed.	32	21·82	60	21·89	80	22·87	43	22·65	215	22·40
	Girls'	37	22·21	59	23·00	90	22·93	29	23·25	218	22·87
13 +	Co-ed.	32	20·67	60	20·11	80	20·66	43	21·93	215	20·76
	Girls'	37	20·26	59	20·75	90	20·40	29	21·23	218	20·59

TABLE 19.5 *Neuroticism—mean scores (H.S.P.Q.)*

Senior girls

		Classes 1 and 2		Classes 3, 4 and 5		All*	
Age	Schools	N	Mean	N	Mean	N	Mean
15 +	Co-ed.	61	21·81	54	20·77	115	21·32
	Girls'	61	21·41	59	20·67	121	21·02
17 +	Co-ed.	61	21·66	54	20·79	115	21·25
	Girls'	61	21·96	59	20·46	121	21·25

* Includes some unclassifiable.

Table 19.4 shows that the co-educated girls had rather lower neuroticism scores when aged 11 and that this was maintained in every occupational class,[1] but two years later the average of the girls from girls' schools was very slightly lower[2] than that of the co-educated girls and consistent for three occupational class groups but not for class 2. In Table 19.5 the senior girls' groups reverse this process, those from girls' schools starting at age 15 with slightly lower neuroticism scores than the co-educated (non-significant), and finishing up at 17 years of age with identical

[1] Not statistically significant.
[2] Far from statistically significant.

averages overall and inconsistent differences within the two social class groups.

The results from the more specialized test—the Maudsley—do not change the picture much; they give the co-educated girls a slightly lower average score for neuroticism both at 15 and 17 years of age, but the difference is too small to be reliable and is again inconsistent for the two occupational class groups (Table A.36).

The overall picture, therefore, is that both junior and senior boys in the sample of twelve co-educational schools were lower in neuroticism score than their counterparts in boys' schools, but for the girls the emphasis must be on the near equality of the two groups.

Introversion–extroversion

The same two tests yielded also measures of introversion–extroversion, and the writer was interested in seeing whether the two types of school had any clearly discernible and consistent influence on the pupils in this direction. It could be theorized, for example, that educating the two sexes together would make them less shy of each other and perhaps more extroverted; on the other hand we have seen from this study that *deprivation* of the company of the opposite sex may be a strong driving force impelling pupils to overcome such shyness. Little work has been done on these and related topics, and the writer has been working on such a variety of problems relating to co-education that he does not pretend to have done more here than make a preliminary survey. As the results do not show clear and consistent differences between the co-educational and single-sex schools they are presented concisely and with little comment.

BOYS

The co-educated junior boys were slightly more extroverted as measured by the H.S.P.Q. than the boys from boys' schools, both at 11 and 13 years of age, but the differences were in the opposite direction for children from both occupational classes 2 and 4/5, and were therefore lacking in consistency and reliability (Table A.37). In the case of senior boys the scores of the opposing groups were virtually equal both at 15 and 17 years of age.

When tested by the Maudsley Personality Inventory the extroversion scores of the senior boys from boys' schools at 15 years of age were slightly higher than those of the co-educated boys, though the difference was far from statistically reliable and at 17 years of age had virtually disappeared. The distribution of scores was similar for the two groups, both at 15 and at 17 years of age and they threw up approximately the same number of high scorers (scores over 39).

GIRLS

The junior co-educated girls were slightly more extroverted than those from the girls' schools at 11 years of age as measured by the H.S.P.Q., but by the time they were 13 years old the difference was minimal. There were no consistent occupational class trends (Table A.38). The two senior girls' groups recorded almost the same average score at 15 years of age and two years later the girls from girls' schools were slightly more extroverted. Here there was a slight tendency for the extroversion scores of the girls from occupational classes 1 and 2 to be lower than those of girls from classes 3, 4 and 5 (Table A.39).

The picture obtained from the Maudsley test for the senior girls emphasized this occupational class trend without reaching a difference which was statistically reliable. The 15-year-old girls

TABLE 19.6 *Introversion–extroversion—mean scores*
      (*Maudsley*)

Senior girls

Age	Schools	Classes 1 and 2		Classes 3, 4 and 5		All*	
		N	Mean	N	Mean	N	Mean
15 +	Co-ed.	61	27·80	54	29·72	115	28·70
	Girls'	61	30·15	59	30·02	121	30·07
17 +	Co-ed.	61	27·67	54	30·11	115	28·82
	Girls'	61	29·92	59	31·56	121	30·71

* Includes some unclassifiable.

from girls' schools were rather more extroverted than the co-educated girls and this difference had increased a little two years later (Table 19.6). Once again, however, the variability of score within each group was so high that we cannot rely on the clear difference between the groups being reproduced at another testing. It is true that for this group of senior girls the difference was obtained in both the tests and at ages 15 and 17, and this is strong support for the reliability of the result. On the other hand no such difference between the co-educated and single-sex educated groups

281

of junior girls was found either when 11 or when 13 years old. There was approximately the same number of high scores on both sides at 15 plus, but rather more at girls' schools than at co-educational schools at 17 plus (31 to 21).

Comment

Taking an overall view these tests of introversion–extroversion revealed no decided or consistent difference between the pupils from co-educational schools and those from single-sex schools. This is somewhat fortunate as the interpretation of the significance of such a difference might have been exceptionally difficult. However, the possibly greater extroversion of the senior girls in girls' schools needs further inquiry.

Shyness and leadership

Two of the items on the Maudsley test were pre-selected for a separate analysis of scores because they might have provided an elementary useful lead to research on two of the many problems related to the advantages and disadvantages of co-education, namely shyness in the company of the opposite sex and the possibly reduced opportunities of leadership for girls in co-educational schools.

The first of these questions was, 'Are you inclined to be shy in the presence of the opposite sex?' In none of the four groups of pupils tested—boys aged 15 and aged 17 and two comparable groups of girls—were the differences between co-educated and single-sex educated pupils sufficiently large to be statistically reliable, and most of them were far from being so. Contrary to expectations the 15-year-old boys in boys' schools confessed to being only a little more shy of the opposite sex than did those from co-educational schools, and at 17 years of age there was even a minimal difference in the opposite direction. Rather more co-educated girls than girls from girls' schools said they were shy in the presence of the opposite sex at age 15, but the difference had disappeared two years later. If these small differences in favour of the single-sex schools are confirmed, a tenable theory (as mentioned previously) is that there are conflicting forces at work and depriving each sex of the company of the other acts as a driving force in the overcoming of shyness—a force which may even be stronger than the overcoming of shyness by the natural meeting of the sexes for work at school. However, it should be remembered that the samples of *ex-pupils* are quite sure that mingling with the opposite sex at school helped them with their relationships with members of that sex after they had left school.

The other question was, 'Do you generally prefer to take the lead in group activities?' Again none of the differences between co-educational and single-sex school groups were large enough to be reliable, but the trend was that although at 15 years of age rather more boys from boys' school than from co-educational schools said they preferred to take the lead, this became equality two years later, with co-educational boys from occupational classes 1 and 2 having an advantage. With the girls there was a decided difference between those from different occupational classes, the co-educated girls from classes 1 and 2 being rather more ready to take the lead than their rivals from the girls' schools, but the reverse being the case with girls from occupational classes 3, 4 and 5, this even approaching statistical significance (Table 19.7). Those who do further research into this matter will need to take more account of the nature of the entry into the two types of school. It is, for example, regretted that the merging of the five occupational classes into two may have hidden the real differences of class between co-educational and single-sex schools within these two groups.

The smallness of the numbers within each of the occupational class groupings makes further comment inadvisable except that if additional research confirms that girls of occupational classes 3, 4 and 5 are more reluctant to take the lead in co-educational schools than in girls' schools, then co-educational schools would need to take preventative action as part of their regular policy.

TABLE 19.7 *'Do you generally prefer to take the lead in group activities'*

Maudsley question 28 (senior girls)

	15 plus						17 plus					
	Co-ed. schools			Girls' schools			Co-ed. schools			Girls' schools		
	N*	Yes	No	N*	Yes	No	N*	Yes	No	N*	Yes	No
Social classes 1 and 2	61	19	42	61	15	42	61	25	33	61	19	39
Social classes 3, 4 and 5	54	13	37	59	21	35	54	15	37	59	26	30
Totals	115	32	79	120	36	77	115	40	70	120	45	69

* The totals include a few who marked 'Doubtful'.

20

The amalgamated schools

In the preceding volume it was shown that the students who attended amalgamated schools usually gave rather less favourable estimates relating to these schools than other comparable students gave about the normal co-educational schools they attended. An attempt is made here to summarize the evidence relating to the topic, including that of the first volume *in so far as this involves a comparison with the normal co-educational school.* Throughout the chapter differences between the two types of school are not 'statistically significant' unless this is stated. Some differences which are not statistically significant are mentioned because they form a consistent logical pattern and therefore have an added reliability. As the sample of men from amalgamated schools, however, was only twenty-four their results are not dependable, though they receive some support from the general character of the women's results, where the sample from amalgamated schools numbered ninety-three.

In the earlier research the amalgamated ex-pupils gave a slightly lower estimate for the friendliness of their teachers than did those seniors who were in the other co-educational schools. (Men from amalgamated schools, incidentally, regarded their men teachers as pleasanter than their women teachers to an extent almost statistically significant.)

With regard to discipline there was little difference between the two groups of women, but the men from amalgamated schools provided a much larger proportion of the three 'lax discipline' categories than was warranted by their proportion in the total sample of students from 'co-educational last' schools. The women from amalgamated schools also found their teachers rather less pleasant, including their male teachers, although in reply to another question they considered the presence of male teachers to be as highly favourable as did their parent sample. The corresponding sub-group of men pronounced their men teachers less pleasant than did the other students from normal co-educational schools (though some 83 per cent of the former endorsed the 'fairly pleasant' category or better), but there was very little difference between these groups when they assessed their women teachers. However, in reply to the related item, 'The presence of the opposite sex of teacher has a good influence', the men from amalgamated schools gave less favourable estimates than their opposite numbers.

Readers who would like additional evidence about the effect of amalgamation should consult Chapter 11 of the previous volume (Dale, 1969) where there is a comparison of the estimates of ex-pupils whose single-sex schools became co-educational with those of ex-pupils whose co-educational schools were divided into single-sex ones. This theme would be out of place in this chapter, which is confined to a comparison of the amalgamated with the other co-educational schools.

We have already seen in Chapter 2 that both men and women from amalgamated schools did not give quite as high estimates of their happiness there as the remaining co-educated seniors gave about their schools. In the case of the question on 'school atmosphere the ex-pupils of amalgamated schools considered it to be less pleasant than did the co-educated seniors, the difference being almost statistically significant for men and highly significant for women (Table 20.1).

TABLE 20.1 *School atmosphere: Amalgamated v. other co-educated seniors*

'Both schools' survey

Estimates	Men				Women			
	Normal co-ed. schools		Amalgamated		Normal co-ed. schools		Amalgamated	
	N	%	N	%	N	%	N	%
Very pleasant	35	43·8	8	33·3	109	40·8	24	25·8
Pleasant	39	48·8	10	41·7	117	43·9	44	47·3
Neutral	3	3·7	3	12·5	31	11·6	12	12·9
Rather unpleasant	3	3·7	2	8·3	10	3·7	13	14·0
Very unpleasant	0		1	4·2	0		0	
Totals	80	100	24	100	267	100	93	100

After the survey of pupil–teacher relations followed by the more general 'school atmosphere', we now come to an examination of pupil–pupil relationships, still comparing amalgamated with the normal type of co-educational school. Here the same trends continue. Both male and female ex-pupils from amalgamated schools liked the presence of the opposite sex less than did the ex-pupils from normal co-educational schools, and this difference was statistically significant in both cases.[1] It will avoid misunderstanding if it is pointed out that even in the amalgamated schools some 87 per cent of the women liked the presence of the opposite sex (with only 2 pupils out of 92 disliking it) and 79 per cent of the men similarly (with 2 out of 24 against). However, in answer to the overlapping item, 'The presence of the opposite sex of pupil had a good influence,' the difference between the amalgamated pupils and the rest was not as large, that for the women being slight, though both were still in the same direction.

The question of the influence of the opposite sex was pursued in a little more detail. For example, one of the items asked, 'Do you consider that the influence of the girls on the boys in this school was, in general, Very good/Good/Fairly good/No effect/Bad/Very bad?' For the two men's groups there was little difference between their judgments (92 per cent of the 'amalgamated' men thought the influence to be 'fairly good', 'good' or 'very good'), but the women from amalgamated schools judged the influence of the girls to be not as good as did the women from the rest of the 'co-education last' group (though 70 per cent said 'good', with 20 per cent undecided).

The opposite question about the influence of the boys on the girls again yielded only a little difference between the judgments of *men* from 'amalgamated' and the other co-educational schools, with a slight advantage to the latter. In the case of the *women* those

TABLE 20.2 *Influence of boys on girls*

Both schools survey (women)

Preferences	Normal co-educational schools		Amalgamated schools	
	N	%	N	%
Very good	26	10·1	6	6·6
Good	101	39·2	28	30·7
Fairly good	85	32·9	27	29·7
Neutral	29	11·2	13	14·3
Bad	17	6·6	17	18·7
Very bad	0		0	
Totals	258	100	91	100

NOTE: The difference between the two distributions is statistically significant beyond the ·025 level.

[1] Highly significant for the women and at ·025 level for the men.

from normal co-educational schools were much more sure of the good influence of the boys;[1] but even in the amalgamated schools some 66 per cent of the women ex-pupils placed this influence in the three 'good' categories (see Table 20.2).

To conclude this section the results are presented from two items of the 'Both schools' questionnaire which dig a little deeper into the problem. The first of these was, 'In your co-educational school was the general attitude of most of the pupils (of your own sex) towards the opposite sex "antagonistic"?' The respondents could choose between True/Partly true/False/Doubtful. It will be seen from Table 20.3 that both the women and the men from the amalgamated schools thought the sexes were more antagonistic there than the remaining ex-pupils of other co-educational schools judged to be so in their schools, the differences being statistically significant. The cause would probably be resentment of the 'intruders' and perhaps opposition to drastic change.

TABLE 20.3 *Antagonism between the sexes*

'Both schools' survey

Reply	Men				Women			
	Normal Co-ed. schools		Amalgamated		Normal Co-ed. schools		Amalgamated	
	N	%	N	%	N	%	N	%
True	0	0	0	0	2	0·8	4	4·5
Partly true	5	6·8	10	(41·7)	36	14·3	17	19·3
False	51	69·9	11	(45·8)	163	65·0	48	54·6
Doubtful	17	23·3	3	(12·5)	50	19·9	19	21·6
Totals	73	100	24	100	251	100	88	100

NOTE: The differences between the distributions for the 'normal' and the amalgamated schools are statistically significant for both men and women.

The second item substituted the phrase 'girl/boy-crazy' for 'antagonistic', and in spite of the antagonism (which was true for only one-quarter of the 'amalgamated' women), the women from amalgamated schools were somewhat more boy-crazy at school[2] than were women from normal co-educational schools. There was again little discernible difference between the men's groups. The latter finding is a little surprising but it should be noted that only two of the men (one from each group) gave the extreme answer that it was 'true' the boys were 'girl-crazy', though a quarter of both groups endorsed 'partly true'. (For the boys' schools, the

[1] The difference is statistically significant.
[2] The difference was statistically significant.

answer 'true' was given by nearly 14 per cent of the seniors, while nearly another 50 per cent endorsed 'partly true'.)

From the above items it was an easy transition to the question, 'In which school do you consider the pupils had the healthier attitude towards sex?' The ex-pupils were asked to underline one of the following: Doubtful/Don't know/Single-sex school/Co-educational school. The general results have already been given in another chapter, but here we are interested in the amalgamated schools, who were part of the sample of co-educational schools.

The women from the amalgamated schools produced a distribution of judgments which was almost identical to that of the women who were seniors in other co-educational schools. In both groups some 79 per cent said the pupils in the co-educational schools had the healthier attitude, with only 3 to 5 per cent endorsing girls' schools. The men from amalgamated schools were, however, less certain than those from the other co-educational schools that the pupils in their schools had a healthier attitude than those in their single-sex schools—75 per cent (amalgamated) to 85 per cent (co-educational), the difference between the percentages being made up not by the 'single-sex school' category but under 'doubtful' and 'don't know'.

Finally, was the proportion of pupils who preferred their co-educational school greater among the 'amalgamated' sub-group than among those who attended normal co-educational schools as seniors? This has been reported in Chapter 11 but is summarized here for completeness. The women from the normal co-educational schools were much more certain that they preferred their co-educational school to their girls' school[1] (Table A.20), the preference 'mixed much' being made by 71 per cent of them compared with 60 per cent of those from the amalgamated sample. Again, most of the differences between these percentages did not go to preference for the girls' schools, but were placed in the 'doubtful' or 'don't know' categories.

The men from amalgamated schools had the same trend but the smallness of the numbers made the result statistically not significant (see Table A.20).

Administrators will naturally have realized that the upheaval and resentment occasioned by the sudden combining of two single-sex schools into one co-educational establishment would create problems for some time. The data confirm the existence of these usually temporary problems and suggest perhaps a little more precisely the nature of some of them. The findings indicate that where two junior comprehensive single-sex schools feed a co-educational senior comprehensive school some of these difficulties

[1] The difference being statistically significant.

288

will be perpetuated, and the school may well be less successful on the social and emotional side than would a school where the boys and girls had grown up together—though other influences would play their part.

For male pupils the numbers are small for reliability, yet it looks as if further research might well show that the girls are more affected by such a reorganization than the boys, and women teachers more than the men.

21

Conclusion

As the present volume and its predecessor *Mixed or Single-sex School?* are separate parts of the same work, this conclusion seeks to integrate the findings of both. The two books analyse and appraise the experience of teachers, ex-pupils and pupils of co-educational and single-sex schools mainly through their own reports. The research has concentrated on respondents' attitudes to their schools and to varying aspects of school life, with a brief look into a few effects of the schooling on their lives afterwards. The most important samples used are those of teachers and of ex-pupils who had each taught or been taught in both kinds of school.

The previous volume was concerned with teachers and pupil–teacher relationship. Teachers in secondary grammar schools were seen to be strongly in favour of co-education, and those teaching in co-educational schools almost unanimously preferred them to single-sex schools. The principal opposition was shown to come from two sources, namely those teachers who had had no direct experience of co-education and were essentially basing their attitudes on ignorance and a stereotyped prejudice, and those women who understandably feared that their opportunities for promotion to headships would disappear if all schools were co-educational. A few teachers thought that the interests of the sexes diverged too much for them to be taught together, and others that academic standards might suffer. Support for co-education was mainly for social reasons, including preparation for life in a bisexual world and the good influence that each sex of pupil and of teacher was believed to have on the conduct of the other. Additional reasons were the fresh life given to school societies, the invigorating effect of increased breadth of interests, the stimulation provided by the greater variety in school life and the beneficial results of a friendly academic rivalry between the sexes.

In order to counter the objection that many of these teachers had taught in only one type of school and therefore knew little about the other, two special samples of teachers, almost 500 in all, who had taught in both types of school were separated out from the others and their returns reclassified. They were strongly in favour of co-education; in one sample the majority was 60 per cent of those teachers who themselves were educated in single-sex schools and 79 per cent of those educated in co-educational schools; in the second sample (analysed differently) those in favour were 93 per cent of men and 97 per cent of women teaching in co-educational schools, 80 per cent of those in boys' schools and 64 per cent in girls' schools, with small percentages undecided. In another inquiry only 9 per cent of staff in University Departments of Education were in favour of single-sex and 'dual' schools.

What is the significance of these results? There are certain limitations of the new evidence which should be mentioned. The teachers are from maintained day grammar schools only, so that the findings cannot be said to be directly applicable to independent schools or to boarding schools, and one can only theorize that if co-education is preferable in grammar schools it would probably also be preferable in secondary modern, technical, bilateral and comprehensive schools.

Some critics may say that teachers prefer co-educational schools not for any purely educational reasons but because they themselves feel happier in such schools. Although almost all the reasons given by the teachers for their preferences were educational in the widest sense, this factor might indeed have affected the preference. However, even if this were true it seems pertinent to ask whether it is not desirable to have a happy staff in a school and whether this happiness might not conceivably be communicated to the pupils, creating thereby an atmosphere which would be conducive to good attainment in the narrow sense of education and better adjusted pupils in its wider sense.

Yet we should recognize that the judgments made by the teachers depend in part upon the established ethos of the society in which they live, and if they had been living in Victorian times, with its fears about the unchaperoned social mixing of the sexes, they might have been swayed in the opposite direction. On the other hand it could be argued that if there had been many more co-educational schools in Victorian times society would not have been so frightened at the idea of educating the two sexes together!

At the present day a noteworthy aspect of the swing towards co-education is that it is occurring in spite of the entrenched prestige of the single-sex 'public' schools, including the direct grant schools, in spite of the single-sex education of most teachers, in spite of there being a majority of teachers teaching in single-sex grammar schools, and in spite of an 'establishment' which is largely the product of single-sex schools. The force of tradition is incredibly strong, yet these teachers have in this one aspect decided for change, and an educational revolution is now taking place in the schools of England by which it seems probable that most of the children will soon be educated in co-educational secondary schools.

The next section summarizes the main findings of the previous volume about the relations between pupils and teachers in co-educational compared with single-sex maintained grammar and technical schools. These results were obtained mainly through questionnaires answered by several large samples of ex-pupils (including a sprinkling who had been taught in comprehensive and bilateral schools). The most important of these samples was that used in the 'Both schools' survey, consisting of some 800 students who had each attended both a co-educational and single-sex secondary school (excluding secondary modern). These students, both men and women, judged the teachers in their co-educational school to be friendlier and more helpful than those in their single-sex schools. The students also thought there was a greater tendency for some teachers in their co-educational schools rather than boys' and girls' schools to have 'a powerful influence for good' (though with equality for senior boys).

The consensus of the findings about the discipline in these schools is that the ex-pupils considered that both boys' and girls' schools tended towards strictness, an appreciable number being judged 'too strict', this becoming over-severity and harshness in a minority of schools, whereas in their co-educational schools the discipline was mostly reported 'satisfactory', but the group judging it 'too lax' was greater than that judging it to be 'too strict'. In the ensuing discussion the theory was put forward that this difference in the conduct of school affairs is probably caused by one type of community having both sexes and the others only one— that boys and girls and also men and women, in such an institution as a school, have an ameliorating effect on each other's conduct and that this makes it possible for authority to use a lighter form of control in a co-educational school than is found practicable in a single-sex school. Hence it is easier for teachers in co-educational schools to appear more friendly and helpful than they do in single-sex schools, where there is more of a barrier between teacher and pupil. Linking up with this theme is the strong liking expressed by girls in co-educational schools for being taught by men.

In reply to some more detailed questions affecting aspects of the pupil–teacher relationship the female ex-pupils of the 'Both schools' survey thought there was much more 'unnecessary fuss about small details' in their girls' schools than in their co-educational, and both males and females in the sample considered that the staffs of their single-sex schools were more 'out of touch with modern adolescents'. The women, whether they attended their girls' school first or last, and those men who had attended their boys' school first, endorsed more frequently for their single-sex schools than for the others that they 'felt grown-up and were treated like children'.

A chapter in the first volume was devoted to a special analysis of the replies of students who had attended an 'amalgamated' school. The results from such schools were not as favourable as were those from the normal co-educational schools in which boys and girls had grown up together from the age of eleven. The estimates from the whole co-educational group were therefore depressed a little in the comparison with single-sex schools. The influence of amalgamated schools persists throughout the results given in the present volume, as demonstrated in a recent chapter. However, another feature which emerged was that the amalgamation affected the girls more than the boys and the women teachers more than the men. Three of the findings were, first, that the pupils from the amalgamated schools were rather less happy than the corresponding group of seniors who had grown up with the opposite sex at school since the age of eleven, though the difference was not sufficiently large to be statistically reliable; second, that the pupils' attitude to sex was reported as being not as healthy in amalgamated schools as in the normal co-educational type (though still healthier than in single-sex schools), and finally that the ex-pupils of the amalgamated were not quite as pronounced in their preference for these (as against their single-sex ones) as were the normally co-educated pupils for their schools.

Returning to the comparison between co-educational and single-sex schools, the chief findings of this volume are outlined in the next few pages. The ex-pupils of the co-educational schools reported themselves as having been happier at school than did those from single-sex schools and they also found the school atmosphere pleasanter. Usually these results are more consistent and stronger for the women than for the men. The reasons both sexes give are that the social life with two sexes is better, it is a more natural preparation for life in the adult world, relations with the staff and between the staff are pleasanter, and the atmosphere is less tense. With regard to academic work they find it more enjoyable in a mixed school and like the friendly rivalry with the opposite sex, though others emphasize the good academic standard of their single-sex school.

In the Schools project the 17-year-old co-educated girls gave higher estimates than those in girls' schools for 'kindness' as opposed to 'unpleasantness' (highly significant), for 'enthusiasm' as opposed to 'apathy' (approaching significance), and for 'variety' as opposed to 'monotony' (substantial but not statistically significant). In the 'Check' questionnaire more of the 13-year-old co-educated girls than of their opposing group estimated their school to be 'lively' as opposed to 'dull'.

In these 'life in school' aspects the co-educated boys, surprisingly, had a bigger advantage than the co-educated girls. The 13-year-old boys believed their schools to be more lively as opposed to more dull, to have more variety as opposed to monotony, and possibly to show more enthusiasm than did the boys from boys' schools. Also the 17-year-old co-educated boys rated their schools as more lively and more enthusiastic.

In this section it appeared likely that pupils from working-class homes found school life in the single-sex schools, on the average, more dull and monotonous, less enthusiastic, more unpleasant and with more cliques than did their fellow-pupils from the higher social classes. This tendency was less certain among co-educated girls and absent among co-educated boys. As this finding is only a by-product of the research a concentrated effort on this aspect might be rewarding.

One of the most startling differences between the men's groups was that whereas almost half of the men in the 'Both schools' survey judged bullying to be frequent or very frequent in their boys' schools, only one-fifth of them made the same estimate for their co-educational schools. The verdict of the women was similar. Following the same general theme, both sexes found the prefects to be 'more officious' in their single-sex than their co-educational schools.

Men and women also judged the education provided in their single-sex schools to be 'narrower' than in their co-educational schools, nor were there as many enjoyable out-of-school activities. In both these cases the difference between the two senior boys' groups was smaller than for junior boys or for girls in general.

In the area of pupil interaction both male and female ex-pupils were strongly of the opinion that it was easier to make friends in their co-educational than in their single-sex schools, and the women thought the girls in the latter were more 'spiteful' and more 'quarrelsome'.

In Chapter 9 the outline case-studies of those girls who had described themselves as 'unhappy' or 'rather unhappy' at school yielded some interesting results. It was demonstrated that the unhappy girls in the co-educational schools were of lower average intelligence than their opposite numbers in the single-sex schools and that their difficulty in coping with their studies was a powerful factor in this unhappiness. By far the more important reasons for unhappiness among the co-educated girls were out-of-school or home difficulties and the above-mentioned lack of ability, with teachers' discipline almost the least important whereas the girls from girls' schools placed dislike of school first, with teachers' discipline second, work difficulties almost equal to this, and out-of-school and home difficulties fourth. A specially intriguing point is that at both junior and senior level the unhappy girls from girls' schools had higher extroversion scores than did those at co-educational schools. Interestingly, hints of this difference are seen between the *boys' main* groups. This finding could not be followed up but it is suggested tentatively either that deprivation of the company of the opposite sex drives these pupils of single-sex schools into slightly increased extroversion, or that those girls in girls' schools who are highly extroverted are more likely to become unhappy at school than similar girls in co-educational schools.

The characteristically stricter discipline of the one-sex school is shown also in the attitude of these schools towards out-of-school conduct. Both male and female ex-pupils judged this interest as 'excessive' or 'rather strict'—mostly the latter (though the difference between the opposing groups of male ex-pupils was not statistically significant), whereas half of the co-educated men and women, for both first and last schools, estimated the interest to be 'just right', with the remaining half spread equally on both sides of this middle line. This was, of course, the judgment of the consumers—though of former consumers who as student teachers were already becoming those who directed the consuming!

A schooling in which boys and girls spend many years at school with the opposite sex, compared with a schooling which segregates boy from girl, would naturally produce a decided difference in attitude in each towards the other. This result was, however, not attained in answer to all the questions in this area. For example, when they were asked if they thought of the opposite sex as being Very superior/Superior . . . Very inferior, the two main groups of women in the Second College survey produced results which were almost identical, though the men from boys' schools did give just a hint of more extreme opinions in both directions. Yet in the replies about the pleasantness or unpleasantness of the attitude of the pupils towards the opposite sex both male and female students of the 'Both schools' survey were sure that the pleasanter attitude was in their co-educational schools. At the same time they reported much more timidity towards the opposite sex among pupils in single-sex schools. Again the latter were more 'preoccupied with the opposite sex' and also more 'boy-girl crazy'.

It is sometimes said that boys do not like the presence of girls in school. The falsity of this argument was demonstrated by the co-educated ex-pupils, as only three males (out of 186) and six females (out of 657) agreed with the statement, in spite of the existence of a number of amalgamated schools in the sample. They also considered that the presence of the opposite sex of teacher had a good influence, but here the male approval (though moderately favourable) was shown to be diminished by the influence of the amalgamated schools.

Ex-pupils of the 'Both schools' survey asserted strongly that the two sexes had a good influence on each other, improving the boys' appearance, manners and turbulent behaviour, and making them work harder, while on the other side improving the atmosphere among girls, widening their interests and making more normal the interest of the girls in boys.

One of the crucial questions which lies hidden in the minds of parents and of some teachers and educationists is whether the presence of boys and girls together in co-educational schools would encourage an excessive interest in sex, and create an unhealthy atmosphere. The ex-pupils who attended both a co-educational and single-sex school have given a very clear reply. Seventy-six per cent of the women believed the attitude towards sex to be healthier in their co-educational school than in their girls' school, only 7 per cent believing the opposite. This is such an important aspect of the problem that three of the reasons given by the women and reported earlier in the text are repeated:

'When you see boys every day the novelty wears off.'

'Boys were part of everyday life in the school and at times were completely forgotten about.'

'Mixing with the opposite sex one comes into closer contact than in the single-sex school—it changes one's ideas completely—found I had more respect towards them and a healthier attitude towards sex.'

The judgment of the men was the same as that of the women. The difference in attitude between the two types of school, for both men and women, was greater than for any other topic explored. A moment's reflection on the problem makes it clear that the propinquity of the sexes in co-educational schools makes it essential for this attitude to be good if the schools are to be viable, whereas the segregation of the sexes in single-sex schools makes a less healthy attitude tolerable as far as the running of the school is concerned, because the consequences in boy–girl relationships are to be seen only away from the school premises if they are known at all. Unfortunately we simply do not know whether the deprivation of

296

the companionship of the opposite sex experienced by pupils in single-sex schools and the consequently less healthy attitude to sex has worse effects outside school than in the case of co-educated pupils.

As was to be expected the topic 'preparation for the adult world' yielded considerable advantage to the co-educational schools. Whereas only some 10 per cent of the ex-pupils of girls' schools, in the Second College survey, said their school life was helpful in their relations with men, the proportion from the co-educated women was three-quarters. Many more of the latter also found it easier to work with men in the adult world. The men's results followed the same pattern except that in addition the men from co-educational schools found it easier to work under the direction of a woman than did the men from boys' schools. In the Schools project the 17-year-old girls from co-educational schools were also more certain than their counterparts that their school 'prepared them sufficiently for the adult world'. The differences between the boys' groups for this question fell a little short of statistical significance, the co-educated boys finding their schooling more helpful.

Marriage would seem a far cry from school—though not as far these days as it used to be. Yet it would seem possible that the two methods of education under consideration—co-education and its opposite—might have very different effects on the social and emotional development of children and even affect the relative happiness of children when later they marry. There have indeed been hints of this possibility in the preceding paragraphs, though it would be folly not to recognize that even if co-education has an influence here it is unlikely that it will be as powerful as a number of other forces.

An amusing beginning in this area was made by the finding that the women of the Second College survey were slightly more keen to marry if they had been educated in a single-sex school, while the reverse was true for the men! Though the differences are not statistically reliable they are not insignificant, and it may be that deprivation of the company of the male sex makes women a little keener on marriage, but men deprived of women (more doubtfully) a little less keen. The same result was obtained from a question on the desire to have children.

Atherton carried this work further by asking a very large sample of married people whether their mixed or single-sex schooling had helped or hindered them in their everyday relations with the opposite sex. His results were overwhelmingly in favour of the co-educational schools. In answer to another question, 'Do you think the type of school (mixed or single-sex) helped or hindered you in making a happy marriage?' his sample again gave a decisive judgment for the co-educational school.

The most important part of his work, however, was that in which he used a self-rating scale of marital happiness, as outlined in Chapter 17, and found that among those who had attended secondary school for five years or more, the co-educated had a better score than those educated in single-sex schools. It is self-evident that in this difficult area of research the finding needs replication before it can be accepted with confidence, but a relevant point is that there appear to be no research findings at present which are in opposition to Atherton's work.

Finally, which schools did the samples prefer? We have seen the views of the teachers and must now consider those of the ex-pupils (the question was omitted from the questionnaire used in the Schools project). In each case there was a decided preference for the co-educational schools, and this was most marked in the two samples, one large and one small where the ex-pupils had attended both a co-educational and a single-sex school and were able to compare their experiences in the two schools. They prefer these schools because—in their own words—there is a natural friendliness between the sexes, and they educate each other; they find the atmosphere pleasant and relaxed, enjoy the social life of the school, the friendliness of the teachers, the broad balanced outlook, and the preparation for the adult world. They also stress that work is more enjoyable, with more interesting and lively lessons and more variety.

A rather small minority preferred the single-sex school, usually for academic reasons, but sometimes because of friendly staff, small school, tradition, etc. Whether they are teachers, pupils or ex-pupils, as soon as they have experienced a co-educational school most of them will have a strong tendency to prefer co-education. Opposition comes mainly from those ignorant of it, and co-education is unthinkingly confused in the minds of some of these teachers and pupils with differences due to the rather lower-social-class intake of some co-educational schools.

Here and there in this work teachers in single-sex schools, particularly women in girls' schools, have been severely criticized by some of their ex-pupils. More than once the writer has shown that this is a minority opinion and that most of these College of Education students give due acknowledgment to the effort and influence of their secondary school teachers. Yet a difference in important aspects of school atmosphere does exist between the two types of school, and this difference could be due entirely to the presence of both sexes in one type of school and the absence of one sex in another type. We must also remember that these researches have been examining average tendencies, and in the endeavour to single out differences between co-educational and single-sex schools other factors in the well-being of a school have rarely been mentioned. Perhaps the most important of these, in the present form of administration used in schools, is the personality and character of the head, but factors such as the calibre of the staff, type and position of buildings, undeniably have a strong influence. On the pupils' side the nature of the school intake, e.g. its ability and its social class, will also be a force of consequence. The result is that there is a wide range of quality within any one type of school and an overlap between types, so that the achievement of a school —in its widest sense—by no means depends only upon whether it is co-educational or single-sex, though these researches have illustrated the importance of this difference in organization.

In the last half of the nineteenth century a few prophetic voices urged the value of co-education, but they were indeed voices crying in the wilderness. The examples of Scotland and the United States were ignored, as were the pleas in the twentieth century of Badley, Pekin and Curry. Victorian and Edwardian society was afraid of the idea, the uncritical worship of the public schools— single-sex by historical evolution—was at its height, and it would have been heresy—as it still is in some circles—to have speculated to what extent the academic achievements and widely acclaimed 'character training for leadership' were due to a combination of special selection of pupils (e.g. in Direct Grant schools) and the pupils' high social class. It was taken for granted—without any scientific examination of the case—first, that the academic achievement was good and second, that it was good because of special merit in the teaching, and these beliefs became connected with a vaguer belief that high achievement and single-sex schooling went hand in hand. It was also assumed—again without any serious examination of the facts—that the acclaimed character training was inclusive of all desirable aspects of personality development, and again, more vaguely, that this was best achieved in a single-sex school. Many teachers in girls' grammar schools tended to think of nearby co-educational schools as 'inferior' and this attitude became linked with the idea that these schools were inferior because they were co-educational, though the weaknesses of which these teachers were critical could have arisen because of the difference in social class intake between the contrasted schools.

Today we now know more facts with which to make a more rational appraisal of the position. The research set out in this volume and in its predecessor has shown that co-educational and single-sex schools are communities with very different atmospheres, with the co-educational school providing the happier, more balanced, more interesting and more complete education. This research does not cover all aspects that need to be covered, nor has the writer been able—for lack of time and resources—to include a sufficient analysis of the more objective evidence which is mentioned elsewhere—the comparative incidence of delinquency, of truancy, homosexuality and schoolgirl pregnancies, etc. Nor has he been able to do more than touch upon the question whether the differences between co-educational and single-sex schools create long-lasting differences in attitudes, personality and social development. It seems likely that the products of co-educational schools have for at least some years after leaving school a more natural and easier relationship with the opposite sex, find it easier to work with the opposite sex and rate themselves as rather more happily married, than do the products of single-sex schools. The writer would be the first to say that we need more evidence on these points, but at the present this is the only evidence that exists.

The Introduction briefly examined how in the last two or three decades the western educational world has slowly moved towards co-education. In Britain more pupils are now in co-educational secondary schools than in single-sex ones. So far so good—the progress appears to be in the right direction. It will not, of course, remove all our troubles—co-education is no panacea for all the ills of the secondary school system, as administrators and teachers in U.S.A. will know. In particular, the success of schools with their pupils depends in part on the attitudes and values inculcated in the children by their parents and by society itself.

Each type of institution, however, is liable to develop its special kind of failing. In this research a few failings of co-educational schools have been mentioned sufficiently frequently by respondents to persuade the writer that they need some consideration. One is the inequality of the status of women on the staff of some of these schools, not indeed in the relationship between male and female assistants, which is usually cordial, but in the fact that not only is the head almost invariably a man (which is accepted by most female critics as necessary in view of the attitude of society, though some relaxation in favour of women is needed), but in some schools *the second in command is also a man*—the senior master. This relegates the senior mistress to third in the hierarchy and this 'image of women' is bad for the girls. Moreover, this accentuates the promotion problem which leads so many headmistresses and some of their staff to oppose co-education; in a world of co-educational schools run in this way they would not only be unable to obtain headships, they would not even be second in command. As mentioned earlier, the best way to deal with this injustice would be to have a headmaster who—in deference to public opinion and because of the scarcity of suitable female applicants—would *usually* be first in command, but also a *headmistress* rather than senior mistress, who would *usually* be second in command rather than first, but would have with the headmaster a right to a seat on the governors' committee. In conjunction with this reform is the necessity to make sure that a reasonable balance of male and female teachers is achieved—a number of schools have now a heavy imbalance of men, and this impairs the true atmosphere of a co-educational school.

A third complaint of women teachers is that the head, being a man, is inclined to sacrifice the interests of the girls to those of the boys, and it is sometimes added that this comes from his lack of experience in co-educational schools before he was appointed. This is something which has not been investigated, but is mentioned as a possible danger—and a possible hint to those organizing training courses for heads that the special needs of co-educational schools ought to be kept in mind.

No mention has been made of parents. This does not mean that the writer is indifferent to them, but they fall outside the limit of this research. In fact the making of a comparison between co-educational and single-sex schools needs either specialized know-ledge, which has become available only in the last twenty years and then only in learned journals that are not readily available to parents, or needs actual experience in both kinds of school, and even this is a limited basis for a single individual to make an appraisal. An individual who has no such specialized knowledge or experience may think that he or she is making a judgment about co-education when in reality it is based on the building and its situation, the tradition of the school or its clientele. The net result is that wherever parents' views are ascertained the majority is in favour of the established order, whether it be single-sex or co-educational. It is indeed a tribute to the existing grammar schools of whichever type, that the parents are ready to fight for the local school if there is any proposal to change it from one type to the other. On the other hand, this is a state of affairs which is not of much help to the administrators. It is likely that parental opinion, with that of the teachers (who are, after all, often parents) and student teachers (who will in a few years become parents), is moving slowly towards co-education, but the change will inevitably lag behind the opinion of those people who are themselves working in education.

This brings to an end the reporting of the writer's investigation into those aspects of the comparison between co-educational and single-sex secondary schools which are related to the social and emotional well-being of the pupils. In the next volume it is hoped to present evidence which will help educationists to compare the influence of the two types of schooling on the academic attainment of the pupils.

Finally, although this book has co-education as its main theme, the writer hopes that it will be useful in other contexts. The evidence that has been gathered together about pupil–teacher relationships, about the happiness and unhappiness of pupils, the good and the bad influence of teachers and the anxiety of pupils, bears directly on other central issues of education.

Appendix 1

The questionnaires[1]

[SECOND COLLEGE SURVEY]

Research questionnaire I

For ex-pupils of Secondary Grammar Schools
This questionnaire forms part of a research project on a subject about which there is a great need for reliable information. The compiler asks for the generous co-operation of all those who are invited to assist in the inquiry; it is hoped that they will feel that they are contributing their quota towards the advance of knowledge in this particular field. Great care will be taken to ensure the anonymity of all individuals and of all educational institutions which may take part. You are particularly asked not to put your name on the form.
Sincere thanks to all those who help.

Old Scholars of Secondary Grammar, Comprehensive and Grammar-Technical Schools
All questions relating to school refer to the *secondary school*. Please tick which ever answer is corret. If you attended more than one grammar school, please number your ticks where necessary throughout the questionnaire, using (1) for your first school, (2) for your second, and so on. If your school changed from mixed to single-sex or vice versa, while you were at school, consider this as two separate schools, and instead of numbering your ticks (1) and (2) mark them with M (Mixed) and S (Single-sex).

Please state your sex: Male/Female
Age (unless you prefer not to give it)   .... years
Occupation of father ....
Number of brothers ....
Number of sisters   ....
Type of Secondary Grammar School attended:
(1) Co-educational/Single-sex[2], for   .... years

---

[1] Only those parts of the questionnaires are given which have relevance to the material in this book.
[2] 'Dual' schools, with girls under a headmistress in one part of the building, and boys under a headmaster in another part of the building, are classed as 'Single-sex', but in such cases please add a D to your tick.

(Answer (2) and (3) if you attended more than one secondary grammar school.)
(2) Co-educational/Single-sex, for .... years
(3) Co-educational/Single-sex, for .... years

Was your life in school, viewed as a whole,
Very happy/Happy/Jogging along/Rather unhappy/Very unhappy?
Comment briefly if you wish, ...
e.g. giving reasons for your opinion ....
....
Do you think the school atmosphere was
Very pleasant/Pleasant/Neutral/Rather unpleasant/Very unpleasant?
If in your secondary grammar school career you attended more than one school, and changed from a mixed to a single-sex school, or vice versa, which did you prefer?
Single-sex school very much/Single-sex school a little/No preference/
Mixed school a little/Mixed school very much
If you attended a single-sex school would you have preferred it to have been a mixed school?
Yes/No/Undecided
If you attended a mixed school would you have preferred it to have been single-sex?
Yes/No/Undecided
Did your school life help or hinder you in your relations with the opposite sex?
Very helpful/Helpful/No effect/Slight hindrance/Great hindrance
Do you find it easy to work with the opposite sex?
Very easy/Easy/Fairly easy/Doubtful/A little difficult/Difficult/Very difficult
Do you think you would find it easy, in general, to work under the direction of a member of the opposite sex?
Very easy/Easy/Fairly easy/Doubtful/A little difficult/Difficult/Very difficult
Comment if you wish ....
....

(When answering the question below, please analyse your attitude very carefully, and give a frank answer)
In your attitude to the opposite sex do you think of them, in general, as being

Very superior/Superior/Equal/Inferior/Very inferior?
Comment if you wish ....
....
(For the unmarried)
Do you wish to marry, provided you can find a suitable partner?
Very much/Much/A little/Undecided/A little opposed/Much
opposed/Very much opposed
If you do not wish to marry, please comment ....
....
If you marry—or if you are married—do you wish to have children?
Very much/Much/A little/Undecided/A little opposed/Much
opposed/Very much opposed
If you do not wish to have children of your own, it would be helpful
if you would give your reasons.
....
....

['BOTH SCHOOLS' SURVEY]

Research questionnaire II

FORM B. *For students who have attended both a co-educational and a
single-sex grammar, or comprehensive, or grammar technical school
in Britain*
This questionnaire forms part of a research project on a subject
about which there is a great need for reliable information. The
project is financially supported by the Department of Education
and Science. The compiler asks for the generous co-operation of
all those who are invited to assist in the inquiry; it is hoped that
they will feel that they are contributing their quota towards the
advance of knowledge in this particular field. Great care will be
taken to ensure the anonymity of all individuals and of all educational institutions which may take part. You are particularly asked
not to put your name on the form.
Sincere thanks to all those who help.

Please answer these preliminary questions. (In ink please—not
pencil)
Age ...... years   Sex ... Male/Female
How long have you been a student in a College of Education
(or Training College)?   ...... years ...... months
Occupation of Father or Guardian (former occupation if unemployed or deceased). Please give this as fully as you can, e.g. not
merely MINER but *Miner-Deputy* or *Cutter*; not ENGINEER but

Maintenance Engineer or *Graduate Engineer*; not MANAGER but *Manager of small shop*; not FARMER but *Tenant Farmer* or *Smallholder*; not just CIVIL SERVANT but *Civil Servant—Clerk* or *Executive*; not just FACTORY WORKER but *Fitter*, or *Works Labourer*, or *Machine Operator*.

OCCUPATION..

All questions refer to your *secondary schools*
If while you were at school your school changed from a mixed to a single-sex school, or vice versa, consider this as two separate schools. If one school you attended was secondary modern exclude this from your answers.

When answering the following questions please underline the answer which is correct for you, e.g. Co-educational

Type of Secondary (or Comprehensive etc.) school attended, in *chronological order.*
(1) Co-educational/Single-sex   ... years (approx.)
(2) Co-educational/Single-sex   ... years (approx.)
(3) Co-educational/Single sex   ... years (approx.)
If you were a boarder write 'B' after the school where you boarded.
If you attended a Comprehensive school write 'C' after this school.

Your co-educational school

If you attended more than one co-educational secondary school (apart from secondary modern) please give answers for each of these schools and distinguish between them by numbering each answer, (1) for the first co-educational school you attended and (2) for the second. Please give these numbers even where the answer is the same for both schools.
Underline the answer which is correct for you.

  1. Was your life in your co-educational school, viewed as a whole,
     1. Very happy/2. Fairly happy/3. Jogging along/4. Rather unhappy/5. Very unhappy?
     Please give your reasons ....
     ....
     ....

  7. Do you think the school atmosphere in your co-educational school was 1. Very pleasant/2. Pleasant/3. Neutral/4. Rather unpleasant/5. Very unpleasant?
     Give the most important reason for your answer ....
     ....
     ....

8. Do you agree or disagree with the following statements about your co-educational school? *Underline* your answers.
   (2) Pleasant situation of the school.
      1. Agree strongly/2. Agree/3. Doubtful/4. Disagree/5. Disagree strongly.
   (3) Presence of the opposite sex of teacher had a good influence.
      1. Agree strongly/2. Agree/3. Doubtful/4. Disagree/5. Disagree strongly.
   (4) Presence of the opposite sex of pupil had a good influence.
      1. Agree strongly/2. Agree/3. Doubtful/4. Disagree/5. Disagree strongly.
   (6) There were enjoyable out-of-school activities (other than games).
      1. Agree strongly/2. Agree/3. Doubtful/4. Disagree/5. Disagree strongly.
   (7) There was unnecessary fuss over small details, e.g. hair, uniform, etc.
      1. Agree strongly/2. Agree/3. Doubtful/4. Disagree/5. Disagree strongly.
   (8) The prefects were officious.
      1. Agree strongly/2. Agree/3. Doubtful/4. Disagree/5. Disagree strongly.
   (9) I disliked the social image the school tried to capture.
      1. Agree strongly/2. Agree/3. Doubtful/4. Disagree/5. Disagree strongly.
   (10) I felt I didn't belong socially.
      1. Agree strongly/2. Agree/3. Doubtful/4. Disagree/5. Disagree strongly.
   (11) The staff were out of touch with modern adolescents.
      1. Agree strongly/2. Agree/3. Doubtful/4. Disagree/5. Disagree strongly.
   (13) The education I got was extremely narrow.
      1. Agree strongly/2. Agree/3. Doubtful/4. Disagree/5. Disagree strongly.
   (14) The school tried to dominate my whole life.
      1. Agree strongly/2. Agree/3. Doubtful/4. Disagree/5. Disagree strongly.
   (15) I felt I was grown up and was treated like a child.
      1. Agree strongly/2. Agree/3. Doubtful/4. Disagree/5. Disagree strongly.
   (16) I felt that the school created a gap between myself and my home.
      1. Agree strongly/2. Agree/3. Doubtful/4. Disagree/5. Disagree strongly.

13. Within your co-educational school did you find it easy or difficult to make friends?
    1. Very easy/2. Fairly easy/3. Neither easy nor difficult/4. A little difficult/5. Very difficult.
    Comment if you wish...
    ....

14. In your co-educational school was the general attitude of most of the pupils (of your own sex) towards the opposite sex
    1. Pleasant/2. Fairly pleasant/3. Neutral/4. A little unpleasant/5. Unpleasant?
    Comment if you wish...
    ....

15. In your co-educational school was the general attitude of most of the pupils (of your own sex) towards the opposite sex
    Antagonistic?   1. True/2. Partly true/3. False/4. Doubtful
    Indifferent?   1. True/2. Partly true/3. False/4. Doubtful
    Normal Interest?   1. True/2. Partly true/3. False/4. Doubtful
    Rather preoccupied
      with opposite sex?   1. True/2. Partly true/3. False/4. Doubtful
    Girl/Boy crazy?   1. True/2. Partly true/3. False/4. Doubtful
    Timid?   1. True/2. Partly true/3. False/4. Doubtful

16. The presence of the opposite sex of pupils in my school was
    1. Liked very much/2. Liked/3. Tolerated/4. Disliked/5. Disliked intensely.

20. Do you consider that the influence of the girls on the boys in this school was, in general,
    1. Very good/2. Good/3. Fairly good/4. No effect/5. Bad/6. Very bad
    Please comment ....
    ....
    ....

21. Do you consider that the influence of the boys on the girls in this school was, in general,
    1. Very good/2. Good/3. Fairly good/4. No effect/5. Bad/6. Very bad?
    Please comment ....
    ....

22. Do you think that the school's concern with the out-of-school conduct of the pupils was
    1. Excessive/2. Rather strict/3. Just right/4. Rather insufficient/5. Much too lax?

    Comment if you wish...
    ....

23. WOMEN ONLY
    Do you think that the girls in your form, considered as a whole, were
    1. Spiteful/2. A little spiteful/3. Neutral/4. Rather nice/5. Very nice?

    Comment if you wish...
    ....

24. WOMEN ONLY
    Did the other girls in your form quarrel
    1. Very often/2. Fairly often/3. Sometimes/4. Seldom/5. Never?

25. WOMEN ONLY
    In your co-educational school would you say that a group or groups of girls 'made life unpleasant' for some girls (or girl)
    1. Very frequently/2. Frequently/3. Not so frequently/4. Infrequently/5. Not at all?

    Please comment ....
    ....

26. MEN ONLY
    In your co-educational school would you say bullying by boys occurred
    1. Very frequently/2. Frequently/3. Not so frequently/4. Infrequently/5. Not at all?

    Please comment ....
    ....

WOMEN STUDENTS ONLY
A. In your co-educational school would you say bullying of girls by girls occurred
    1. Not at all/2. Infrequently/3. Not so frequently/4. Frequently/5. Very frequently?

    Comment if you wish...
    ....
    ....

Your single-sex school

If you attended more than one single-sex secondary school (apart from secondary modern) please give answers for each of these schools and distinguish between them by numbering each answer, (1) for the first single-sex school you attended and (2) for the second. Please give these numbers even where the answer is the same for both schools.

[The questions under this heading were exactly the same as for the co-educational school except when not applicable.]

WOMEN AND MEN STUDENTS

48. Which did you prefer, the mixed or single-sex school?
Single-sex school much/Single-sex school a little/No preference/
Mixed school a little/Mixed school much.
State the most important reason for your preference:
....
....
....

49. Has your study and experience in your training for the teaching profession changed your opinion about co-educational secondary schools? *Underline* which statement applies:
Made no change.
Strengthened preference for single-sex secondary schools.
Strengthened preference for co-educational secondary schools.
Changed my preference from co-educational to single-sex secondary schools.
Changed my preference from single-sex to co-educational secondary schools.
Comment if you wish ....
....

50. In which school do you consider the pupils had the healthier attitude towards sex?
Doubtful/Don't know/Single-sex school/Co-educational school
Comment if you wish ....
....
....

[SCHOOLS PROJECT]

Age...   Sex...Boy/Girl (Please tick)

Name of school..................................... Date..............
Please answer the following questions according to the instruction given. *Do not* write your name on this sheet. Your answers will be kept strictly private, so please be *completely frank and truthful.*

Here is a list of statements about school. Underneath each statement is a list of opinions. Underline the opinion with which you agree.
  6. Altogether my life at school is:
     1. Happy/2. Fairly happy/3. Jogging along/4. Rather unhappy/5. Unhappy.
     Please comment ....
     ....

ALL QUESTIONS ON THIS PAGE ARE TO BE ANSWERED BY 'GIRLS ONLY'
Here are some statements about boys of your own age. *Underline* the opinion which in general is true for you.

26. Boys are much too noisy.
     1. Agree strongly/2. Agree/3. Doubtful/4. Disagree/5. Disagree strongly

27. Boys cannot be trusted.
     1. Agree strongly/2. Agree/3. Doubtful/4. Disagree/5. Disagree strongly

28. Boys are unpleasant.
     1. Agree strongly/2. Agree/3. Doubtful/4. Disagree/5. Disagree strongly

29. Boys are nicer than girls.
     1. Agree strongly/2. Agree/3. Doubtful/4. Disagree/5. Disagree strongly

30. Boys are cleverer than girls in school work.
     1. Agree strongly/2. Agree/3. Doubtful/4. Disagree/5. Disagree strongly

31. Boys are better leaders than girls.
     1. Agree strongly/2. Agree/3. Doubtful/4. Disagree/5. Disagree strongly

32. Boys are not as catty as girls.
     1. Agree strongly/2. Agree/3. Doubtful/4. Disagree/5. Disagree strongly

33. Boys are braver than girls.
     1. Agree strongly/2. Agree/3. Doubtful/4. Disagree/5. Disagree strongly

34. Boys are cruel.
    1. Agree strongly/2. Agree/3. Doubtful/4. Disagree/5. Disagree strongly

35. Boys are interested in the wrong things.
    1. Agree strongly/2. Agree/3. Doubtful/4. Disagree/5. Disagree strongly

36. I would prefer to be a boy.
    1. Agree strongly/2. Agree/3. Doubtful/4. Disagree/5. Disagree strongly

38. When I meet boys at a party I don't know what to say.
    1. Very true/2. Often true/3. Sometimes true/4. Seldom true/ 5. Not true

    Please comment ....
    ....

39. I feel very awkward whenever I am with boys.
    1. Very true/2. Often true/3. Sometimes true/4. Seldom true/ 5. Not true

40. I feel perfectly at ease when talking with boys.
    1. Very true/2. Often true/3. Sometimes true/4. Seldom true/ 5. Not true

41. I prefer talking to boys rather than to girls.
    1. Very true/2. Often true/3. Sometimes true/4. Seldom true/ 5. Not true

    Please comment ....
    ....

FOR ALL PUPILS
Which of the following words *best* fits your school life? Try to choose one of the first two alternatives, even if it doesn't fit exactly. Use 'neither' only as a last resort.

45. 1. lively/2. dull/3. neither

46. 1. variety/2. monotony/3. neither

47. 1. enthusiasm/2. apathy/3. neither

48. 1. kindness/2. unpleasantness/3. neither

49. 1. friendly individuals/2. cliques or gangs/3. neither

ALL QUESTIONS ON THIS PAGE ARE TO BE ANSWERED BY 'BOYS ONLY'
Here are some statements about girls of your own age. *Underline* the opinion with which you agree.

61. Girls are nicer than boys.
    1. Agree strongly/2. Agree/3. Doubtful/4. Disagree/5. Disagree strongly
62. Girls are catty and spiteful.
    1. Agree strongly/2. Agree/3. Doubtful/4. Disagree/5. Disagree strongly
63. Girls cannot be trusted.
    1. Agree strongly/2. Agree/3. Doubtful/4. Disagree/5. Disagree strongly
64. Girls are kinder than boys.
    1. Agree strongly/2. Agree/3. Doubtful/4. Disagree/5. Disagree strongly
65. Girls are interested in unimportant things.
    1. Agree strongly/2. Agree/3. Doubtful/4. Disagree/5. Disagree strongly
66. Girls are boring.
    1. Agree strongly/2. Agree/3. Doubtful/4. Disagree/5. Disagree strongly
67. Girls are cleverer than boys in school work.
    1. Agree strongly/2. Agree/3. Doubtful/4. Disagree/5. Disagree strongly
68. Girls giggle and talk too much.
    1. Agree strongly/2. Agree/3. Doubtful/4. Disagree/5. Disagree strongly
69. Girls are more sensible than boys.
    1. Agree strongly/2. Agree/3. Doubtful/4. Disagree/5. Disagree strongly
70. I would prefer to be a girl.
    1. Agree strongly/2. Agree/3. Doubtful/4. Disagree/5. Disagree strongly
71. Girls do not bully each other as much as boys do.
    1. Agree strongly/2. Agree/3. Doubtful/4. Disagree/5. Disagree strongly.
    Please comment ....
    ....

[Questions 72 to 75 were the same as Questions 38 to 41, but with 'girls' inserted instead of 'boys' and vice versa.]

FOR ALL PUPILS
93. I look forward to coming to school each day.
    1. Agree strongly/2. Agree/3. Doubtful/4. Disagree/5. Disagree strongly

94. Apart from employment do you think your school prepares you sufficiently for the adult world?
    1. Agree strongly/2. Agree/3. Doubtful/4. Disagree/5. Disagree strongly
96. Do you find the other pupils, in general,
    1. Very friendly/2. Friendly/3. Indifferent/4. Unfriendly/ 5. Very unfriendly?
97. Do you consider that the atmosphere of the school is
    1. Very pleasant/2. Pleasant/3. Neutral/4. Rather unpleasant/ 5. Very unpleasant?

[SCHOOLS PROJECT]

'*Check Questionnaire*'

Name of school .... Grammar/High School
Occupation of Father or Guardian (former occupation if unemployed or deceased). Please give this as fully as you can, e.g. not merely MINER but *Miner-Deputy* or *Cutter*; not ENGINEER but *Maintenance Engineer* or *Graduate Engineer*; not MANAGER but *Manager of small shop*; not FARMER but *Tenant Farmer* or *Smallholder*; not just CIVIL SERVANT but *Civil Servant-Clerk* or *Executive*; not just FACTORY WORKER but *Fitter*, or *Works Labourer*, or *Machine Operator*
OCCUPATION..
Please answer the following questions according to the instructions given.
Do not write your name on this sheet. Your answers will be kept strictly private, so please be *completely frank and truthful*.
Read the following items and *underline* the answer which is true for you.
3. I look forward to coming to school each day.
   1. Agree strongly/2. Agree/3. Doubtful/4. Disagree/5. Disagree strongly
4. Do you find the other pupils, in general,
   1. Very friendly/2. Friendly/3. Indifferent/4. Unfriendly/ 5. Very unfriendly?
5. Do you consider that the atmosphere of the school is
   1. Very pleasant/2. Pleasant/3. Neutral/4. Rather unpleasant/ 5. Very unpleasant?
6. Altogether my life at school is:
   1. Happy/2. Fairly happy/3. Jogging along/4. Rather unhappy/5. Unhappy

Which of the following words best fits your school life? Try to choose one of the first two alternatives, even if it doesn't fit exactly. Use 'neither' only as a last resort.

11. 1. lively/2. dull/3. neither
12. 1. variety/2. monotony/3. neither
13. 1. kindness/2. unpleasantness/3. neither
14. 1. friendly individuals/2. cliques or gangs/3. neither

Modified Boxall Anxiety Test[1]

Here is a list of statements. *Underline* either 'YES' or 'NO' for each one according to whether or not it is true for you. Answer *all* the questions.

ALL ABOUT SCHOOL

1. I feel all funny inside if I have to stand up and speak in front of the class. YES/NO

2. I get very worried if I see a new kind of sum on the blackboard and I do not know how to do it. YES/NO

3. It worries me if some of my sums are wrong. YES/NO

4. My teacher makes me frightened when he or she is cross with the class. YES/NO

5. At home I often worry about school. YES/NO

6. I am very worried if I promise to bring to school a book and then forget. YES/NO

7. I dread making a mistake when reading aloud to the class. YES/NO

8. I don't like other children to know if I get a bad mark for arithmetic. YES/NO

9. I do not like having new teachers. YES/NO

10. Shivers go up and down my spine if I hear that a child in school is to be severely punished. YES/NO

11. I feel so awful if I haven't got gym shoes for P.T. lessons. YES/NO

12. I go all hot and cold inside if I think that I am late for school. YES/NO

13. I dread the thought of my parents coming and talking to my teacher. YES/NO

[1] Revised by the writer.

14. I should hate to go into a new class with strange children. YES/NO
15. I am miserable if my teacher grumbles at me. YES/NO
16. I dread the thought of examinations. YES/NO
17. I hate it if my teacher looks over my shoulder while I am writing. YES/NO
18. I dread having to see the school doctor. YES/NO
19. I get all dithery and muddled if my mathematics teacher asks sudden questions. YES/NO
20. I hate having to go back to school when I have been away. YES/NO
21. I think that coming back to school after the holidays is frightening. YES/NO
22. I am sure that I would go white if I got a message that I am to go to see the headmaster/headmistress. YES/NO
23. Sometimes I have horrid dreams about school. YES/NO

Appendix 2

Some additional tables

TABLE A.1 *Occupational Class composition of the longitudinal sample*

Schools project

		Occupational class of pupils' parent											
		1		2		3		4		5		Totals*	
		N	%	N	%	N	%	N	%	N	%	N	%
Girls aged 11 + and 13 +	Co-ed. schools	32	14·9	60	27·9	80	37·2	33	15·3	10	4·7	215	100
	Girls' schools	37	17·0	59	27·0	90	41·2	23	10·6	6	2·8	218	100
Girls aged 15 + and 17 +	Co-ed. schools	24	20·9	37	32·2	39	33·9	12	10·4	3	2·6	115	100
	Girls' schools	28	23·1	33	27·3	41	34·0	9	7·4	9	7·4	121	100
Boys aged 11 + and 13 +	Co-ed. schools	28	12·4	57	25·2	106	47·0	22	9·7	12	5·3	226	100
	Boys' schools	27	12·3	78	35·5	88	39·9	16	7·3	8	3·6	220	100
Boys aged 15 + and 17 +	Co-ed. schools	20	14·9	36	26·9	60	44·8	10	7·5	7	5·2	134	100
	Boys' schools	31	22·6	39	28·5	52	37·9	12	8·8	3	2·2	137	100

* Includes a few unclassifiable. The analysis is based on occupations and follows the classification used in the Early Leaving Report, viz.: Class 1 Professional, managerial, executive; Class 2 Clerical occupations; Class 3 Skilled occupations; Class 4 Partly skilled; Class 5 Unskilled.

TABLE A.2 *Average intelligence scores (H.S.P.Q. 'B' Factor)*

Schools project longitudinal sample (maximum 10)

		Co-educational schools		Single-sex schools	
		N	Mean	N	Mean
1964					
Boys aged	11 +	226	7·23	220	7·23
	15 +	134	8·15	137	8·19
Girls aged	11 +	215	7·11	218	7·27
	15 +	115	8·24	121	8·27
1966					
Boys aged	13 +	226	7·55	220	7·56
	17 +	134	8·39	137	8·33
Girls aged	13 +	215	7·38	218	7·80
	17 +	115	8·44	121	8·56

NOTE: The co-educated girls have a lower score than those from girls' schools at all four ages: one of these differences (at 15 plus) can obviously be dismissed but that at 13 plus is statistically significant.

TABLE A.3 *Happiness of female ex-pupils (first schools): Analysis by parental occupational class*

'Both schools' survey

Estimates of happiness in school	Replies about first co-educational schools						Replies about first girls' schools					
	Occupational classes						Occupational classes					
	1		2		3, 4, 5		1		2		3, 4, 5	
	N	%	N	%	N	%	N	%	N	%	N	%
Very happy	76	49·7	39	63·0	45	56·3	49	21·9	24	29·6	28	28·9
Fairly happy	55	35·9	18	29·0	24	30·0	85	38·0	32	39·5	35	36·1
Jogging along	10	6·5	2	3·2	5	6·2	46	20·5	15	18·5	17	17·5
Rather unhappy	11	7·2	2	3·2	6	7·5	39	17·4	8	9·9	16	16·5
Very unhappy	1	0·7	1	1·6	0	0	5	2·2	2	2·5	1	1·0
Totals	153	100	62	100	80	100	224	100	81	100	97	100

TABLE A.4 *Happiness of female ex-pupils (last schools): Analysis by parental occupational class*

'Both schools' survey

Estimates of happiness in school	Replies about last co-educational schools						Replies about last girls' schools					
	Occupational classes						Occupational classes					
	1		2		3, 4, 5		1		2		3, 4, 5	
	N	%	N	%	N	%	N	%	N	%	N	%
Very happy	118	60·2	37	50·0	40	45·5	34	27·2	13	22·8	20	28·0
Fairly happy	60	30·6	28	37·8	38	43·2	37	29·6	25	43·8	30	40·0
Jogging along	11	5·6	5	6·8	4	4·5	27	21·6	14	24·6	12	16·0
Rather unhappy	6	3·1	4	5·4	5	5·7	24	19·2	5	8·8	11	14·7
Very unhappy	1	0·5	0	0	1	1·1	3	2·4	0	0	1	1·3
Totals	196	100	74	100	88	100	125	100	57	100	74	100

TABLE A.5 *Pupil happiness and school situation (females): Analysis by first and last school and occupational class*

'Both schools' survey

Happiness estimates of those who agree strongly on pleasant situation of school	Replies about first schools												Replies about last schools											
	Co-educational Occupational classes						Girls' Occupational classes						Co-educational Occupational classes						Girls' Occupational classes					
	1 and 2		3, 4, 5		All*		1 and 2		3, 4, 5		All*		1 and 2		3, 4, 5		All*		1 and 2		3, 4, 5		All*	
	N	%	N	%	N	%	N	%	N	%	N	%	N	%	N	%	N	%	N	%	N	%	N	%
Very happy	40	59·7	15	62·6	56	60·9	32	39·0	12	44·5	44	40·0	64	68·0	22	59·5	86	65·2	21	36·8	9	37·5	30	36·6
Fairly happy	24	35·8	5	20·8	29	31·5	29	35·4	11	40·7	40	36·4	28	29·8	10	27·0	38	28·8	21	36·8	10	41·7	31	37·8
Jogging along	0	0	2	8·3	2	2·2	12	14·6	2	7·4	14	12·7	1	1·1	2	5·4	4	3·0	11	19·3	2	8·3	14	17·1
Rather unhappy	3	4·5	2	8·3	5	5·4	9	11·0	1	3·7	10	9·1	1	1·1	3	8·1	4	3·0	3	5·3	3	12·5	6	7·3
Very unhappy	0	0	0	0	0	0	0	0	1	3·7	2	1·8	0	0	0	0	0	0	1	1·8	0	0	1	1·2
Totals*	67	100	24	100	92	100	82	100	27	100	110	100	94	100	37	100	132	100	57	100	24	100	82	100

* Includes a few unclassifiables. Those percentages which are based on small numbers are liable to large fluctuations.

TABLE A.6 *Pupil happiness and school situation (females): Analysis by first and last schools**

'Both schools' survey

Estimates of happiness in school	Replies about first schools												Replies about last schools											
	Co-educational						Girls'						Co-educational						Girls'					
	Pleasant school situation						Pleasant school situation						Pleasant school situation						Pleasant school situation					
	Agree		Doubtful		Disagree†		Agree		Doubtful		Disagree		Agree		Doubtful		Disagree		Agree		Doubtful		Disagree	
	N	%	N	%	N	%	N	%	N	%	N	%	N	%	N	%	N	%	N	%	N	%	N	%
Very happy	74	55·3	20	46·5	13	44·9	34	20·6	18	28·1	5	7·7	81	48·2	21	53·8	7	33·3	30	24·2	3	12·0	5	17·9
Fairly happy	42	31·3	14	32·6	12	41·4	74	44·9	17	26·6	22	33·8	66	39·3	12	30·8	11	52·4	47	38·0	9	36·0	5	17·9
Jogging along	9	6·7	5	11·6	1	3·4	32	19·4	15	23·4	17	26·2	13	7·7	3	7·7	1	4·8	23	18·5	8	32·0	9	32·1
Rather unhappy	9	6·7	3	7·0	2	6·9	23	13·9	14	21·9	16	24·6	6	3·6	3	7·7	2	9·5	23	18·5	5	20·0	7	25·0
Very unhappy	0	0	1	2·3	1	3·4	2	1·2	0	0	5	7·7	2	1·2	0	0	0	0	1	0·8	0	0	2	7·1
Totals	134	100	43	100	29	100	165	100	64	100	65	100	168	100	39	100	21	100	124	100	25	100	28	100

* The social class analysis is not given as the data showed no consistent trend.
† Combines 'Disagree' with 'Disagree strongly'.

TABLE A.7 *Happiness in school (girls)*

Schools project (longitudinal)

Estimates of happiness in school	Replies from 11 plus girls				Replies from 13 plus girls			
	Co-educational schools		Girls' schools		Co-educational schools		Girls' schools	
	N	%	N	%	N	%	N	%
Happy	129	60·0	116	53·9	102	47·7	103	47·9
Fairly happy	69	32·1	74	34·4	82	38·3	77	35·8
Jogging along	14	6·5	18	8·4	24	11·2	23	10·7
Rather unhappy	3	1·4	6	2·8	6	2·8	7	3·3
Unhappy	0	0	1	0·5	0	0	5	2·3
Totals	215	100	215	100	214	100	215	100

TABLE A.8 *Happiness in school (boys)*

Schools project (longitudinal)

Estimates of happiness in school	Replies from 11 plus boys				Replies from 13 plus boys			
	Co-educational schools		Boys' schools		Co-educational schools		Boys' schools	
	N	%	N	%	N	%	N	%
Happy	110	48·9	83	38·2	96	42·6	72	33·3
Fairly happy	88	39·1	98	45·1	90	40·0	98	45·4
Jogging along	24	10·7	29	13·4	35	15·6	38	17·6
Rather unhappy	2	0·9	6	2·8	2	0·9	7	3·2
Unhappy	1	0·4	1	0·5	2	0·9	1	0·5
Totals	225	100	217	100	225	100	216	100

TABLE A.9 *Happiness in school* (*girls*)

Schools project (*longitudinal*)

Estimates of happiness in school	Replies from 15 plus girls				Replies from 17 plus girls			
	Co-educational schools		Girls' schools		Co-educational schools		Girls' schools	
	N	%	N	%	N	%	N	%
Happy	63	54·7	63	52·5	61	53·0	48	40·0
Fairly happy	41	35·7	37	30·8	34	29·6	48	40·0
Jogging along	8	7·0	17	14·2	16	13·9	22	18·3
Rather unhappy	3	2·6	2	1·7	4	3·5	2	1·7
Unhappy	0	0	1	0·8	0	0	0	0
Totals	115	100	120	100	115	100	120	100

TABLE A.10 *Happiness in school* (*boys*)

Schools project (*longitudinal*)

Estimates of happiness in school	Replies from 15 plus boys				Replies from 17 plus boys			
	Co-educational schools		Boys' schools		Co-educational schools		Boys' schools	
	N	%	N	%	N	%	N	%
Happy	64	48·2	59	43·1	44	33·0	61	44·5
Fairly happy	48	36·1	58	42·3	62	46·7	56	40·9
Jogging along	16	12·0	18	13·1	20	15·0	17	12·4
Rather unhappy	4	3·0	2	1·5	6	4·5	2	1·5
Unhappy	1	0·7	0	0	1	0·8	1	0·7
Totals	133	100	137	100	133	100	137	100

TABLE A.11 *Look forward to coming to school (girls aged 13 plus)*

'*Check*' *questionnaire*

	Replies from girls in			
	Co-educational schools		Girls' schools	
	N	%	N	%
Agree strongly	33	7·3	34	5·1
Agree	219	48·9	305	45·3
Doubtful	153	34·1	251	37·3
Disagree	33	7·3	72	10·7
Disagree strongly	11	2·4	11	1·6
Totals	449	100	673	100

TABLE A.12 *Look forward to coming to school* (*boys' responses*)
Schools project (*1966*)

Estimate	Comment	Co-educational schools	Boys' schools
Agree and Agree strongly	*School*		
	like school much, enjoy, fun	31	25
	like usually, on the whole	18	13
	useful, essential	1	10
	variety of school life	8	1
	boring at home, school better	7	6
	Pupils		
	for friendships	12	11
	Teachers and teaching		
	friendly teachers, good	5	3
	like school work	7	6
	depends on teachers, lessons	6	5
	Personal		
	but don't like getting up		3
	sometimes get very tired	1	1
	but prefer other pastimes		2
	others		3
Totals		96	89
Doubtful	doubtful in general	6	11
	doubtful sometimes	14	13
	depends which day, teacher	12	9
	only useful	2	3
	all right when I get there	7	4
	monotonous, routine, boring	7	6
	no choice		4
	worry about homework, tests	3	
	prefer earn money, do other things	8	5
	dislike getting up, too early	13	7
	others	2	6
Totals		74	68

TABLE A.12 *(continued) Look forward to coming to school (boys' responses)*

Estimate	Comment	Co-educational schools	Boys' schools
Disagree and	*School*		
	hate it, depressing, dread it	2	8
Disagree	sometimes hate it	3	
strongly	dislike school	18	21
	dislike but necessary	4	5
	but don't hate, dislike	5	5
	but enjoy when there	2	
	not normal to look forward to it		1
	Teachers and teaching		
	too boring	7	15
	dislike some teachers	7	8
	depends on the day, teachers	10	9
	dislike tests, homework, examinations		4
	depends if homework done, right	1	2
	depends on mood, weather	2	
	disliked by teachers		1
	Activities		
	prefer leisure activities, games, home	10	3
	Personal		
	dislike getting up early	17	19
	sometimes too tired	2	
	Work		
	rather be working		3
	others	6	11
Totals		96	115

TABLE A.13 *Classification of unhappy pupils' free responses**

	Number of pupils		Teachers'† discipline	Working pupils too hard	General† dislike of school	Work difficulties	Trouble with classmates	General anxiety	Out-of-school or home difficulties
Girls aged 13 plus									
Co-educated	6	Unfavourable	-4	-1	-5	-13	-4	0	-9
		Favourable	+2	0	0	+1	0	0	0
in girls' schools	12	Unfavourable	-28	-4	-22	-14	-7	-7	-4
		Favourable	+7	0	+1	0	0	0	0
Girls aged 15 plus									
Co-educated	10	Unfavourable	0	0	-3	-8	-2	-3	-24
		Favourable	0	0	0	0	0	0	0
in girls' schools	13	Unfavourable	-5	-1	-11	-9	0	-3	-15
		Favourable	0	0	0	0	0	0	0
Combined co-ed. girls	16	Unfavourable	-4	-1	-8	-21	-6	-3	-33
		Favourable	+2	0	0	+1	0	0	0
		Balance	-2	-1	-8	-20	-6	-3	-33
Combined girls in girls' schools	25	Unfavourable	-33	-5	-33	-23	-7	-10	-19
		Favourable	+7	0	+1	0	0	0	0
		Balance	-26	-5	-32	-23	-7	-10	-19

NOTE: The principal reasons given for unhappiness are heavily underlined to facilitate the contrast for the two types of school. The smaller numbers are recorded merely to complete the table. Though the scoring system is arbitrary it should be fair enough for the comparison of the two groups, but it should be noted that the contrasted groups are unequal in numbers.

* Teachers' discipline is scored minus if there is trouble or dislike evident, or if school rules are mentioned as irksome or irritating. Under general dislike are scored boredom with school (-1) and hatred of school or similar phrase (-2). 'Work difficulties' comprises difficulty in studying or understanding, or if, in the Mooney special problem response, dislike of a particular subject is expressed. Those comments showing a general anxiety not traceable to problems at home or school are placed under 'anxiety'. Out-of-school or home difficulties includes trouble about boy-friends. Of the 15-year-old girls two from girls' schools and one from a co-educational school made no comment; they were omitted in calculating the averages. In the table heading, 'unhappy' includes those who said 'rather unhappy'.

† A follow-up test after analysis of variance shows that the difference between the scores of the girls at co-educational schools and those at single-sex schools, for teachers' discipline and dislike of schoo combined, is statistically significant beyond the ·01 level.

TABLE A.14 *Average scores of 'unhappy' and 'rather unhappy' girls*

	Number of pupils	Bristol Social Adjust. Guide	High School Personality Questionnaire				Maudsley		Mooney
			Anxiety* 0–100	Factor H† 0–20	Factor O‡ 0–20	Intelligence 0–10	Neurot. 0–48	Extrov. 0–48	Problems (210 possible)
Co-ed. 15 plus	6	10·3	66·8	4·5	14·6	7·2	37·1	23·8	43·3
Single-sex 15 plus	12	9·0	77·7	6·2	15·5	8·1	39·4	36·3	43·5
							H.S.P.Q. 4–40	7–70	
Co-ed. 13 plus	11	Not given	74·5	4·2	14·3	7·0	21·1	27·5	42·0
Single-sex 13 plus	15	Not given	72·3	5·5	14·4	7·6	22·0	32·8	54·7

* Possible range not given (10 extremely low and 100 extremely high).

† Factor H: Low scoring indicates a person who is withdrawn, retiring in face of opposite sex, aloof, conscientious, considerate and danger-sensitive as opposed to adventurous, likes meeting people, overt interest in opposite sex, genial, frivolous, carefree. It is interesting to note the slight signs of possible differences between 'unhappy' girls in co-educational and girls' schools, but the fewness of the numbers and shortness of the test make statistical analysis unwise. All four groups score below the average for their main groups, the co-educational more so than the others.

‡ Factor O: Low scoring indicates *self-confidence*, cheerfulness, rudely vigorous, no fears, as opposed to worrying, depressed, sensitive, strong sense of duty, *insecure*. Here also the four groups score above the average for their main groups, i.e. in the direction of greater insecurity, etc.

TABLE A.15 *Test scores: unhappy girls in co-educational schools (aged 15 plus in 1964)*

Occu-pational class	Code No.	Intelligence score	Extroversion–introversion (Maudsley)	Neuroticism (Maudsley)	Mooney Problem Check-list	Anxiety (H.S.P.Q.)	Factors H and O (H.S.P.Q.)	Bristol score (teacher's)
3	1	10	25 Normal	41 High	31 Fairly high	82 High	Withdrawn and insecure	9
1	2	9	31 Normal	26 Normal	31 Fairly high	66	Active, social	21 Maladjusted
2	3	9	38 Fairly high	24 Fairly low	5 Very low	41 Low	Active, social	4
1	4	9	32 Normal	44 High	61 High	80 High	A little shy, insecure	6
3	5	9	11 Introverted (low)	47 High	50 High	84 High	Shy and rather insecure	6
2	6	6	30 Normal	19 Low	18 Normal	49	Active, social	None given
4	7	6	8 Low (introverted)	44 High	40 High	72 High	Shy, withdrawn	0
4	8	6	16 Low (introverted)	42 High	39 Fairly high	59	Rather shy	15 Unsettled
3	9	6	29 Normal	44 High	82 Very high	56	Timid	18 Unsettled
3	10	5	32 Normal	33 Normal	36 Fairly high	73 High	Some bitterness, not shy	13 Unsettled
3	11	4	10 Introverted (low)	44 High	83 Very high	73 High	Extremely shy and insecure	11 Unsettled

TABLE A.16 *Test scores: unhappy girls in girls' schools (aged 15 plus in 1964)*

Occupational class	Code No.	Intelligence score	Extroversion–introversion (Maudsley)	Neuroticism (Maudsley)	Mooney Problem Check-list	Anxiety (H.S.P.Q.)	Factors H and O (H.S.P.Q.)	Bristol score (teacher's)
2	1	10	40 High	36 Normal	49 High	74 High	Rather shy	8
5	2	9	33 Normal	36 Normal	47 High	82 High	Rather shy, insecure, depressed	15 Unsettled
4	3	9	24 Normal	44 High	32 Fairly high	78 High	Shy and timid, insecure	8
2	4	9	46 High	44 High	68 Very high	76 High	Fairly normal	17 Unsettled
3	5	9	36 Normal to High	46 High	81 Very high	80 High	Very timid, shy, insecure	2
1	6	9	46 High	46 High	23 Not high	66	Active, friendly	10 Unsettled
2	7	8	33 Normal	44 High	70 Very high	88 Very high	Not shy or timid, insecure	19 Unsettled
1	8	8	44 High	26 Normal	15 Low	82 High	Shy, rather insecure, depressed	5
2	9	8	39 High	43 High	44 High	84 High	Rather shy	3
1	10	8	34 Normal	45 High	62 High	80 High	Shy, timid	7
3	11	7	44 High	32 Normal	41 High	82 High	Not shy or timid, insecure, depressed	17 Unsettled
2	12	7	33 Normal	46 High	21 Not high	64	Friendly, impulsive, little insecure	6
5	13	7	26 Normal	36 Normal	19 Average	64	Rather confident	5
2	14	7	40 High	32 Normal	50 High	81 High	Not shy or timid, a little insecure	9
3	15	6	27 Normal	35 Normal	30	84 High	Not shy, rather insecure	10 Unsettled

TABLE A.17 *Test scores: unhappy girls in co-educational schools (aged 13 plus in 1966)*

Code No.	Occu- pational class	Intelligence score	Extroversion (H.S.P.Q.)*	Neuroticism (H.S.P.Q.)	Anxiety (H.S.P.Q.)	Factors H and O (H.S.P.Q.)	Mooney Problem Check- list	No. of school problems	% school problems to whole	Looks forward to coming to school	Pressure of work worries me
1	2	9	26 Fairly low	20·7	87 Very high	Rather shy and unsettled	37	8	22	Disagree	Agree strongly
2	3	7	21 Low	21·8	78 High	Shy	77	17	22	Doubtful	Agree strongly
3	3	7	37 Normal	18·2	62	A little shy	86	22	26	Disagree strongly	Agree strongly
4	4	7	30 Normal to low	24·4	74 High	A little shy and insecure	26	15	58	Disagree strongly	Agree strongly
5	2	6	25 Fairly low	15·2 Fairly low	62	Shy and insecure	9	3	33	Disagree strongly	Agree strongly
6	2	6	26 Fairly low	26·4	84 High	A little shy	15	5	33	Agree	Disagree strongly

* Note that the tests on extroversion and introversion are different for the two age groups (15 plus and 13 plus).

TABLE A.18 *Test scores: unhappy girls in girls' schools (aged 13 plus in 1966)*

Code No.	Occupa-tional class	Intelli-gence score	Extroversion (H.S.P.Q.)	Neuroticism (H.S.P.Q.)	Anxiety (H.S.P.Q.)	Factors H and O (H.S.P.Q.)	Mooney Problem Check-list	No. of school problems	% school problems to whole	Looks for-ward to coming to school	Pressure of work worries me
1	3	10	30 Fairly low	27·7	67 High	Shy	89	15	17	Disagree strongly	Agree strongly
2	2	9	18 Low	27·0	80 High	Withdrawn and rather insecure	92	20	22	Disagree strongly	Agree
3	3	8	26 Fairly low	23·6	86 Very high	Very shy	59	11	19	Disagree strongly	Agree
4	1	8	27 Fairly low	23·6	86 Very high	A little shy and insecure	26	7	27	Doubtful	Agree strongly
5	2	8	22 Low	29·4 Rather high	74 High	Very shy	95	19	20	Doubtful	Agree strongly
6	3	8	42 Normal	21·5	75 High	Average socially, insecure	26	14	54	Disagree	Agree strongly
7	3	8	28 Fairly low	22·9	79 High	Rather insecure	97	11	11	Disagree strongly	Doubtful
8	5	7	53 High	12·5 Low	65	Active, social	21	9	43	Disagree strongly	Disagree
9	4	7	41 Normal	21·8	58	Average socially	34	10	29	Disagree	Agree
10	4	6	31 Normal	22·4	64	Average socially a little insecure	38	9	24	Doubtful	Agree
11	3	6	38 Normal	16 Fairly low	60	Average socially	53	8	15	Disagree strongly	Agree strongly
12	3	6	37 Normal	15·4 Fairly low	74 High	Rather timid and insecure	26	17	65	Disagree strongly	Agree strongly

TABLE A.19 *School's control of out-of-school conduct*

(*Women's responses, 'Both schools' survey*)

Estimate	Comment	Co-educational schools	Girls' schools
Excessive			2
	because boarding	2	6
	school image too important	4	8
	no talking to boys, parties, etc.		8
	no boy/girl friendships	2	5
	too much interference, out of date petty rules, eating in streets, hats, cafés	6	21
	severe punishment		2
	staff, heads too nosey		3
	others		2
Totals		14	57
Rather strict		8	4
	too much stress image	5	8
	concern about public opinion		7
	hats, cafés, weekends, evenings, Saturday jobs, eating in streets, too much interference	10	23
	when in uniform, buses	9	18
	on smoking, drinking, swearing	1	
	head too strict	7	
	boy/girl relationships	2	
	too concerned private life	2	2
	no talking to boys		3
	strict but necessary	16	7
	but ineffective	1	2
	others	7	5
Totals		68	79

TABLE A.19 *(continued) School's control of out-of-school conduct*

Estimate	Comment	Co-educational schools	Girls' schools
Just right		16	6
	correct stress reputation of school	14	
	when in uniform, to and from school	20	
	sufficient interest, when necessary	23	7
	good behaviour stressed	17	5
	strict but necessary		3
	not dominated; few restrictions, interference	17	
	respect for school	3	3
	no boy/girl friendships	3	2
	out-of-school conduct good		3
	staff not interested		5
	others	10	2
Totals		123	36
Rather insufficient		8	
	only concerned re school reputation	4	
	few rules	3	
	wrong concern—hats, etc.		1
	staff took no interest	11	11
	staff attempts ineffectual	9	4
	head weak, not strict	3	
	rowdy behaviour buses	8	
	only on buses		1
	school poor reputation	2	
	homes too scattered	7	
	but not needed	1	1
	others	7	5
Totals		63	23
Much too lax	poor behaviour in public	2	
	pupils bad discipline		2
	poor behaviour of boys	1	
	no interest unless complaints	13	7
	homes too dispersed	1	
Totals		17	9

TABLE A.20 *School preference: Amalgamated pupils versus the remainder of the 'co-educated last'*

'*Both schools*' *survey*

Preference	Men				Women			
	Normal co-educational		Amalgamated		Normal co-educational		Amalgamated	
	N	%	N	%	N	%	N	%
Single-sex school much	4	5·5	3	(13)	24	9·5	6	6·7
Single-sex school a little	3	4·1	2	(8)	14	5·5	3	3·3
No preference	5	6·8	2	(8)	8	3·2	11	12·2
Mixed school a little	4	5·5	2	(8)	27	10·7	16	17·8
Mixed school much	57	78·1	15	(62)	179	71·1	54	60·0
Totals	73	100	24	100	252	100	90	100

NOTE: The men from amalgamated schools were less in favour of mixed schools than the remainder (non significant): the women were also less in favour than the rest of the 'co-educated last' women (statistically significant).

TABLE A.21 *Attitude to girls pleasant or unpleasant (men's comments)*

'*Both schools*' *survey*

Estimate	Comment	Co-educational schools	Boys' schools
Pleasant		3	2
	good friendly relationship	21	
	taken for granted—normal interest	5	
	no experience of girls' company —immature		2
	mixed in class, but not out of it	2	
	opposite sex completely cut off		3
	travelled with and dated girls		5
	romantic relationship	4	
	interesting discussions	2	
	often wistfully pleasant		2
	sex talk but not unpleasant		1
	friendly rivalry with sister school		2
	young—shyness, avoidance	2	
	depends on individual	1	
	better with girls than boys	2	
Totals		42	17
Fairly pleasant			6
	good friendly relationship	7	
	romantic relationship	1	
	most boys sex-mad		3
	at first shy, avoidance	1	
	bawdy but not excessively		2
	little contact in school hours		2
	varied with age, too young	7	1
	depends on individual	2	
	better with girls than boys	1	
	but annoying distraction	1	
	better than single-sex school	1	
	others	1	3
Totals		22	17

TABLE A.21 *(continued) Attitude to girls pleasant and unpleasant* *(men's comments)*

Estimate	Comment	Co-educational schools	Boys' schools
Neutral		1	1
	good friendly relationship	1	
	opposite sex not discussed much		4
	taken for granted	1	
	unknown factor		5
	romantic relationship	1	
	did not bother with girls		4
	more mature as grew older	1	2
	occasionally smutty talk		1
	boys will talk of girls		1
	shy but interested	1	
	depends on individual	2	
	varied with age	2	
Totals		**10**	**18**
A little unpleasant			3
	only 11-year-olds—normal	2	1
	improved in VIth		3
	at first thought girls foolish	1	
	pupils 'sex starved'		2
	girls looked on purely from sex angle		8
	no positive attitude towards opposite sex		1
	crude conversation, unhealthy		5
	some boasting of sex experience, some depraved		3
	others	1	
Totals		**4**	**26**
Unpleasant	girls all right for sex, otherwise 'sissy'		1
	dirty and unhealthy		2
	scared of girls—immature		4
Totals		**0**	**7**

Appendix 2

TABLE A.22 (*a*) *Normal interest in girls* and (*b*) *Boy–girl crazy*

'*Both schools*' *survey* (*males*)

Estimates of boys' attitudes to girls	Normal interest				Boy–girl crazy			
	Co-educational schools		Boys' schools		Co-educational schools		Boys' schools	
	N	%	N	%	N	%	N	%
True	138	78·0	74	43·8	7	4·0	25	14·1
Partly true	31	17·4	63	37·3	48	27·3	66	37·3
False	4	2·3	15	8·9	86	48·8	63	35·6
Doubtful	4	2·3	17	10·0	35	19·9	23	13·0
Totals	177	100	169	100	176	100	177	100

NOTE: The difference between the co-educational and boys' schools is statistically highly significant for 'normal interest' for both juniors and seniors, but that for 'girl–boy crazy' is only highly significant for the seniors. The differences between the juniors and seniors were surprisingly not very large but they were reversed in the two types of school, the estimates showing less boy–girl craziness in the senior than in the junior co-educational school. This Table omits the junior/senior breakdown.

TABLE A.23 (*a*) *Antagonistic and* (*b*) *Timid, with girls*

'*Both schools*' *survey* (*males*)

Estimates of boys' attitudes to girls	Replies 'Antagonistic'				Replies 'Timid'			
	Co-educational schools		Boys' schools		Co-educational schools		Boys' schools	
	N	%	N	%	N	%	N	%
True	4	2·3	4	2·3	1	0·6	17	9·8
Partly true	34	19·3	35	20·3	52	30·2	69	39·6
False	107	60·8	96	55·9	90	52·3	56	32·2
Doubtful	31	17·6	37	21·5	29	16·9	32	18·4
Totals	176	100	172	100	172	100	174	100

NOTE: The differences between the estimates for the co-educational and boys' schools are highly significant for juniors and seniors for timidity but not for antagonism.

'*Both schools*' survey

Estimate	Type of comment	Co-ed. school	Girls' school
Pleasant	good friendly relationship, normal	89	10
	friendly rivalry	7	
	interesting discussions	8	
	depends on individual boys, age, etc.	15	
	better with boys than girls	2	
	more natural than girls' school	8	
	romantic relationship	8	
	man-mad, boy-crazy	4	23
	boys novelties		12
	some discussed boys all day		5
	some girls showed off	2	
	boys adored by most		7
	more interested in boys than the co-ed.		2
	most had steady boy-friends		5
	boys' school near, mixed frequently		10
	some shy, especially young	3	3
	depended on morals		2
	others, e.g. 'pleasant'	16	8
Totals		162	87
Fairly pleasant	good friendly relationship, normal	29	4
	friendly rivalry	3	
	depended on the boy, age, etc.	21	
	interesting discussions	2	
	tendency to show off	5	
	romantic relationship	5	
	some shy, especially young	2	4
	attitude better in co-ed. school	2	
	boy-crazy groups		14
	boy-crazy individuals	3	
	silly, immature sometimes (because boys taboo)		9
	varied from boy-crazy to naturally interested		3
	good relationship with adjacent boys' school		6
	great excitement if male appeared		3
	mixed groups and boy-friends outside school		5
	too segregated to know		4
	others, e.g. 'fairly pleasant'	23	17
Totals		95	69

Estimate	Type of comment	Co-ed. school	Girls' school
Neutral	normal interest	12	
	interest increased with age	6	19
	annoying distraction	3	
	depends on individual		5
	enforced neutrality, little contact		13
	mild interest in near-by boys' school		2
	'boy-mad' usual with young girls, silly	3	5
	immature, boy-crazy compared with co-ed.		3
	a little in awe of boys, scared		3
	others	10	6
Totals		34	56
A little unpleasant	good friendly relationship	1	
	many girls boy-mad	1	11
	morbid obsession, unhealthy		5
	sex mad, main conversation		3
	many girls boasted about conquests		6
	boasting sexual experience		1
	exhibitionist, flirting, badly behaved		4
	some hysteria when boys visited school		3
	boys taboo, therefore idolized		2
	more rivalry over boys than co-ed.		1
	out of things if no boy-friends		4
	juniors giggled over boys		4
	frightened of them		4
	more unmarried mothers		2
	foul jokes		1
	others, e.g. a little unpleasant	6	10
Totals		8	61
Unpleasant	man-mad, idol worship	1	2
	sexual desire		2
	much giggling and talk about sex and boys, silly		4
Totals		1	8
No estimate	too young		2
	unnatural and unhealthy		1
	went mad when saw a male		2
	others	1	
Totals		1	5

TABLE A.25 (*a*) *Normal interest in boys and* (*b*) *Girl–boy crazy*

'*Both schools*' *survey* (*females*)

Estimates of girls' attitudes to boys	Normal interest				Girl–boy crazy			
	Co-educational schools		Girls' schools		Co-educational schools		Girls' schools	
	N	%	N	%	N	%	N	%
True	506	79·1	260	41·6	33	5·3	179	29·1
Partly true	112	17·5	246	39·4	163	26·3	260	42·1
False	9	1·4	57	9·1	322	52·1	119	19·2
Doubtful	13	2·0	62	9·9	101	16·3	59	9·6
Totals	640	100	625	100	619	100	617	100

NOTE: The difference between the distributions for co-educational and girls' schools is statistically very highly significant for 'normal interest' and for 'girl–boy crazy'. In neither type of school is there much difference between juniors and seniors.

TABLE A.26 (*a*) *Antagonistic and* (*b*) *Timid, with boys*

'*Both schools*' *survey* (*females*)

Girls' attitudes to boys	'Antagonistic'				'Timid'			
	Co-educational schools		Girls' schools		Co-educational schools		Girls' schools	
	N	%	N	%	N	%	N	%
True	9	1·5	11	1·8	14	2·3	84	14·0
Partly true	110	17·8	104	17·1	152	24·8	270	45·0
False	382	61·6	383	63·0	313	51·2	162	27·0
Doubtful	118	19·1	110	18·1	133	21·7	83	14·0
Totals	619	100	608	100	612	100	599	100

NOTE: The difference between the estimates for co-educational and girls' schools is statistically highly significant for 'timidity' for both juniors and seniors, but not for 'antagonism'.

TABLE A.27 *Sufficient preparation for adult world?* (*age 13 plus*)

Schools project—1966 estimates

| Estimates of sufficiency of preparation for adult world | Replies from boys | | | | Replies from girls | | | |
| | Co-ed. schools | | Boys' schools | | Co-ed. schools | | Girls' schools | |
	N	%	N	%	N	%	N	%
Agree strongly	24	10·8	15	7·0	19	8·9	21	9·9
Agree	127	57·2	119	55·7	113	52·8	101	47·4
Doubtful	46	20·7	48	22·4	55	25·7	49	23·0
Disagree	20	9·0	27	12·6	22	10·3	32	15·0
Disagree strongly	5	2·3	5	2·3	5	2·3	10	4·7
Totals	222	100	214	100	214	100	213	100

NOTE: The differences between co-educational and single-sex schools for both boys and girls aged 13 plus are not statistically significant.

TABLE A.28 *Anxiety to School: Mean scores* (*Boxall*) *by parental occupation*

Schools project: longitudinal sample

| Occup. class | Boys in co-ed. schools | | | | Boys in boys' schools | | | |
	N	Age 11+	Age 13+	Change	N	Age 11+	Age 13+	Change
1	28	10·61	10·07	−0·54	26	10·77	10·46	−0·31
2	56	10·82	10·50	−0·32	78	10·71	9·54	−1·18
3	103	11·51	10·31	−1·20	87	12·39	10·60	−1·79
4 + 5	34	11·03	9·79	−1·24	24	12·96	11·42	−1·54
All*	222	11·17	10·27	−0·90	218	11·65	10·35	−1·30

| Occup. class | Girls in co-ed. schools | | | | Girls in girls' schools | | | |
	N	Age 11+	Age 13+	Change	N	Age 11+	Age 13+	Change
1	32	11·59	10·56	−1·03	36	11·53	9·75	−1·78
2	60	11·80	11·97	+0·17	59	11·92	11·41	−0·51
3	79	13·35	12·09	−1·23	90	12·77	11·79	−0·98
4 + 5	40	12·33	12·18	−0·15	29	13·76	12·69	−1·07
All*	211	12·45	11·84	−0·61	217	12·43	11·47	−0·96

* Includes a few unclassifiable.

TABLE A.29 *The drop-out problem*

School Anxiety Test 1964

Comparison of mean scores for leavers and the remainder of the sample

	(Age 11 plus—longitudinal sample)					
	1964 sample		Leavers and absentees		Remainder 1964 sample	
Girls						
co-educated	236	12·32	25	11·2	211	12·45
from girls' schools	238	12·61	21	14·3	217	12·43
Boys						
co-educated	235	11·10	13	9·8	222	11·17
from boys' schools	238	11·73	20	12·55	218	11·65

TABLE A.30 *Anxiety about school*

Longitudinal sample

		Co-educated boys		Boys in boys' schools		Co-educated girls		Girls in girls' schools	
		Yes	No	Yes	No	Yes	No	Yes	No
Teacher makes me frightened when cross with class									
Age	11 +	57	165	72	146	71	140	79	138
Age	13 +	52	170	52	164	72	139	71	145
At home I often worry about school									
Age	11 +	85	134	83	133	72	137	81	134
Age	13 +	105	114	92	124	91	120	97	118
I hate having to go back to school									
Age	11 +	117	99	115	101	103	104	120	93
Age	13 +	123	99	131	86	92	119	106	111
Coming back to school after holidays is frightening									
Age	11 +	61	159	69	148	52	158	51	165
Age	13 +	39	183	57	161	36	175	50	167

The following differences were statistically significant:

1. The drop in score on the frightening effect of the teacher amongst boys in boys' schools between age 11 and 13.
2. The reduction in score of co-educated boys between age 11 and 13 about going back to school being frightening.
3. The reduction for co-educated girls aged 13 compared with those aged 11 on coming back to school being frightening.
Almost significant was the increase in score between age 11 and 13 of boys in boys' schools about hating going back to school.

TABLE A.31 *Mooney Problem Check list: Longitudinal survey 1964–6 (36 schools)*

Girls aged 11 plus and 13 plus—mean scores

Occup. class	N	Age	Health and physical develop- ment	School	Home and family	Money, work and future	Boy– girl	People in general	Self- concern	Overall
Co-educated girls										
1 and 2	92	11+	2·27	2·75	1·26	1·39	1·48	2·47	3·42	15·04
		13+	2·87	5·07	2·54	2·92	4·02	3·46	4·14	25·03
3	80	11+	2·43	3·33	1·65	2·04	2·18	3·51	3·88	19·00
		13+	3·99	6·56	3·90	4·08	5·00	4·35	4·89	32·76
4 and 5	43	11+	2·44	2·72	1·26	1·70	1·93	2·02	3·26	15·33
		13+	3·21	6·05	2·72	3·35	3·88	3·51	5·21	27·93
all	215	11+	2·36	2·96	1·40	1·69	1·83	2·77	3·56	16·57
		13+	3·35	5·82	3·08	3·44	4·36	3·80	4·63	28·49
Girls in girls' schools										
1 and 2	96	11+	2·53	3·07	2·26	2·10	2·43	2·89	4·45	19·73
		13+	3·00	5·64	3·05	3·39	4·08	3·93	4·07	28·05
3	90	11+	2·03	3·22	1·99	1·87	2·93	4·03	17·67	
		13+	3·30	6·24	3·20	3·81	4·62	4·10	4·97	30·24
4 and 5	29	11+	2·55	3·21	1·52	1·59	1·59	3·00	3·72	17·17
		13+	3·72	7·93	3·17	3·41	4·28	4·03	5·62	32·17
all	215	11+	2·33	3·15	1·88	1·99	2·08	2·92	4·18	18·52
		13+	3·22	6·20	3·13	3·57	4·33	4·01	5·06	29·53

All 42 means rise. The greater speed of working of the 13-year-olds may have had something to do with this, but is unlikely to be the whole explanation. In five of the problem areas the increase of mentions between 11 plus and 13 plus is slightly less for the sample from girls' schools, in one area there is virtual equality of increase, and in the remaining area, *the school*, there is a small advantage to the co-educational sample.

TABLE A.32 *Mooney Problem check list: Longitudinal survey 1964–6 (36 schools)*

Boys aged 11 plus and 13 plus—mean scores

Occup. class	N	Age	Health and physical development	School	Home and family	Money, work and future	Boy–girl	People in general	Self-concern	Overall
Co-educated boys										
1 and 2	85	11 +	2·59	4·13	2·55	3·08	2·53	3·32	4·92	23·12
		13 +	3·27	6·07	2·72	3·60	4·53	3·49	4·75	28·44
3	106	11 +	2·44	3·58	2·28	2·74	2·16	3·21	4·25	20·66
		13 +	3·53	6·08	3·52	3·77	3·82	3·97	5·03	29·73
4 and 5	34	11 +	2·00	3·41	2·65	2·56	2·32	3·29	3·50	19·74
		13 +	3·79	6·24	4·18	3·97	4·59	4·41	4·79	31·97
all	225	11 +	2·43	3·76	2·44	2·84	2·32	3·26	4·39	21·45
		13 +	3·47	6·10	3·32	3·74	4·20	3·86	4·89	29·58
Boys from boys' schools										
1 and 2	105	11 +	2·19	3·18	2·11	2·60	2·40	2·82	3·64	18·94
		13 +	3·04	6·17	2·88	3·23	4·07	3·17	4·39	26·94
3	88	11 +	2·83	4·20	2·86	3·19	2·60	3·38	4·52	23·59
		13 +	3·03	6·30	2·72	3·42	4·26	3·45	4·35	27·53
4 and 5	24	11 +	2·96	5·33	3·54	3·00	3·25	4·71	5·21	28·00
		13 +	3·63	7·21	3·21	3·50	3·92	4·38	6·17	32·00
all	217	11 +	2·53	3·83	2·58	2·88	2·58	3·25	4·17	21·83
		13 +	3·10	6·34	2·85	3·34	4·13	3·42	4·57	27·74

Of the 42 means, 37 rise from age 11 to 13, the single-sex educated groups rising less than the co-educated in all sections *except school*, where the trend was slightly reversed. It should be noted that if the co-educated of combined occupational classes 1 and 2 are compared with the single-sex educated of the same classes, the co-educated have rather lower increases than the single-sex educated, and that this trend is reversed in the other two occupational class groups. Without exception the co-ed. means rise with occupational class, but with boys from single-sex schools there is a tendency for them to fall.

TABLE A.32a *Mooney Problem Check list: Special problems. Longitudinal survey 1964-6 (36 schools)—11 plus and 13 plus girls*

Occup. class	N	Age	Health and physical development	School		Home and family	Money, work and future	Boy-girl	People in general	Self-concern	Overall
				N	%*						
Co-educated girls											
1 and 2	92	11+	19	23	25·0	20	3	5	9	13	92
		13+	16	20	20·8	22	7	19	8	4	96
3	80	11+	14	20	24·4	13	4	8	11	12	82
		13+	10	20	20·4	24	13	15	11	5	98
4 and 5	43	11+	15	11	22·4	5	4	2	3	9	49
		13+	6	9	17·6	10	5	8	6	7	51
all	215	11+	48	54	24·2	38	11	15	23	34	223
		13+	32	49	20·0	56	25	42	25	16	245
Girls from girls' schools											
1 and 2	96	11+	23	14	16·3	13	5	4	9	18	86
		13+	10	16	15·8	20	12	19	15	9	101
3	90	11+	11	26	30·6	10	5	3	11	19	85
		13+	11	21	27·6	12	5	9	9	9	76
4 and 5	29	11+	3	10	33·3	5	5	1	2	4	30
		13+	5	6	21·4	5	1	3	5	3	28
all	215	11+	37	50	33·1	28	15	8	22	41	201
		13+	26	43	26·5	37	18	31	29	21	205

* Number of 'School' problems as a percentage of Overall problems.
NOTE: In any section the pupil who had problems was counted only once but the same pupil has sometimes recorded problems in several sections.

TABLE A.33 *H.S.P.Q. Anxiety mean scores with occupational class*
Longitudinal survey

Occup. class	Boys in co-educational schools				Boys in boys' schools				Difference between differences*
	N	Age	Mean	Difference 11+/13+	N	Age	Mean	Difference 11+/13+	
1	28	11+	60·82	−2·86	27	11+	56·41	7.63	+10·49
		13+	57·96			13+	64·04		
2	57	11+	57·56	0·40	78	11+	57·06	4·04	+3·64
		13+	57·97			13+	61·10		
3	106	11+	58·43	1·13	88	11+	60·51	0·48	0·65
		13+	59·56			13+	60·99		
4 + 5	34	11+	58·35	4·24	24	11+	59·79	5·17	+0·93
		13+	62·59			13+	64·96		
all†	226	11+	58·56	0·94	220	11+	58·85	3·19	+2·25
		13+	59·50			13+	62·04		

* A + sign before a difference indicates that the single sex-schools had the greater increase in anxiety.
† Includes a few unclassifiable.

TABLE A.34 *Mooney Problem Check list: Longitudinal survey 1964–6 (36 schools)*

Boys aged 15 plus and 17 plus—mean scores

Occup. class	N	Age	Health and physical develop-ment	School	Home and family	Money, work and future	Boy–girl	People in general	Self-concern	Overall
Co-educated boys										
1 + 2	56	15 +	2·73	5·73	3·13	3·46	4·41	3·52	4·73	27·71
		17 +	2·11	3·86	2·14	3·34	2·73	2·48	3·36	20·02
3, 4 & 5	77	15 +	2·86	6·14	2·58	4·22	4·04	4·05	4·69	28·58
		17 +	2·70	4·68	2·00	4·06	2·96	2·78	3·70	22·88
all	133	15 +	2·80	5·97	2·81	3·90	4·20	3·83	4·71	28·22
		17 +	2·45	4·33	2·06	3·76	2·86	2·65	3·56	21·68
Boys in boys' schools										
1 + 2	70	15 +	3·14	4·83	3·24	4·33	3·57	3·73	5·67	28·51
		17 +	2·69	3·73	2·50	3·57	2·94	2·80	3·96	22·19
3, 4 & 5	67	15 +	3·52	6·27	3·63	5·18	4·46	4·19	5·88	33·13
		17 +	3·07	5·12	3·00	5·06	3·43	3·51	4·36	27·55
all	137	15 +	3·33	5·53	3·43	4·74	4·01	3·96	5·77	30·77
		17 +	2·88	4·41	2·74	4·30	3·18	3·15	4·15	24·81

Every boys' group mean falls between 15 plus and 17 plus, within each type of school and within each occupational class—28 instances. The co-educational means fall rather more than the single-sex though not in all sections, the most favourable to co-education being the school and boy–girl relationship sections. For occupational classes 1 and 2 five means fall more in the co-educational sample and two the reverse, while for classes 3, 4 and 5 the two samples differ little in their change of problem incidence.

Girls aged 15 plus and 17 plus

Mean scores:

Occup. class	N	Age	Health and physical devel.	School	Home and family	Money, work and future	Boy–girl	People in general	Self-concern	Overall
Co-educated girls										
1 + 2	61	15+	2·59	4·66	2·84	3·64	3·49	3·80	4·79	25·80
		17+	2·84	3·61	2·79	3·54	3·03	3·48	4·93	24·21
3, 4 & 5	54	15+	2·28	5·06	2·33	3·37	3·15	4·00	3·93	24·11
		17+	2·48	3·41	1·85	3·37	2·06	2·74	3·85	19·76
all	115	15+	2·44	4·84	2·60	3·51	3·33	3·90	4·38	25·01
		17+	2·67	3·51	2·35	3·46	2·57	3·13	4·43	22·12
Girls in girls' schools										
1 + 2	61	15+	2·16	4·16	1·89	2·97	2·93	2·67	4·02	20·80
		17+	2·62	4·21	2·64	3·87	2·67	3·41	4·23	23·66
3, 4 & 5	59	15+	2·68	5·81	3·08	4·29	3·68	3·51	5·00	28·05
		17+	3·03	4·39	2·90	4·25	2·71	2·80	4·86	24·95
all	120	15+	2·42	4·98	2·48	3·62	3·30	3·08	4·50	24·37
		17+	2·83	4·30	2·77	4·06	2·69	3·11	4·54	24·29

The reduction in problem mentions between 15 plus and 17 plus are greater for the co-educational sample in all sections except self-concern (equality) and health and physical development where the same trend is to be seen in the slightly lower increase for the co-educational. The sections with the largest differences between co-educational and single-sex are 'people in general' and 'school'.

TABLE A.35a *Mooney Problem Check list: Special problems: Longitudinal survey 1964–6 (36 schools)—15 plus and 17 plus girls*

Occup. class	N	Age	Health and physical devel.	School N	School %*	Home and family	Money, work and future	Boy–girl	People in general	Self-concern	Overall
Co-educated girls											
1 and 2	61	15+	6	23	22·1	18	27	13	6	11	104
		17+	4	17	18·9	13	22	16	13	5	90
3, 4 & 5	54	15+	9	20	29·4	12	6	9	4	8	68
		17+	8	15	19·5	13	16	7	6	12	77
all	115	15+	15	43	25·0	30	33	22	10	19	172
		17+	12	32	19·2	26	38	23	19	17	167
Girls from girls' schools											
1 and 2	61	15+	9	18	30·5	7	4	11	4	6	59
		17+	6	16	19·3	13	16	11	7	14	83
3, 4 & 5	59	15+	9	18	25·0	11	9	8	7	10	72
		17+	3	17	28·3	13	14	8	1	4	60
all	120	15+	18	36	27·5	18	13	19	11	16	131
		17+	9	33	23·1	26	30	19	8	18	143

* Number of 'School' problems as a percentage of Overall problems.
NOTE: In any section the pupil who had problems was counted only once but the same pupil has sometimes recorded problems in several sections.

TABLE A.36 *Girls' neuroticism—mean scores* (*Maudsley*)

Age	Schools	Classes 1 and 2		Classes 3, 4 and 5		All	
		N	Mean	N	Mean	N	Mean
15+	Co-ed.	61	28·87	54	31·56	115	30·13
	Girls'	61	29·33	59	31·48	120	30·36
17+	Co-ed.	61	29·02	54	30·74	115	29·83
	Girls'	61	29·93	59	30·19	120	30·06

TABLE A.37 *Introversion–extroversion mean scores* (*H.S.P.Q.*)

Junior boys

Age	Schools	Class 1		Class 2		Class 3		Classes 4 and 5		All*	
		N	Mean	N	Mean	N	Mean	N	Mean	N	Mean
11+	Co-ed.	28	36·79	57	35·95	106	37·49	34	36·56	226	36·82
	Boys'	27	36·11	78	36·28	88	34·83	24	39·00	220	36·05
13+	Co-ed.	28	38·32	57	36·26	106	37·76	34	34·82	226	36·96
	Boys'	27	33·59	78	37·71	88	34·59	24	35·63	220	35·73

* Includes some unclassifiable.

TABLE A.38 *Introversion–extroversion mean scores* (*H.S.P.Q.*)

Junior girls

Age	Schools	Class 1		Class 2		Class 3		Classes 4 and 5		All*	
		N	Mean	N	Mean	N	Mean	N	Mean	N	Mean
11+	Co-ed.	32	38·16	60	38·20	80	36·59	43	38·88	215	37·73
	Girls'	37	35·00	59	39·05	90	36·80	29	35·28	218	36·87
13+	Co-ed.	32	37·81	60	37·58	80	36·56	43	36·49	215	37·02
	Girls'	37	36·57	59	38·27	90	36·21	29	36·28	218	36·87

* Includes some unclassifiable.

TABLE A.39 *Introversion–extroversion mean scores (H.S.P.Q.)*

Senior girls

Age	Schools	Classes 1 and 2		Classes 3, 4 and 5		All*	
		N	Mean	N	Mean	N	Mean
15+	Co-ed.	61	36·30	54	36·72	115	36·50
	Girls'	61	37·49	59	36·66	121	37·04
17+	Co-ed.	61	35·92	54	37·41	115	36·62
	Girls'	61	36·28	59	38·78	121	37·48

* Includes some unclassifiable.

Bibliography

NOTE: A compendious annotated bibliography of books and articles on co-education has been published by Faculté des sciences de l'éducation, Université de Montréal, Montréal, Canada, (1970), entitled *La Coéducation dans les écoles officielles et les écoles Catholiques des 45 pays* by Marcel de Grandpré.

ATHERTON, B. F., (1971), 'The relative merits of co-educational and single-sex schools with particular reference to happiness in marriage of former pupils', M.A. thesis, University College of Swansea.

(1966), 'Co-education and happiness in marriage', *Where?*, 28.

BADLEY, J. H., (1914), *Co-education in Practice*, Cambridge.

(1923), *Bedales: A Pioneer School*, London.

(1929), *Co-education and its part in a complete education*, Cambridge.

BOARD OF EDUCATION, (1926), *The Hadow Report. Report on the education of the adolescent*, H.M.S.O.

BOXALL, JEAN, (1961), 'A study of some of the relationships between anxiety and failure in learning to read', Thesis for the Diploma in the Psychology of Childhood, University of Birmingham.

Bristol Social Adjustment Guide, see STOTT, D. H.

CAMPBELL, DUDLEY, (1874), *Mixed Education of Boys and Girls in America*, London.

CATTELL, R. B. AND BELOFF, H., (1963), 'Jr.–Sr. High School Personality Questionnaire', Form A, (Second Edition), Champaign, Illinois.

COWEN, E. L., et al., (1965), 'The relationship of anxiety in children to school record, achievement and the behavioural measures', *Child Development*, 36, 685–95.

CURRY, W. B., (1947), *Education for Sanity*, London.

DALE, R. R., (1948), 'Co-education: An Enquiry', *Times Educational Supplement*, 28 August 1948.

(1949), 'Co-education and the Modern Age', Association of Assistant Masters, Sept.

(1962a), 'Co-education—I: A critical analysis of research on the effects of co-education on academic attainment in grammar schools', *Educational Research*, 4, 3.

(1962b), 'Co-education—II: An analysis of research on comparative attainment in mathematics in single-sex and co-educational maintained grammar schools', *Educational Research*, 5, 1.

(1964), 'Co-education—III: Research on comparative attainment in English in single-sex and co-educational grammar schools', *Educational Research*, 6, 3.

Bibliography

(1966), 'The happiness of pupils in co-educational and single-sex grammar schools', *British Journal of Educational Psychology*, XXXVI, 1.

(1966a), 'Pupil–teacher relationships in co-educational and single-sex grammar schools', *British Journal of Educational Psychology*, XXXVI, 3.

(1969), 'Anxiety about school among first-year grammar school pupils, and its relation to occupational class and co-education', *British Journal of Educational Psychology*, 39, 1.

(1969), *Mixed or Single-sex School?*, *Vol. I*, London.

DEPARTMENT OF EDUCATION AND SCIENCE, (1969), *Statistics of Education*, Vol. 1, Year 1968: Schools, H.M.S.O.

EYSENCK, H. J., (1959), 'Maudsley Personality Inventory', London.

FURNEAUX, W. D., (1961), *The Chosen Few*, London.

HIGH SCHOOL PERSONALITY QUESTIONNAIRE, JR.–SR., (H.S.P.Q.), *see* CATTELL.

HOWARD, B. A., (1928), *The Mixed School*, London.

LOTZ, H. B., (1953), 'The relationship between emotional and social adjustment of individuals and their attendance at co-educational and single-sex high schools', Ph.D. thesis, New York University.

MCCANDLESS, B. R., AND CASTANEDA, A., (1956a), 'Anxiety in children, school achievement and intelligence', *Child Dev.*, 27, 379–82.

(1956b), 'The Children's form of the Manifest Anxiety Scale', *Child Dev.*, 27, 317–26.

MAUDSLEY PERSONALITY INVENTORY, (H. J. Eysenck), (1959), London.

MINISTRY OF EDUCATION, (1945), Pamphlet No. 1, *The Nation's Schools: their plan and purpose*, H.M.S.O.

MOONEY, ROSS L., and GORDON, L. V., (1950/64 revision), 'Mooney Problem Check List, Junior High School Form', (anglicized version), N.F.E.R. Slough.

MORETON, F. E., (1939), 'Co-education—a statistical enquiry into the attitude of teachers . . . and a comparative study of the emotional development of children . . .', Ph.D. thesis, University of London. (Summarized in *British Journal of Educational Psychology*, 1946, XVI, 2.)

PEKIN, L.B., (1934), *Progressive schools: their principles and practice*, London.

(1939), *Co-education in its historical and theoretical setting*, London.

SARASON, S. B., et al., (1960), *Anxiety in Elementary School Children*, New York.

STEWART, W. A. C., (1967 and 1968), *The Educational Innovators*, 2 vols. (particularly vol. 2, 'The Progressive Schools 1881–1967'), London.

STOTT, D. H., and SYKES, E. G., (1956), 'Bristol Social-Adjustment Guides', No. 1 and No. 2 *The Child in School*.

TYSON, G., (1928), 'Some apparent effects of co-education suggested by a statistical investigation of examination results', M.Ed. thesis, University of Manchester.

INDEX

Social occupational class—*contd.*
school social image, **233–4;**
unhappy pupils, **328–32;** and
working class, 294; *see also*
Anxiety; Bullying; 'Check'
survey; Happiness (school);
Mooney Problem List; Schools
Project
Societies, school, *see* School
Society, influence, 178, 245, 291
Spitefulness, *see* Girls
STEWART, W. A. C., I
Student-teachers as sample, 7,
234, 245
Students, *see* Ex-pupils
Sweden, co-education, I
Teachers: in amalgamated schools,
57, **284–5;** balance of sexes,
2–3; better attitude, 67, 164–5,
167, 292; broader outlook, 164;
'both schools' sample, **290–3;**
fear of, 43, 58, 68, 70, 250,
264–5, 271; female, 48, 171,
296, (and boys), 45; friendly,
36, 38, 41–2, 44–5, 51–8 *passim*,
68, 106, 122, 164; good influence, 292; happiness, 291; male
preferred, 164–5; in mixed
staff, 52, 164, 292–3; old-
fashioned, petty, 43, 46, 110,
269, 293; and mixing, 201, 203;
and out-of-school conduct, **137–
146;** prefer co-education, **290–1;**
quarrel, 155; sex, attitude to,
224; unfriendly, 38, 40–1, 54–6;
unpleasant, 45–6, 107
Technical schools, *see* Schools
Tests: in Schools project, 13; *see
also* individual tests
Third College survey, *see* 'Both
schools'
Three-schools sub-sample, **11–12**

Timidity, *see* Boys; Girls
Tradition, 38, 67, 70, 171
Travel, 54–8 *passim*
Truancy, 260, 300
TYSON, G., 236
Unhappiness, *see* Girls
United States of America, 2, 179,
299, 300
University Departments of
Education: sample, 148; staff
preference, 291
Variety/monotony, **114–17,** 152,
164–6, 290, 294
Violence, 70, 88
Wales: co-education, 2; and
nationality, 76; South, 13, 14;
survey in, **13–14**
West Riding Education Authority,
13–14
WILCOXON Test, 62
Woman, in subjection, 182; *see
also* Girls; Women
Women: attitude to men, 236–41,
297; and authority, 240; and
desire to marry, **253–4;** and
equality of sexes, **182–3;** influence of sexes, **206–8, 211–14;**
wish men superior, 183; work
with men, **236–41,** 297
Work, 152, 164–5, **167–9, 177–8;**
amount of, 36; anxiety and,
262, 266–74 *passim;* competition, 39, 49, 166, 168, 203–14
passim, 290, 293; distractions,
34, 49, 50, 77, 151, 154, 168,
171, 202–14 *passim*, 340; enjoyed, 33, 39, 40, 41, 49, 50, 51,
55, 67, 293; pressure, 33, 37,
39, 40, 44, 46, 50, 107, 123,
131–36 *passim*, 269, 331–2; and
unhappy girls, **120–36;** *see also*
Free responses